TRANSLATING THEORY AND RESEARCH INTO EDUCATIONAL PRACTICE

DEVELOPMENTS IN CONTENT DOMAINS, LARGE-SCALE REFORM, AND INTELLECTUAL CAPACITY

The Educational Psychology Series
Robert J. Sternberg and Wendy M. Williams, Series Editors

Marton/Booth • *Learning and Awareness*

Hacker/Dunlovsky/Graesser, Eds. • *Metacognition in Educational Theory and Practice*

Smith/Pourchot, Eds. • *Adult Learning and Development: Perspectives From Educational Psychology*

Sternberg/Williams, Eds. • *Intelligence, Instruction and Assessment: Theory Into Practice*

Martinez • *Education as the Cultivation of Intelligence*

Torff/Sternberg, Eds. • *Understanding and Teaching the Intuitive Mind: Student and Teacher Learning*

Sternberg/Zhang, Eds. • *Perspectives on Cognitive, Learning, and Thinking Styles*

Ferrari, Ed. • *The Pursuit of Excellence Through Education*

Corno, Cronbach, Kupermintz, Lohman, Mandinach, Porteus, Albert/The Stanford Aptitude Seminar • *Remaking the Concept of Aptitude: Extending the Legacy of Richard E. Snow*

Dominowski • *Teaching Undergraduates*

Valdés • *Expanding Definitions of Giftedness: The Case of Young Interpreters From Immigrant Communities*

Shavinina/Ferrari, Eds. • *Beyond Knowledge: Non-Cognitive Aspects of Developing High Ability*

Dai/Sternberg, Eds. • *Motivation, Emotion, and Cognition: Integrative Perspectives on Intellectual Functioning and Development*

Sternberg/Preiss, Eds. • *Intelligence and Technology: The Impact of Tools in the Nature and Development of Human Abilities*

Patrick C. Kyllonen, Richard D. Roberts, and Lazar Stankov, Eds. • *Extending Intelligence: Enhancement and New Constructs*

Zhang/Sternberg, Eds. • *The Nature of Intellectual Styles*

Constas/Sternberg, Eds. • *Translating Theory and Research Into Educational Practice: Developments in Content Domains, Large-Scale Reform, and Intellectual Capacity*

For a complete list of LEA titles, please contact Lawrence Erlbaum Associates, Publishers, at www.erlbaum.com.

TRANSLATING THEORY AND RESEARCH INTO EDUCATIONAL PRACTICE

DEVELOPMENTS IN CONTENT DOMAINS, LARGE-SCALE REFORM, AND INTELLECTUAL CAPACITY

Edited by

Mark A. Constas
Robert J. Sternberg

2006
LAWRENCE ERLBAUM ASSOCIATES, PUBLISHERS
Mahwah, New Jersey   London

Copyright © 2006 by Lawrence Erlbaum Associates, Inc.

Lawrence Erlbaum Associates, Inc., Publishers
10 Industrial Avenue
Mahwah, New Jersey 07430
www.erlbaum.com

Cover design by Tomai Maridou

Library of Congress Cataloging-in-Publication Data

Translating theory and research into educational practice : develop-
    ments in content domains, large scale reform, and intellectual
    capacity / edited by Mark A. Constas, Robert J. Sternberg.
        p. cm. — (The educational psychology series)
    Includes bibliographical references and index.
ISBN 0-8058-5147-X (cloth : alk. paper)
ISBN 0-8058-5148-8 (pbk. : alk. paper)
1. Education—Research. 2. Educational psychology. I. Constas,
    Mark A. II. Sternberg, Robert J. III. Series.
LB1028.T695 2006
370'.72—dc22   20005052305
                                                            CIP

Books published by Lawrence Erlbaum Associates are printed on
acid-free paper, and their bindings are chosen for strength and
durability.

Printed in the United States of America
10 9 8 7 6 5 4 3 2 1

Contents

Preface

The desire to translate research and theory into practice is shared by many who hope to narrow the gap between the theoretical knowledge and empirical findings of researchers and the practical needs of front-line professionals. Although this has been a longstanding goal in the field of education (see Condliffe-Lagemann, 2000), interest in research-based practice has increased greatly over the past few years. What does it mean for an educational program to be research based? What steps need to be taken by researchers and practitioners to create better connections among theory, research, and educational practice? What challenges might one encounter in the effort to establish such connections? What are some of the common themes found across programs of research that are concerned with translating research into practice? In this volume, focusing on questions such as these, we bring together a collection of well-known researchers who have substantial experience in trying to establish connections between the knowledge produced by the research community and the practices employed in school settings. Authors who have contributed to this volume have spent a considerable amount of energy exploring the practical difficulties, political challenges, and theoretical implications related to the effort to apply theory and findings from research to a diverse range of educational settings.

The book is organized into three principal parts, with each part introduced by a brief commentary that highlights some of the significant points of the chapters contained in each part of the book. In Part I of the book—which includes chapters by Alan Schoenfeld (chap. 1, this volume); Shirley Magnussen and Ann Marie Palincsar (chap. 2, this volume); Jack Fletcher, Barbara Foorman, Carolyn Denton, and Sharon Vaughn (chap. 3, this volume); and Robert Calfee, Roxanne Greitz Miller, Kim Norman,

Kathy Wilson, and Guy Trainin (chap. 4, this volume) report on attempts to use educational theory and research to improve student learning and achievement in content domains (e.g., mathematics and science) and in skill areas (e.g., reading). The first chapter in this part, by Schoenfeld, provides insights into the theoretical foundations, political obstacles, and practical complexities he has witnessed in his many years of work in the field of mathematics education. (As a chronicle of approximately 40 years of reform efforts in mathematics education, Schoenfeld examines how issues such as the deprofessionalization of teachers, national and local politics, and an inadequate research development infrastructure have inhibited efforts to translate theory and research into practice.) In the chapter by Magnussen and Palincsar, the authors focus on science education and integrate what is known about scientific practice, learning, and the sociocultural context of education. Magnussen and Palincsar's work is significant because it demonstrates how theory and research might influence practice, and it also illustrates how the knowledge of practice might influence theory. In a third chapter by Fletcher et al., the authors describe their large-scale effort to translate and integrate research and theory related to reading instruction. The description of how research, theory, policy, and legislation can work together or against each other provides readers with interesting insights about the conditions needed to effectively translate research into practice. Fletcher et al. demonstrate how efforts to connect research and practice remain challenging even when the research evidence is clear as is the case for early reading instruction. In the final chapter in this first part of the book (chap. 4, this volume), Calfee et al., describe the challenges and documents the successful strategies have used to promote literacy through selected professional development activities. The chapter by Calfee et al., (chap. 4, this volume) is significant because it raises questions about translation of research and theory into practice by posing a series of challenging questions about how to define and judge the quality of research. By interrogating long-held views about the conceptual, methodological, and empirical foundations of education research, Calfee et al. give a new way to approach the problem of translating research and theory into educational practice.

In Part II of the book, the authors focus on the challenges of large-scale reform. This section includes chapters by James Comer and Edward Joyner (chap. 7, this volume), Robert Slavin (chap. 5, this volume), James Edward Zigler and Matia Finn-Stevenson (chap. 8, this volume), and Christine Finnan and Henry Levin (chap. 6, this volume). Describing their efforts to translate theory and research into practice in the School Development Project, Comer and Joyner illustrate the ways in which principles of human development may be applied to educational settings. Comer and Joyner argue that failures related to attempts to translate theory and research into practice can be remedied if we pay closer attention to research knowledge derived from studies of child and adolescent development. Zigler and Finn-Stevenson describe their work with the School of the 21st Century (21C), a school-based program that has been implemented in approximately 1,300 schools across the country. Different than most educational programs, 21C has focused its reform agenda on the provision of quality child care. By demonstrating important connections between early-childhood care provisions and development in early childhood, Zigler and Finn-Stevenson illustrate the value of drawing upon research and theory outside of the field education. In the chapter by Slavin, he describes the development of Success For All (SFA), a school-improvement program that has its roots in the theory and research on cooperative learning. As both a report on the achievements and an analysis of remaining challenges of SFA, Slavin offers practical advice and theoretical insights about the dynamic interaction of theory, research, and practice. As the final chapter in this second part of book, Finnan and Levin describe the ways in which the Accelerated Schools Project (ASP) has developed and implemented a transformative response to the practical challenges found in schools that serve "disadvantaged" student populations. Over a period of nearly 20 years, ASP has been implemented in more than 1,000 schools across the United States and in a number of school settings outside of the United States. Finnan and Levin use this broad implementation experience to describe their efforts to translate theory and research into practice.

All efforts to enhance learning are based, either implicitly or explicitly, on a theory of how the mind works and on how intellectual skills and abilities may be most effectively developed. Recognizing the foundational importance of theories of intellect, the authors in Part III of this book explore the ways in which different models of intelligence have informed educational practice. In the first chapter in this part, Robert J. Sternberg et al. (chap. 9, this volume) demonstrate how efforts to develop interventions of increasing scale (e.g., from schools to districts to regions) has led their team of investigators to develop and apply the notion of contextual variation to their work on successful intelligence. In this chapter, Sternberg et al. provide empirical data on the effects that educational context has had, and will continue to have, on the implementation of instructional interventions. The chapter by Sternberg et al. is significant because the authors approach the frequently noted but rarely examined notion of educational context as a research construct, a construct that they argue should be subject to focused empirical investigation. In the chapter by Joseph Renzulli (chap. 10, this volume), he documents his work in the area of gifted education, which combines an analysis of theoretical developments and empirical analysis of research on giftedness and creativity with a description of the professional challenges he has encountered in his effort to close the gap between research and practice.

Renzulli's chapter is significant because he raises important issues about the way in which attempts to translate theory and research into practice are of practical concern. Renzulli also shows how theoretical developments are mediated by the dynamics of political context(s) (e.g., within schools and school districts, within states, and within the research community itself). In the chapter by Mindy Kornhaber and Howard Gardner (chap. 11, this volume), the authors describe a scenario in which the theoretical propositions that form the basis of multiple intelligences (MI) have been implemented without formal organizational supports and outside of the ambitions of the researchers themselves. Kornhaber and Gardner provide an analysis that describes the features of MI that may have led to this phenomenon of self-implementation and offer solutions to the problem of implementation variation. Chapter 11 is significant because Kornhaber and Gardner describe a relatively rare phenomenon, a self-implementing theory, and provide an analysis that is instructive for others who are interested in translating research and theory into educational practice.

Understanding how to build productive connections between research and practice remains a problem for the field of education. *Translating Theory and Research Into Educational Practice* offers a richly detailed account of the challenges encountered and the strategies applied in relation to this problem. Many of the authors from all three parts of the book have committed between 10 and 40 years to narrowing the gap between research and practice. Viewed as a collective effort to translate theory and research into educational practice, the interventions and programs the authors describe across the volume represent nearly 200 years of work. As a compendium of successful strategies, we believe this book may help others identify ways to make their own research more useful to practice communities. As an analysis of persistent, seemingly intractable problems encountered when attempting to connect educational theory and research to the everyday work of teachers in classrooms and schools, the authors in this book demonstrate areas in which additional work is needed. The description of successful strategies and the analysis of seemingly intractable problems the authors provide throughout the book will hopefully spur the interest of researchers who hope to understand how the research community may better respond to the needs of educational professionals.

REFERENCES

Condliffe-Lagemann, E. (2000). *An elusive science: The troubling history of educational research*. Chicago: University of Chicago Press.
The Elementary and Secondary Education Act of 2001, Publ. Law No. 107-110.

List of Contributors

Damian Birney, School of Psychology, University of Sydney

Robert C. Calfee, Graduate School of Education, University of California, Riverside

James Comer, Yale University Child Study Center School Development Program, Yale University

Mark A. Constas, Department of Education, Cornell University

Carolyn Denton, Department of Special Education, University of Texas, Austin

Christine Finnan, Department of Elementary and Early Childhood Education, College of Charleston

Matia Finn-Stevenson, Edward Zigler Center for Child Development and Social Policy, Yale University

Linda Jarvin, The PACE Center, Yale University

Jack M. Fletcher, Center for Academic and Reading Skills, University of Texas Health Sciences Center

Barbara Foorman, Center for Academic and Reading Skills, University of Texas Health Sciences Center

Roxanne Greitz Miller, School of Education, University of California Riverside

Elena Grigorenko, PACE Center, Yale University

Linda Jarvin, PACE Center, Yale University

Edward Joyner, Comer School Development Project, Yale University

Alex Kirklik, University of Illinois, Urbana-Champaigne

Mindy Kornhaber, School of Education, Pennsylvania State University

Henry Levin, School of Education, Stanford University

Shirley Magnussen, School of Education, University of Michigan

Kim Norman, Elementary and Bilingual Education, California State University, Fullerton

Anne Marie Palincsar, School of Education, University of Michigan

Joseph Renzulli, Department of Psychology, University of Connecticut

Alan Schoenfeld, Graduate School of Education, University of California, Berkeley

Robert E. Slavin, Success for All Foundation and Johns Hopkins University

Robert J. Sternberg, School of Arts and Sciences, Tufts University

Guy Trainin, School of Education, University of Nebraska, Lincoln

Sharon Vaughn, Department of Special Education, College of Education, University of Texas, Austin

Kathy Wilson, School of Education, University of Nebraska, Lincoln

Edward Zigler, The Bush Center in Child Development and Social Policy, Yale University

I

TRANSLATION OF RESEARCH AND THEORY IN CONTENT AREAS AND SKILL DOMAINS

Commentary

Mark A. Constas and Robert J. Sternberg

The need to translate educational theory and research into practice in content and skill areas has existed for generations. The importance of developing a coherent, effective response to this need has increased significantly over the past few years, as national indicators (e.g., National Center for Educational Statistics, 2003) and international comparisons (e.g., Gonzales, Guzman, & Jocelyn, 2004) have revealed less than ideal outcomes. In the four chapters in this first part of the book, the authors describe comprehensive programs of research in science education, mathematics education, and reading. In the first chapter, Schoenfeld, (chap. 1, this volume) helps describe the challenges of translating research and theory into practice in the field of mathematics education. Schoenfeld's analysis of the tensions between research and practice brings into sharp focus the intersection, and seeming inseparability, of theoretical perspectives and political reactions related to mathematics education. In the chapter by Magnusson and Palincsar (chap. 2, this volume), the authors offer insights about how a multidisciplinary framework related to guided instruction in science has been used to support their attempts to translate theory and research into practice. One of the driving forces behind the work of Magnusson and Palincsar is a concern for building better, more authentic connections between how children are taught science and how scientists themselves engage in the practice of science. Focusing on reading, in the chapter by Fletcher, Foorman, Denton, and Vaughn (chap. 3, this volume), the authors describe the difficulties of translating theory and research into practice

3

even when the foundation of knowledge is fairly well established. Fletcher et al.'s chapter is important because they examine the ways in which theory, research, policy, and legislation exert a combined effect on attempts to bring about meaningful change in instruction. In the final chapter, Calfee, Miller, Norman, Wilson, and Trainin (chap. 4, this volume) describe the demands of trying to influence practice in the area of literacy, in support of basic reading and in support of reading and writing in science. Chapter 4 is significant because Calfee et al. not only offer insights about how to think about education for literacy but also raise questions about the way in which the field of educational research is structured as a scientific enterprise.

As a collection of chapters focused on the investigation of content and skill domains in education, the work of Fletcher et al. (chap. 3, this volume) and of Schoenfeld, Calfee et al., and Magnusson and Palincsar (chaps. 1, 4, and 2, respectively, this volume) introduces provocative questions and offers sound practical advice about how researchers may more effectively engage with and solve problems of practice. The authors in this part of the book explore new ways to conceive of studies and new ways to develop implementation strategies as we seek to translate theory and research into practice in content and skill domains of mathematics, science, and reading.

MATHEMATICS EDUCATION AT THE CROSSROADS OF THEORY AND POLITICS

In Schoenfeld's chapter (chap. 1, this volume), he provides a historical description of the achievements and persistent challenges for the field of mathematics education as it seeks to translate educational theory and research into practice. Beginning with the surge of interest in mathematics and science education in the Sputnik in the 1960s, Schoenfeld shows how varying conceptions of core knowledge, heuristic understanding, and metacognition have influenced the field of mathematics education. Portrayed as a series of "crisis-response" cycles, the field of mathematics education has been the subject of active debate among policymakers, practitioners, and researchers. Schoenfield describes how various school-reform efforts and content standards have shaped instructional practice. Like many content domains, mathematics has been the subject of heated political debate. As Schoenfeld demonstrates, educational research and theory are just two of many forces that act on the practice of mathematics education. Schoenfeld's analysis of the standards-based curriculum that followed the National Council of Teachers of Mathematics (NCTM) standards illustrates both the successes and remaining challenges in the field of mathematics education. A valuable feature of Schoenfeld's chapter is that he connects his analysis of theoretical issues to a broader set of political transitions related to shifting funding priorities and political transitions at the national level. As Schoenfeld (chap. 1, this volume) argues, somewhat discouragingly (but realistically!), "education is still much more hostage to politics than it is to incremental improvement through research-based means" (p. xx). Schoenfeld cites a range of structural features, institutional practices, and professional pressures that mitigate against the possibility of creating well-established sustained effort to more effectively and more consistently translate educational theory and research into practice. With reference to structural issues, Schoenfeld argues that an "engineering infrastructure" is needed for the field of education, an infrastructure that will support research development work in education. What is perhaps most distinctive of Schoenfeld's analysis is that he provides a comprehensive description and insightful analysis of the disciplinary developments, political forces, and practical constraints that have the shaped the field of mathematics education over the past 40 years. Schoenfeld's chapter is valuable because he gives us an opportunity to understand the social dynamics and politicized history of the contentious debates and competing reform efforts within which efforts to improve mathematics education have taken place.

BRIDGING THE GAP BETWEEN SCIENTIFIC PRACTICE AND SCIENCE EDUCATION

In the second chapter in this first part of the book, Magnusson and Palincsar (chap. 2, this volume) describe their work on guided-inquiry science instruction. With its integration of philosophy of science, cognitive psychology, curriculum theory, and sociocultural theory, Magnusson and Palincsar demonstrate the value of adopting an interdisciplinary approach. By integrating knowledge of how scientists work with a conception of curriculum that is directly linked to inquiry, Magnusson and Palincsar argue for an approach to science education that builds on what we know about the process of scientific inquiry. By attaching this vision of science education to advances in cognitive psychology, Magnusson and Palincsar demonstrate how an understanding of text comprehension needs to be an integral part of our efforts to translate educational research and theory into practice in the domain of science education. The inclusion of a sociocultural perspective highlights the importance of understanding how cognition and curriculum are inextricably linked to community, participation, and culture. Here, Magnusson and Palincsar use Vygotsky's (1978) notion of the zone of proximal development to create a coherent theoretical framework within which their efforts to translate theory and research into practice may be conceptualized and enacted. The instructional manifestation of this conceptualization is found in "notebook texts," a pedagogical translation of the notebooks kept by practicing scientists. Magnusson and Palincsar provide a demonstration of how notebook texts are linked to research and theory. The chapter by Magnusson and Palincsar is distinctive because they show, in explicit terms, how each component of their intervention design was derived from a particular theoretical perspective. There is also a logical symmetry to the way they approach the task of translating research and theory into practice in science education. Magnusson and Palincsar begin with analysis of the practices of scientists and end with an intervention design that focuses on the practices of students as nascent scientists. Theory occupies the middle ground that connects these two varieties of practice. In this way, we believe the chapter by Magnusson and Palincsar exerts a positive stress on the title of this volume. Following their lead, we might have titled the book *Translating Practice Into Theory!*

CHANGE IN READING RESEARCH AND READING THE DYNAMICS OF CHANGE

In the chapter by Fletcher et al. (chap. 3, this volume), the authors describe how advances in research in reading have influenced areas of practice both in schools and in the broader public sphere. Referring to work carried out in Texas, Fletcher et al. demonstrate how a well established body of knowledge from reading research has affected educational practice, state legislation, and national legislation related to reading instruction. Different from many other areas of research that have relevance for education practice, the body of knowledge on which effective practices might be based for reading has grown consistently over the past few decades. The momentum associated with this growth has spawned a series of legislative actions that are designed to facilitate and even mandate efforts to translate research into practice. One would think that the existence of convergent findings supported by strong political will would greatly enhance the probability of implementation. Fletcher et al. demonstrate that a solid research base augmented by political support provides no guarantee of success.

Focused on the problem of how to translate their research into practice at varying levels of scale (e.g., school, collections of schools, school districts, regions), Fletcher et al. (chap. 3, this volume) show the importance of understanding the dynamics of change and describe the way in which epistemological issues, social investments, fiscal resources, and limitations in the research base influence our ability to translate research into practice. One of the most valuable and clearly ambitious aspects of Fletcher et al.'s analysis is that they urge investigators to reconceptualize the problem as the intersection of epistemological conflicts and methodological variations related to reading research and instruction. Fletcher et al. argue for the reconciliation of the well-worn methodological dichotomies (quantitative vs. quantitative) and for the integration of epistemological oppositions. As an illustration of their position, Fletcher et al. review the work on the Texas Reading Initiative. Their work provides a compelling demonstration of how the formation of collaborative partnerships and the provision of support for teacher participation have facilitated efforts to translate research into practice. By describing major problems encountered in their experiences with the Texas Reading Initiative, Fletcher et al. provide us with a series of recommendations based on many years of theoretical and practical work focused on translating educational theory and research into practice.

QUALITIES OF EDUCATIONAL RESEARCH AND THE DEMANDS OF PRACTICE

Focusing on literacy, both for basic reading and for scientific literacy, Calfee et al. (chap. 4, this volume) describe the ways in which their work on three professional-development projects has brought into focus critical issues related to the translation of research into practice. Calfee et al. provide an analysis that urges the research community to reconceptualize fundamental views about research practice, research standards, and research applications. The analysis of research practices presented in Calfee et al.'s chapter portrays research as another instance of complex learning rather than as a purely technical approach to knowledge production. The discussion of standards has implications for how the notion of "rigor" might be defined as investigators work to conceptualize the problem of translating theory and research into educational practice. Researchers in many fields of study use the term *rigor* to signify that the particular research study has adhered to the highest standards. Questions raised about the "demands of practice." introduced by Calfee et al. move the discussion of research rigor beyond the technical conventions of research methods. The idea calls for fundamental reconfiguring of the epistemological principles on which research practices are based. According to Calfee et al., work that meets the demands of practice displays methodological qualities and a high degree of conceptual coherence. As a theoretically oriented approach to the problem of translating research into practice, Calfee et al. also emphasize the importance of generalizability as a central concept for research that aims to have an impact on practice settings. One of the strengths of this chapter is that Calfee et al. provide a framework of issues within which recommendations for how to focus and improve our attempts to translate theory and research into practice may be developed. Key elements of this framework include redefinition of instruction as learning, a focus on sustained engagement with schools, a reconsideration of what counts as evidence at varying levels of scale (e.g., locally, nationally), and a call for adequate support for educational research. On a more practical level, Calfee et al.'s work helps think about ways to establish connections at various points (e.g., teachers, schools, school districts). In many respects, the chapter by Calfee et al. is of foundational importance because it raises fundamental questions about the set of assumptions upon which our practices as researchers are based.

REFERENCES

Gonzales, P., Guzman, J. & Jocelyn, L. (2004). *Highlights from the trends in international mathematics and science study*. Washington, DC: National Center of Education Statistics, U.S. Department of Education.

National Center for Educational Statistics. (2003). *National assessment of educational progress*. Washington, DC: U.S. Department of Education.

Vygotsky, L. S. (1978). *Mind in society: The development of higher psychological processes* (M. Cole, V. John-Steiner, S. Scribner, & E. Souberman, Eds.). Cambridge, MA: Harvard University Press.

1

Notes on the Educational Steeplechase: Hurdles and Jumps in the Development of Research-Based Mathematics Instruction

Alan H. Schoenfeld
University of California, Berkeley

PART 1: A SUCCESS STORY (OF SORTS)

I start with a look on the bright side. A case can be made that a significant proportion of mathematics instruction in the United States has been changed for the better as a result of basic research in mathematical thinking, learning, and problem solving. In fact, mathematics may be the poster child for changes in practice influenced by basic research. I can tell this story autobiographically, for I experienced it firsthand—first as a student, then as a researcher, then as change agent. I begin with my school years. I was one of the happy (and therefore rare) products of what is now called the "traditional curriculum." The four major influences shaping curricular design at that time were

- The assumption that mathematics is a hierarchical domain with a ladder of skills that is well defined. It was assumed that such a hierarchy should define curricular structure. Addition and subtraction preceded multiplication and division, which preceded algebra, and so on up the ladder.

- The assumption, consistent with the organization of Bloom's (1956) *Taxonomy of Educational Objectives,* that mastery at any one particular level was critical for advancement to the next level.
- The assumption that "learning mathematics" and "mastering various mathematical facts, concepts, and procedures" are more or less synonymous.
- The assumption that tools had to be mastered before they could be used. Acquiring skills came first; then there was the possibility of using them in applications and problem solving.

The major theories shaping instruction at that time were behaviorism (I earned lots of gold stars for doing my work correctly) and associationism or connectionism (basically, the idea that repeated practice strengthens bonds between ideas—the theoretical underpinnings of "drill and practice"). Although I thrived on the traditional curriculum and went on to earn my PhD in mathematics, I was a rarity statistically speaking.

Mathematics was viewed by almost everyone as being both distasteful and difficult. On average, once mathematics became optional in the curriculum (about ninth grade), students dropped out of the mathematical pipeline at the rate of 50% per year. In 1989, millions upon millions of ninth graders were enrolled in mathematics courses. Hundreds of thousands were enrolled as college freshmen, and fewer than a thousand earned PhDs (many of these foreign nationals). The 50% annual attrition rate was an average across the population. Dropout rates from mathematics were much higher for African Americans, Latinos, Native Americans, and female students. In 1989,[1] for example, White male students constituted 40% of the U.S. population, Asians 2%; White male students and Asians constituted 78% of those earning PhDs. The curriculum was failing across the boards but even more so for some segments of the U.S. population (Madison & Hart, 1990; National Research Council [NRC], 1989). In a call for change, a 1989 report from the National Research Council, *Everybody Counts,* made the case as follows:

> Mathematics is the worst curricular villain in driving students to failure in school. When mathematics acts as a filter, it not only filters students out of careers, but frequently out of school itself.... Low expectations and limited opportunity to learn have helped drive dropout rates among Blacks and Hispanics much higher—unacceptably high for a society committed to

---

[1]As indicated in the body of this chapter, 1989 was a watershed year for curricular change. The National Council of Teachers of Mathematics' (1989) *Curriculum and Evaluation Standards for School Mathematics* catalyzed the development of a number of "reform" curricula, which differed in philosophy and pedagogy from the established "traditional" curricula.

equality of opportunity. It is vitally important for society that all citizens benefit equally from high quality mathematics education. (p. 7)

Now I turn to the research that catalyzed change. The simple version of the story is that things began to change with the onset of the "cognitive revolution" (see, e.g., Gardner, 1985; Neisser, 1967, is considered the book that established cognitive psychology as a discipline.). Through the 1970s, conceptions of "subject matter understanding" were focused almost exclusively on content—on the specific mathematics (or history, or literature, etc.) that students were to learn. Over the course of the 1970s and 1980s, research in cognitive science in general and in mathematical thinking and learning in particular resulted in a radical rethinking of what it means to develop expertise in subject matter. By the mid-1980s, there was an emerging consensus (de Corte, Verschaffel, & Greer, 1996; Greeno, Pearson, & Schoenfeld, 1997; Schoenfeld, 1985) that the following can be fundamental determinants of individuals' performance in various intellectual domains:

- Core knowledge—knowledge of important facts, mastery of standard procedures, understanding of fundamental concepts, and familiarity with paradigmatic ways of operating in the domain (e.g., Greeno et al., 1997; Kilpatrick, 1985, 1992; Silver, 1987).
- The ability to implement problem solving strategies, also known as "heuristic strategies." These are not rules or algorithms that guarantee that a problem will be solved. Rather, they are rules of thumb, suggestions for making progress on difficult problems (Charles & Silver, 1989; Lester, 1994; Pólya, 1945; Schoenfeld, 1985; Silver, 1985).
- Effective metacognitive skills including monitoring and self-regulation (Brown, 1987; Flavell, 1976; Lester, 1985, 1994).
- Beliefs about, for example, oneself, the nature of the domain (a.k.a. epistemology), and appropriate ways of engaging with the subject matter (Greeno, Collins, & Resnick, 1996; Koehler & Grouws, 1992; Lampert, 1990; Schoenfeld, 1985; Shaughnessy, 1985; Silver, 1985).

By way of illustration, I briefly describe the role of each of these categories in mathematics and in writing.

Core Knowledge

There is, of course, a huge literature on knowledge acquisition and access. Simply put, knowledge is necessary for competent performance. General skills can carry you only so far; if you don't have the tools of the trade, you won't do very well at it. However, as the discussion of the next three categories indicates, they are only part of the story.

Heuristic Strategies

Various strategies in mathematics (e.g., draw a diagram, try to solve an easier related problem and then use either the result or the method to solve the original problem, establish subgoals, decompose the problem into subproblems) enable problem solvers to make progress on problems for which they do not initially have a way of solving. Strategies such as prewriting, "free writing," and using topic sentences enable writers to generate and organize text. Research over the third quarter of the 20th century established that such problem-solving strategies could be taught and that they enhanced problem-solving performance.

Metacognition

Effective monitoring and self-regulation during problem solving are major components of competent performance. Roughly speaking, these aspects of metacognition concern the effectiveness with which one employs the resources (specifically, knowledge and time) at one's disposal during problem solving. A major finding of the 1970s was that people often failed at tasks despite knowing the material. Suppose, for example, that someone makes a poor choice of direction in trying to solve a mathematics problem and pursues that direction doggedly. Whether the person has the knowledge to solve the problem is irrelevant: The useful knowledge lies inaccessible while the wrong problem-solving direction is being pursued. The same is the case with an author who loses track of the audience or with the main line of argument in what is being written. Large chunks of text may need to be discarded if the purpose of writing them was lost during the writing process.

Beliefs

Various kinds of beliefs shape the ways that individuals perform in a domain. Americans tend to believe, for example, that one's ability to do mathematics is innate and therefore not modifiable by effort. The Japanese tend to believe that mathematics learning is a function of effort—that anyone can do well at mathematics if the appropriate hard work is done. Needless to say, people will approach learning and problem solving differently if they believe that effort makes a difference. Clearly someone who believes that "writing is putting down on paper what's in your head" will go about producing text differently than someone who believes that writing is a process that involves planning and multiple revisions. Other beliefs about subject matter are learned from experience with the domain and shape how people go about working in the domain. Lampert (1990) summarized the case with regard to mathematics as follows:

> Commonly, mathematics is associated with certainty; knowing it, with being able to get the right answer, quickly (Ball, 1988; Schoenfeld, 1985b; Stodolsky, 1985). These cultural assumptions are shaped by school experience, in which *doing* mathematics means following the rules laid down by the teacher; *knowing* mathematics means remembering and applying the correct rule when the teacher asks a question; and mathematical *truth is determined* when the answer is ratified by the teacher. Beliefs about how to do mathematics and what it means to know it in school are acquired through years of watching, listening, and practicing. (p. 33; italics in original)

In short, an outcome of research in the 1970s and 1980s was that *content* (the classic view of subject matter), *process* (ways of engaging in the subject matter), and *belief systems/epistemology* (one's set of understandings regarding the nature of the enterprise) are all important outcomes of instruction—and thus important goals for it.

This research made its way into the practical arena largely by a series of historical accidents. Over the course of the 20th century, attention to mathematics education had waxed and waned. During periods of calm, issues of mathematics and science instruction pretty much faded from public view; but during periods of "crisis," they tended to become front-page items. In the mid-1950s, for example, the Soviet Union's success in sending the satellite sputnik into space catalyzed a great deal of activity in science and mathematics including various "hands on" science curricula and the "new math." Federal investments in science and mathematics instructional development flourished in the 1960s but then diminished through the 1970s for a number of reasons. One was apparent success. Our national space program got stronger after the post-sputnik years, and although the cold war continued, the atmosphere of crisis no longer obtained. A second was politics. One of the National Science Foundation (NSF)-supported curricula developed in response to sputnik was a hands on elementary school science and social science curriculum called Man: A Course of Study (MACOS). The first responses to MACOS were extraordinarily positive, and the curriculum was distributed widely. Lappan (1997) describes what happened afterwards:

> By the early 70s however, the mood of the country was changing. Distrust of federally funded materials was increasing.... "The first sign of impending trouble appeared in Lake City, a small market town in northern Florida (population 10,000), in the fall of 1970. Shortly after school opened in September, Reverend Don Glenn, a Baptist minister who had recently moved to Lake City visited his daughter's sixth-grade class." ... The school was under a court ordered integration plan. The teachers had chosen the materials because they felt they might help ease racial tensions.... Glenn claimed that the materials advocated sex education, evolution, a "hippie-yippee philosophy," pornography, gun control, and Communism. With support of a local radio station he broadcast four hour-long programs criticizing MACOS. This set off a growing series of attacks on MACOS over several years that led to a full

scale Congressional debate of MACOS in both houses in 1975. NSF launched
an internal review of its Education Directorate activities including an audit of
the fiscal management of the project at EDC [the Educational Development
Center, which produced MACOS]. While the audit revealed little to complain about, the damage in a sense was done. Dow quotes the former acting
assistant director for science education, Harvey Averch, "It was the worst political crisis in NSF history." (Dow, 1991, p. 229) (Lappan, 1997)

The upshot of the MACOS controversy was that until the appearance of the
National Council of Teachers of Mathematics (NCTM) *Curriculum and
Evaluation Standards for School Mathematics* (1989), there was negligible support for curriculum development at NSF. This story is important in two
ways. First, it establishes the context for the next period of crisis and response. Second, it documents the importance of politics, writ large, on the
processes of education. Those are part of the current context as well.

To continue the narrative, in the 1980s, the nation was responding to yet
another crisis, this one economic. The U.S. economy was faltering as the
Japanese and other Southeast Asian economies flourished. The most prom-
inent national report, commissioned by U.S. Secretary of Education T. H.
Bell in 1981, was *A Nation at Risk* (National Commission on Excellence in
Education, 1983). Here is how the report began:

> Our Nation is at risk. Our once unchallenged preeminence in commerce, in-
> dustry, science, and technological innovation is being overtaken by competi-
> tors throughout the world. This report is concerned with only one of the
> many causes and dimensions of the problem, but it is the one that undergirds
> American prosperity, security, and civility. We report to the American peo-
> ple that while we can take justifiable pride in what our schools and colleges
> have historically accomplished and contributed to the United States and the
> well-being of its people, the educational foundations of our society are pres-
> ently being eroded by a rising tide of mediocrity that threatens our very fu-
> ture as a Nation and a people. (National Commission on Excellence in
> Education, 1983, p. 1)

It was within this political and economic context that the NCTM, a professional organization of teachers, decided in the mid-1980s to produce and
recommend a set of (national) desiderata for mathematics curriculum and
evaluation. At the time, no such frameworks existed in the United States.
(In some countries, e.g., France and Japan, there is a national curriculum:
The subject matter content that students encounter is specified by the min-
istry of education. In the United States, there was [and is] no national curriculum and no national examinations in mathematics. Some of the 50 states
had frameworks for mathematics, but most did not. The nation contained
some 15,000 school districts, which had varied degrees of autonomy in selecting curricular goals and instructional materials. There were varied degrees of accountability to state frameworks and assessments. However,

there was a practical constraint: The de facto curriculum was the curriculum presented in commercially available texts, which were homogeneous.) Given the post-MACOS history at NSF described previously, there was no chance that NCTM's effort could be federally funded. NTCM invited some other organizations to participate and then put together a team of two dozen writers whose charge was to construct a vision of mathematics education for the nation.

The result, *Curriculum and Evaluation Standards for School Mathematics* (NCTM, 1989), known as the *Standards,* had profound impact on American education, catalyzing the "standards movement" in a wide range of disciplines. However, I take things one at a time. The *Standards* were written by NCTM for its members (mathematics teachers) and a somewhat broader constituency, those interested in mathematics education. They are not a research document: 258 pages of curriculum goals and examples are buttressed only by a page and a half of references, most of which are general. The language of cognitive science and the research-based warrants for the vision presented are not to be found in the *Standards.* However, they were very much in the mix as the *Standards* were crafted. The preceding two decades of mathematics education research shaped the *Standards* in profound ways. Gone was the simple-minded notion of mathematics as a hierarchically ordered discipline that students were to march through in straightforward ways, mastering the content at level n before moving on to level $n + 1$. In its stead was a much richer view of mathematics, one that was to prove controversial. That view, in the light of *A Nation at Risk* (National Commission on Excellence in Education, 1983) and national statistics on mathematics enrollments, was more democratically oriented—the goal was high-quality mathematics for all, not just the elite. Equally important, it reflected current research views that processes (such as reasoning, communication, and problem solving) and worldview (including disposition toward mathematics) were outcomes every bit as much to be desired as mastery of mathematical content. In a radical departure from past practices, the *Standards* identified the following as the first four standards for mathematics teaching and learning at every grade level:

- Mathematics as problem solving.
- Mathematics as communication.
- Mathematics as reasoning.
- Mathematical connections.

Within the context of these process goals came the delineation of specific content to be learned. Applications and problem solving were no longer seen as activities to be engaged in after the content was mastered; instead, they were seen as possible contexts for the learning of mathematics.

The *Standards* (NCTM, 1989) had far more impact than its authors had dared imagine. They exemplified the potential for consensus in important subject areas at a time of national crisis. Within short order, the standards movement was born: the NRC orchestrated the creation of the *National Science Education Standards* (ultimately published in 1995 by the National Research Council), and disciplines as diverse as history and English worked on standards of their own. This burgeoning sense of mathematical consensus, along with the recognition that the commercial sector was not likely to produce curricular materials consistent with the *Standards,* led the NSF to support mathematics curriculum development once again. The NSF issued requests for proposals (RFPs) for the development of curricula and assessments aligned with the *Standards*.

The RFPs went out in the early 1990s. NSF provided support for a small number of grants to develop innovative curricula aligned with the *Standards* (NCTM, 1989). Typically, funding was in the form of an n-year grant to produce n years of curriculum—for example, 5 years of curriculum in 5 years. (For a list of those curricula and links to their sites, go to the Mathematically Sane Web site, at <http://mathematicallysane.com/links/nsfprojects.asp>; for a detailed assessment of the curricula, see Senk & Thompson, 2003.) In effect, the curricula were finished in the late 1990s. Preliminary testing of those materials was done during the development and small-scale implementation of the final versions of the curricula. The results of large-scale testing of the curricula are just beginning to accumulate.

Figures on textbook adoptions are difficult to construct because of publishers' proprietary data, but those who are familiar with the textbook market estimate that *Standards* (NCTM, 1989) based curricula account for roughly 10% to 15% of current textbook adoptions. Overall, the evidence in favor of well-designed curricula aligned with the research-driven view embodied in the *Standards* is compelling. As I noted previously, most of the test results are preliminary. However, they are quite consistent.

Senk & Thompson (2003) provide the first comprehensive review of "reform" curricula in mathematics, with chapters describing evaluations of each of the major curricula and summary chapters providing across-the-board commentary. The results described have to be taken with a grain or two of salt, for many of the studies reported were conducted by the curriculum developers in "beta testing" environments rather than in regular field conditions. Nonetheless, many of the studies included comparisons with traditional curricula, and the pattern of findings is clear. Putnam (2003) summarized the results of the elementary curriculum evaluations as follows:

> Students in these new curricula generally perform as well as other students on traditional measures of mathematical achievement, including computa-

tional skill, and generally do better on formal and informal assessments of conceptual understanding and ability to use mathematics to solve problems. These chapters demonstrate that "reform-based" mathematics curricula can work. (p. 161)

Analogously, Chappell (2003) discusses the evaluations of three middle school reform curricula:

> Collectively, the evaluation results provide converging evidence that *Standards*-based curricula may positively affect middle-school students' mathematical achievement, both in conceptual and procedural understanding…. They reveal that the curricula can indeed push students beyond the "basics" to more in-depth problem-oriented mathematical thinking without jeopardizing their thinking in either area. (pp. 290–291)

The story is the same at the high school level, according to Swafford (2003):

> Taken as a group, these studies offer overwhelming evidence that the reform curricula can have a positive impact on high school mathematics achievement. It is not that students in these curricul[a] learn traditional content better but that they develop other skills and understandings while not falling behind on traditional content. (p. 468)

The trends reported here are clear and strong, but one must issue a methodological caveat. Many of the tests used in the studies reported were developed by the curriculum developers. Some standardization of testing for the broad range of content and processes now deemed appropriate as outcomes of mathematics instruction and adherence to rigorous methodological protocols must take place before such findings can be considered definitive. (See the discussion later in this chapter of the 2004 NRC report "On Evaluating Curricular Effectiveness: Judging the Quality of K–12 Mathematics Evaluations" (Confrey & Stohl, 2004) and the What Works Clearinghouse.)

An intensive series of studies in the city of Pittsburgh, Pennsylvania, indicates that when *Standards*-based curricula are implemented in consistent ways (i.e., where curriculum, assessment, and professional development are all aligned), the "performance gap" between Whites and underrepresented minorities can be narrowed. (See Briars, 2001; Briars & Resnick, 2000; Schoenfeld, 2002.) A series of comparison studies in Massachusetts, using the statewide assessment as the measure of performance, shows that fourth and eighth graders using reform texts "outperformed matched comparison groups who were using a range of textbooks commonly used in Massachusetts…. These performance gains … remained consistent for different groups of students, across mathematical topics and different types of questions on the state test (Riordan & Noyce, 2001, pp. 392–393). Also, in the largest study conducted to date, the ARC Center, an NSF-funded project, examined reform mathematics programs in elementary schools in Massachusetts, Illinois, and Washington state. The study included more than 100,000 students, comparing schools implementing *Standards*-based curricula with nonusing comparison schools carefully matched by reading level, socioeconomic status, and other variables:

> Results show that the average scores of students in the reform schools are significantly higher than the average scores of students in the matched comparison schools. These results hold across all racial and income subgroups. The results also hold across the different state-mandated tests, including the Iowa Test of Basic Skills, and across topics ranging from computation, measurement, and geometry to algebra, problem solving, and making connections. The study compared the scores on all the topics tested at all the grade levels tested (Grades 3–5) in each of the three states. Of 34 comparisons across five state-grade combinations, 28 favor the reform students, six show no statistically significant difference, and none favor the comparison students. (COMAP Center, October 2005)

I sum up the narrative at this point. If one views the preceding story through rose-colored glasses, there is reason to be happy. Fundamental research on the nature of mathematical thinking, teaching, and learning has had a profound and beneficial impact on mathematics instruction in the United States. The NCTM (1989) *Standards* bear the indelible stamp of that research. Somewhere between 10% and 15% of current textbook sales are of *Standards*-based curricula, and what reliable evidence there is suggests that these curricula represent a significant improvement over traditional curricula. In a rational world, the pathway would be clear.

However, this is not a rational world, and there is more than one reason to view the history (and the future) not through rose-colored glasses but through a lens darkly. These comments serve as an introduction to Part 2 of this chapter, in which I explore the hurdles and jumps of the educational steeplechase.

Note that the successful importation of research ideas into curriculum development and implementation described previously depended on at least one major historical accident. The NCTM (1989) *Standards* and their enormous impact are a historical anomaly; never before had a grass roots document had such a strong impact. As I noted previously, the *Standards* catalyzed the standards movement nationwide. For reasons I elaborated in Part 2 of this article, the creation of *Standards*-based curricula would not have been undertaken by commercial publishers; some sort of catalyst, such as NSF funding, was necessary for their creation. In the post-MACOS, pre-*Standards* world, NSF support for the development of a nationally distributed science or mathematics curriculum was unthinkable. A wonderful accident of timing—the fact that people perceived themselves as a nation at risk and that there appeared to be a consensus regarding new directions in mathematics instruction—allowed the NSF to decide to fund the curriculum development efforts, but this isn't all. It happens that the leaders of the *Standards* writing team were deeply conversant with major ideas from the research literature regarding the nature of mathematical competency.[2] Those ideas informed the vision statement that was the *Standards*. Had the writing team been differently constituted, the outcome might have been very different. Had NSF not supported *Standards*-based curricula, the impact of the research might be much much less.

It is also important to note that the current political context is changing significantly. It is not at all clear that the hard-won gains of 25 years, resulting in 10% to15% of the current textbook market, will withstand the current emphasis on high-stakes assessments that tend to have a rather strong skills orientation. Just as in the days of the MACOS controversies, education is still much more hostage to politics than it is to incremental improvement through research-based means.

PART 2: JUMPS AND HURDLES

In this section, I discuss a series of systemic obstacles to the effective linkage of research (R) and practice (P), which I shall delineate by R↔P. A much more expansive treatment of some aspects of this topic can be found in Burkhardt and Schoenfeld (2003).

By way of preface, I note that there is a substantial research–practice divide at this time. For the most part, researchers write for other researchers rather than for practitioners; and when they do write with practice in mind, it is rare that what is written can support robust practical implementation. A much more serious engineering enterprise needs to be put in place.

The difficulty is that educational research and development (R&D) lacks well-established mechanisms for taking ideas from laboratory scale to widely used practice. Much research in education is either in the humanities tradition or (more recently) in the tradition of the sciences. The main product of such research is insight. Much less of educational research is in the engineering tradition in which scholars (individually or collectively) take it on themselves the charge of converting insights into robust practical applications. The field lacks an "engineering infrastructure" and we lack the social infrastructure that would support it. There are numerous barriers to progress.

---

[2]I say "It happens" advisedly: In the history of NCTM, like that of many teachers' organizations, there has been significant distrust between the teaching and research communities. It was by no means a given that the authors of a practice-oriented volume would be familiar with state-of-the-art research, much less that they would be accepting of the epistemological shift it represented.

To begin, consider the task of taking insights from educational research and converting them into effective instruction. Just whose job is it? It's not the responsibility of the typical faculty member—indeed, at major research universities, faculty members are likely to lose credit for diverting themselves from research if they devote themselves to creating instructional materials or refining them in practice. There are some academic "development houses," for example, the Lawrence Hall of Science and TERC. However, the total number of people involved in the direct R↔P process is small (numbered in the hundreds) compared to the number of researchers (numbered in the tens of thousands). The balance works the other way in the communications and pharmaceutical industries. The incentive there is financial: Good products sell, and they bring in money. The R↔P infrastructure pays for itself.

One might think that the publishing industry would be on the lookout for good research ideas and be ready to capitalize on them. After all, it works that way in major R&D industries such as pharmaceuticals and consumer electronics. Why not education? The answers are simple: costs and standards for evaluation. The costs are obvious. Employing the engineering approach calls for multiple iterations of design, field testing, evaluation, and refinement. These are expensive both in terms of implementation—nothing like that is done on a large scale today—and in terms of time, for it delays going to market. Such procedures fly in the face of current instructional design. In mathematics, books are often sold as series. A series of elementary texts covers kindergarten through fifth or sixth grade, for example, or a middle school series covers Grades 6 through 8. No single author could produce such a series on a reasonable time frame. So, the work is farmed out: An editorial team creates design specs and cuts the work into small pieces, which are then produced by individuals and pieced together at the end. The process is efficient. But does it produce high quality materials?

The sad truth is that it doesn't matter that much whether the end product is really good—especially when most of the major text series look the same. The reason that quality doesn't really matter (in terms of student performance) is that there are no standards for the evaluation of instructional materials. If you want to buy a cell phone or a stereo system, you can look at *Consumer Reports* or a specialty magazine devoted to such issues. If a manufacturer markets a shoddy product, those magazines make it known in no uncertain terms—and the market responds. Or if a product represents a significant advance, the independent evaluators say so, and it makes a difference. But there is no educational analog. A recent report from the National Research Council (Confrey & Stohl, 2004) documents the lack of available data evaluating both reform and traditional curricula. The federally funded What Works Clearinghouse, or WWC, (see http://www.whatworks.ed.gov/) represents a well-structured attempt to comb the literature for such evidence. However, to date, fewer than a dozen studies of middle school mathematics (the first mathematics topic examined by WWC) have been found that meet WWC's very rigorous statistical criteria. Moreover, the findings of some of those studies have been challenged with regard to the inferences that can be drawn from them. (See Schoenfeld, in press, for detail.)

In sum, there are not yet available reports that say how well students will do on various tests of skills, concepts, and problem solving if they use this instructional program rather than that one. In the absence of meaningful evaluative mechanisms, why should publishers invest in a costly development process? Slick advertising or new surface features are much more likely to bring in customers.

As suggested above, the academic value system works against development. Because insight tends to be valued more than engineering, faculty are more likely to devote their attention to exploring novel ideas than to mining good ideas for what they are worth in practice. Good curricular engineering demands replication and refinement. Typical design questions are: Under what conditions do these materials work? and, What kinds of support structures are needed in what contexts? Answering such questions is very time-consuming. While such efforts do result in improved instructional materials, they are rarely seen as more than drone-like research (if they count as research at all). For their own good, researchers may shy away from such activities. Because what they produce is typically not seen as a contribution to knowledge, good designers may not be tenurable in universities. Answering such questions also calls for teams. The current reward structure, in the social sciences, at least (medicine, engineering, and "big science" are different!) undervalues team efforts. Being the third or fourth author on a paper doesn't count for very much; researchers would be better off, career-wise, going solo.

In short: building teams is difficult, and teams tend to be ephemeral (i.e., supportable by soft money only) in academia. There are no significant commercial incentives for investing in research ideas and refining them carefully. And the reward system tends to undermine both collaboration and personal investment in activities that are not seen as "creative." (A brief fiscal coda here: the serious engineering approach, which calls for large teams that are relatively stable over time, costs a substantial amount of money. As I have noted elsewhere (Schoenfeld, 1999), the pharmaceutical and communications industries spend on the order of 10-20% of their income on R&D. The relative investment in education is laughable. In 1998 the U. S. House Committee on Science wrote: "currently, the U.S. spends approximately $300 billion a year on education and less than $30 million, 0.01 percent of the overall education budget, on education research.... This minuscule investment suggests a feeble long-term commitment to improving our educational system" [p. 46]. Of course, investments in medical R&D were negligible a century ago as were investments in web-based applications a few decades ago. Research success breeds funding, so there's hope if the field gets its act together—but there is a long way to go.)

A second set of issues one must confront concerns the current state of theory and the need to develop a reasonably stable theoretical base for applications. (See Burkhardt & Schoenfeld, 2003, for more detail.) It is sad to say, but the theoretical state of the field (in all of the social sciences, not just education and psychology) and the current state of theoretical disputation seriously undermine the R↔P process. There is a tendency in the field toward grand (and almost always undersubstantiated) theories and claims for them. This happens consistently at the "big theory" level: The behaviorists, constructivists, cognitive scientists, and sociocultural theorists all claim to explain everything. A little theoretical humility goes a long way—and it's honest besides. One thing the research community has to understand it that such disputations, which are highly public (see, e.g., Anderson, Reder, & Simon, 1996), harm the field; if outsiders don't see the field as having reached consensus, how can they trust statements about "what works"? In fields such as physics, there is also disputation—but it's kept below the radar screen, so when physicists go to congress for funding, they speak in harmony if not with one voice. "Let a thousand voices bloom" is not smart funding policy, nor is it smart intellectually. The fact is that most of the big theories have "applicability conditions": They only apply some of the time, and the trick is to figure out when. Although some version of constructivism is undoubtedly true—humans do not perceive reality directly (otherwise we would not be susceptible to optical illusions), and hence we interpret what we see—that statement is too vague and general to be of practical help in instructional contexts. Even if one is a dyed-in-the-wool constructivist, one must remember that in some cases, for example, the mastery of rote skills, behaviorism does a darned good job of saying how much practice will yield mastery. The serious job of theory refinement is to say how well a theory works in which contexts. (Even Newton's laws of gravity, which apply just fine at a human scale, fail at subatomic and galactic scales.) The serious job of materials development is to find out how well a particular set of materials work in specific kinds of instructional contexts. Global statements regarding particular instructional treatments should be seen as advertising, not as research-based claims.

The preceding arguments, although aimed at big theories, also apply to the work of individuals. It takes a great deal of work to nail down the domain of application of an idea. For obvious reasons in terms of the reward structure, most papers are concerned with staking out theoretical territory rather than cleaning up that territory. Thus, many studies identify a phenomenon and document how it works in some context; it is then suggested that the phenomenon is general, but the follow-up work is not done. The result is that the knowledge base is not solid enough to support the practical development of instructional materials. Part of the problem here is a lack of standardization: so many studies use "home-grown" measures that it is often difficult to compare and contrast different studies. Authors of research papers rarely describe the methods employed (or the constructs investigated!) with sufficient precision that others could use the same techniques. Hence the task of replication, a scientific necessity, is not only unfashionable and given little credit, it is much more difficult than it ought to be.

I now turn to the outside world—first schools and then politics—to identify additional factors that complexify the work of educational researchers. A third major factor that makes the R↔P process so difficult is that the lives of teachers allow them little time or opportunity to engage with systematic research-based improvement (or, for that matter, any substantial form of professional development) in meaningful ways. It is known that one standard model of influencing practice in which researchers or others write papers, and teachers are supposed to read and implement them, doesn't work very well. Typically researchers write papers for each other in language at best partly accessible to nonspecialist audiences, but even when groups write specifically for teachers, the effects are usually minimal. The conditions of meaningful implementation are far too subtle to be conveyed by a simple text. (You might find it interesting to read a "how to" manual written by someone who has won Formula 500 automobile races. Yet would you feel qualified to enter a race?) Moreover, this model presumes that teachers have the time to read, reflect on what they read, and adapt what they understand to practice. The reality—the contexts of professionalism—are otherwise.

Lortie (1975) described the "egg crate" character of much teaching in the United States—the idea being that teachers are isolated from each other, with each in a somewhat insulated container apart from his or her colleagues. Lortie's description, written a quarter century ago, still rings true. As an illustration, I tell one story of many that I might tell about my experiences in a local school district. Just before the end of the 2002 school year, the district decided to discontinue its practice of tracking students in middle school mathematics. To meet the (recently imposed) California Mathematics Standards, it also decided to have all eighth-grade students enroll in algebra. The goal of insuring that all eighth graders will meet state standards is laudable. The decision to end tracking did, however, disrupt the fabric of instruction: A large number of students finishing seventh grade had been enrolled in middle school mathematics, a course taken by those who had been deemed "not ready for prealgebra." These students would be enrolled in algebra in Fall 2002 without having studied prealgebra. On reflection, the district decided to create a new course for these eighth graders called Algebra 1A. The course would cover one semester of algebra in a year, filling in prealgebraic knowledge where necessary. If this plan succeeded, the students would end the year a semester behind those on a regular schedule as opposed to a year behind.

This is a noble experiment, undertaken in good faith by the district's teachers. It overlapped with the professional development efforts by the Diversity in Mathematics Education (DiME) project, because a very large proportion of the students at risk mathematically are members of underrepresented minority groups. Hence DiME thought it would fit with our agenda; we planned to address the Algebra 1A course in our meetings. Instead, discussions of the Algebra 1A course became our agenda for the first few meetings. The reason is simple. At each of the middle schools in the district, teachers were struggling to make the course work. Prerequisite skills were a problem, getting collaborative groups to work was a problem, pacing was a problem, discipline was a problem, and so on. When the DiME group, which is district wide, had its first meeting, none of the teachers had had the opportunity to talk with teachers from any of the other schools about the challenges they faced and the solutions they tried. Given that opportunity, they were going to take advantage of it.

The point is that teachers in our district—which is a good district—had no time in their ordinary professional lives for even the most basic communication with each other regarding pressing professional matters. They lack access to "teacher friendly" distillations of research or other mechanisms that can help them come to grips with findings from research, and they face increased accountability pressures from high-stakes testing mandates. In such a context, it is unreasonable to expect teachers to take advantage of advances in the knowledge base, which come from a universe that is (at least) one step removed from their everyday realities.

Finally, there are issues of politics—exacerbated by the fact that just about anyone, having gone through the schools, feels competent to say what should be happening in them. Can you imagine an elected medical board having control over what took place in local hospitals? Yet that is what local school boards do. Some are progressive, some are neutral in their effects, and some ... downright pathological. I spare you the horror stories, but they are easy to come by.[3]

Alas, politics at the state and national levels are not necessarily any better. California, for example, is undertaking a return to the traditional curriculum. In the name of high standards, the traditional curriculum has been condensed so that algebra is now mandated in eighth grade. The content of the mandated curriculum (as prescribed in the California Mathematics Standards) is much what it was when I went to school. The new

---

[3]The MACOS story started locally and then went national. It is a paradigmatic example of educational pathology.

textbooks aligned with the California Standards—the only ones whose purchase the state supports fiscally—are as devoid of the process side of mathematics (problem solving, reasoning, connections, communication) as were the textbooks I studied from. History will repeat itself if one allows it to—and the historical data I cited previously (significant attrition rates in mathematics, especially for poor children and minorities) suggest that California's students will be facing hard times. Indeed, things may be worse this time around due to newly imposed high-stakes testing. The consequences of not passing the tests will be retention in grade or, in the case of high school, not being granted a diploma. I examine what the literature says about these issues and about the impact of high-stakes tests in general.

First, consider retention. A summary of the literature may be found in Dawson (1998). The survey indicates that there may be some short-term benefits of being held in grade for some students. However, it is difficult to predict which students will profit from retention. Moreover, the benefits seem to vanish with time. The long-term impact of retention is much more clear:

> No researcher has found long-term, substantial benefits to the practice of retention. No study has shown that students who are retained do better in high school or after high school than students who are not retained on any measure, even when controlling for important factors such as school achievement, ability, demographic variables, etc. Studies looking at the relationship between retention and school dropout have consistently demonstrated that students who are retained are far more likely to drop out of school prior to graduation than students who are not retained. (Dawson, 1998, p. 3)

If anything, the presence of high school exit examinations is likely to increase dropout rates. Why should a student who sees himself or herself as having little chance of passing the exam stay in school? Second, consider high-stakes tests. Someone who reads the previous paragraph might simply say that the author has "low standards"—after all, shouldn't a student learn substantive content to graduate from high school? That raises the question of whether high-stakes tests maintain high standards as their advocates assert.

Amrein and Berliner (2002) provide the most comprehensive evidence to date regarding the impact of high-stakes tests. Amrein and Berliner examined data from 18 states that have high-stakes tests and looked for their impact by examining student performance on four commonly used standardized tests (ACT, SAT, NAEP [National Assessment of Educational Progress], and AP [advanced placement] tests) that overlapped in content with the state tests. Amrein and Berliner's (2002) criterion: "If scores on the transfer measures went up as a function of a state's imposition of a high-stakes test we considered that evidence of student learning in the domain and support for the belief that the state's high-stakes testing policy was promoting transfer, as intended" (p. 1). Amrein and Berliner's (2002) findings were the following:

> In all but one analysis, student learning is indeterminate, remains at the same level it was before the policy was implemented, or actually goes down when high-stakes testing policies are instituted.... At the present time, there is no compelling evidence from a set of states with high-stakes testing policies that those policies result in transfer to the broader domains of knowledge and skill for which high-stakes test scores must be indicators. Because of this, the high-stakes tests being used today do not, as a general rule, appear valid as indicators of genuine learning, of the types of learning that approach the American ideal of what an educated person knows and can do. (Amrein & Berliner, 2002, p. 1)

These two examples (the wide-scale implementation of retention in grade and high-stakes testing) are emblematic of the relationship between educational research and high-visibility politics. To put things simply, in today's climate, political rhetoric trumps educational research, independent of the merits of the rhetoric.

Is this cause for despair? I don't think so. Is it cause for a call to arms? In my opinion, yes. However, the solution is not to shout "listen to us!" more loudly than at present—that is not likely to do much good. Rather, researchers need to address the fundamental problems identified in this chapter:

- We need to decrease the distance between research and practice and between researchers and practitioners—we need to build an engineering infrastructure for educational R↔P.

Suggestions for how to deal with this issue are discussed at some length in Burkhardt and Schoenfeld (2003). There Burkhardt and Schoenfeld argue that it is possible to define a rigorous chain of experimental work that proceeds from small-scale research and design through large-scale curricular implementation, and they give an example of how one might proceed in that direction.

- We need to work toward enabling conditions that support greater professionalism for teachers.

This is partly a matter of public relations; the public is not knowledgeable about either what it means to understand certain subject matter deeply or about what it takes to teach effectively. It is also a matter for negotiation when university researchers arrange partnerships with collaborating school districts. One condition for entering into such partnerships can be that the district provide teachers opportunities to learn as a part of their professional development. Another, which would make it worth the district's while to collaborate, is that the researchers agree to focus on issues that are of central importance to the district.

- We need to work toward creating contexts within universities that support the creation and stability of large research teams that can grapple with mid-level theoretical and pragmatic issues.

The success of these attempts will depend on changes in the value and reward systems. Currently, major universities reward published papers but devalue theoretically driven instructional design and the empirical work that fine tunes it—even though such work can be as creative and intellectually demanding as the production of research.

- We need to do better at theory refinement and to stop counterproductive theoretical disputations—"my theory's better than your theory" arguments do nobody any good.

This too is a matter of community values. At present, academia is largely an individualistic, entrepreneurial enterprise; theoretical disputes are often rewarded by increased visibility. There can and should be a wider range of activities that merit respect and rewards within academia. See Burkhardt and Schoenfeld (2003) for details.

- We need to be smarter about communicating the results of educational research and the consequences of ignoring it.

I see these as essential and doable tasks. If we set our minds to them and produce results along the way, we can (a) shorten the 25-year time scale that characterized the positive example given in Part 1 of this chapter, and (b) increase the credibility of educational research and the funding it attracts. Nothing breeds success like success.

REFERENCES

Amrein, A. L., & Berliner, D. C. (2002, March 28). High-stakes testing, uncertainty, and student learning. *Education Policy Analysis Archives, 10*(18). Retrieved March 7, 2003, from http://epaa.asu.edu/epaa/v10n18/

Anderson, J. R., Reder, L. M., & Simon, H. A. (1996). Situated learning and education. *Educational Researcher, 25*(6), 5–11.

Bloom, B. S. (1956). *Taxonomy of educational objectives. Handbook I: Cognitive domain. Handbook II: Affective domain.* New York: McKay.

Briars, D. (2001, March). *Mathematics performance in the Pittsburgh public schools.* Paper presented at a Mathematics Assessment Resource Service conference on Tools for Systemic Improvement, San Diego, CA.

Briars, D., & Resnick, L. (2000). *Standards, assessments—And what else? The essential elements of standards-based school improvement.* Unpublished manuscript.

Brown, A. (1987). Metacognition, executive control, self-regulation, and other more mysterious mechanisms. In F. Reiner & R. Kluwe (Eds.), *Metacognition, motivation, and understanding* (pp. 65–116). Hillsdale, NJ: Lawrence Erlbaum Associates.

Burkhardt, H., & Schoenfeld, A. (2003). *Improving educational research: Toward a more useful, more influential, and better funded enterprise.* Manuscript submitted for publication.

Chappell, M. (2003). Keeping mathematics front and center: Reaction to middle grades curriculum projects' research. In S. Senk & D. Thompson (Eds.), *Standards-oriented school mathematics curricula: What does the research say about student outcomes?* (pp. 285–296). Mahwah, NJ: Lawrence Erlbaum Associates.

Charles, R., & Silver, E. A. (Eds.). (1989). *The teaching and assessing of mathematical problem solving.* Hillsdale, NJ: Lawrence Erlbaum Associates.

COMAP Center (The Consortium for Mathematics and Its Applications). (2005). A report of the tri-state student achievement study was retrieved October 7, 2005 from http://www.comap.com/elementary/projects/arc/tri-state%20achievement.htm

Confrey, J., & Stohl, V. (Eds.). (Committee for a Review of the Evaluation Data on the Effectiveness of NSF-Supported and Commercially Generated Mathematics Curriculum Materials, National Research Council. (2004). *On evaluating curricular effectiveness: Judging the quality of K–12 mathematics evaluations.* Washington, DC: National Academy Press.

Dawson, P. (1998). A primer on student grade retention: What the research says. *National Association of School Psychologists Communiqué* [online]. Retrieved October 31, 2005, from http://www.nasponline.org/publications/cq268retain.html

de Corte, E., Verschaffel, L., & Greer, B. (1996). Mathematics teaching and learning. In D. Berliner & R. Calfee (Eds.), *Handbook of educational psychology* (pp. 491–549). New York: Macmillan.

Flavell, J. (1976). Metacognitive aspects of problem solving. In L. Resnick (Ed.), *The nature of intelligence* (pp. 231–236). Hillsdale, NJ: Lawrence Erlbaum Associates.

Gardner, H. (1985). The mind's new science: A history of the cognitive revolution. New York: Basic Books.

Greeno, J. G., Collins, A. M., & Resnick, L. B. (1996). Cognition and learning in D. C. Berliner & R. C. Calfee (Eds.) *Handbook of educational psychology* (pp.15–46). New York: Simon & Schuster.

Greeno, J. G., Pearson, P. D., & Schoenfeld, A. H. (1997). Implications for the National Assessment of Educational Progress of Research on Learning and Cognition. In *Assessment in transition: Monitoring the nation's educational progress, background studies* (pp. 152–215). Stanford, CA: National Academy of Education.

House Committee on Science. (1998). *Unlocking our future: Toward a new national science policy. A report to Congress by the House Committee on Science.* Washington, DC: Author.

Kilpatrick, J. (1985). A retrospective account of the past twenty-five years of research on teaching mathematical problem solving. In E. A. Silver (Ed.), *Teaching and learning mathematical problem solving: Multiple research perspectives* (pp. 1–16). Hillsdale, NJ: Lawrence Erlbaum Associates.

Kilpatrick, J. (1992). A history of research in mathematics education. In D. Grouws (Ed.), *Handbook for research on mathematics teaching and learning* (pp. 3–38). New York: Macmillan.

Koehler, M. S., & Grouws, D. (1992). Mathematics teaching practices and their effects. In D. Grouws (Ed.), *Handbook of research on mathematics teaching and learning* (pp. 115–126). New York: Macmillan.

Lampert, M. (1990). When the problem is not the problem and the solution is not the answer: Mathematical knowing and teaching. *American Educational Research Journal, 17,* 29–64.

Lappan, G. (1997). Lessons from the sputnik era in mathematics education. Paper presented at a symposium at the National Academy of Sciences, Reflecting on sputnik: Linking the past, present, and future of educational reform. Retrieved March 12, 2003, from http://www.nas.edu/sputnik/papers.htm

Lester, F.. (1985). Methodological considerations in research on mathematical problem-solving instruction. In E. A. Silver (Ed.), *Teaching and learning mathematical problem solving: Multiple research perspectives* (pp. 41–69). Hillsdale, NJ: Lawrence Erlbaum Associates.

Lester, F. (1994). Musings about mathematical problem-solving research: 1970–1994. *Journal for Research in Mathematics Education, 25,* 660–675.

Lortie, D. (1975). *Schoolteacher: A sociological study.* Chicago: University of Chicago Press.

Madison, B. L., & Hart, T. A. (1990). *A challenge of numbers: People in the mathematical sciences.* Washington, DC: National Academy Press.

Mathematically Sane. (2005). http://www.mathematicallysane.com/home.asp. A list of the curriculum projects funded by the National Science Foundation was retrieved October 7, 2005, from http://www.mathematicallysane.com/links/nsfprojects.asp

National Commission on Excellence in Education. (1983). *A nation at risk: The imperative for educational reform.* Washington, DC: U.S. Government Printing Office.

National Council of Teachers of Mathematics. (1989). *Curriculum and evaluation standards for school mathematics.* Reston, VA: Author.

National Research Council. (1989). *Everybody counts: A report to the nation on the future of mathematics education.* Washington, DC: National Academy Press.

National Research Council. (1995). *National science education standards.* Washington, DC: National Academy Press.

Neisser, U. (1967). *Cognitive psychology.* Englewood Cliffs, NJ: Prentice Hall.

Pólya, G. (1945). *How to solve it.* Princeton, NJ: Princeton University Press.

Putnam, R. (2003). Commentary on four elementary mathematics curricula. In S. Senk & D. Thompson (Eds.), *Standards-oriented school mathematics curricula: What does the research say about student outcomes?* (pp. 161–178). Mahwah, NJ: Lawrence Erlbaum Associates.

Riordan, J., & Noyce, P. (2001). The impact of two standards-based mathematics curricula on student achievement in Massachusetts. *Journal for Research in Mathematics Education, 32,* 368–398.

Schoenfeld, A. H. (1985). *Mathematical problem solving.* Orlando, FL: Academic.

Schoenfeld, A. H. (1999). Looking toward the 21st century: Challenges of educational theory and practice. *Educational Researcher, 28*(7), 4–14.

Schoenfeld, A. H. (2002). Making mathematics work for all children: Issues of standards, testing, and equity. *Educational Researcher, 31*(1), 3–15.

Schoenfeld, A. H. (in press). What doesn't work: The challenge and failure of the What Works Clearinghouse to conduct meaningful reviews of studies of mathematics curricula. *Educational Researcher.*

Senk, S., & Thompson, D. (Eds.). (2003). *Standards-oriented school mathematics curricula: What does the research say about student outcomes?* Mahwah, NJ: Lawrence Erlbaum Associates.

Shaughnessy, M. (1985). Problem-solving derailers: The influence of misconceptions on problem-solving performance. In E. A. Silver (Ed.), *Teaching and learning mathematical problem solving: Multiple research perspectives* (pp. 399–415). Hillsdale, NJ: Lawrence Erlbaum Associates.

Silver, E. A. (1985). Research on teaching mathematical problem solving: Some underrepresented themes and needed directions. In E. A. Silver (Ed.), *Teaching and learning mathematical problem solving: Multiple research perspectives* (pp. 247–266). Hillsdale, NJ: Lawrence Erlbaum Associates.

Silver, E. A. (1987). Foundations of cognitive theory and research for mathematics problem-solving. In A. Schoenfeld (Ed.), *Cognitive science and mathematics education* (pp. 33–60). Hillsdale, NJ: Lawrence Erlbaum Associates.

Swafford, J. (2003). Reaction to high school curriculum projects' research. In S. Senk & D. Thompson (Eds.), *Standards-oriented school mathematics curricula: What does the research say about student outcomes?* (pp. 457–468). Mahwah, NJ: Lawrence Erlbaum Associates.

What Works Clearinghouse. (2005). A description of What Works project and a series of mathematics study and topic reports. Retrieved October 7, 2005, from http://www.whatworks.ed.gov/

The Application of Theory to the Design of Innovative Texts Supporting Science Instruction

Shirley J. Magnusson
California Polytechnic State University

Annemarie Sullivan Palincsar
University of Michigan

The curriculum reform of the 1960s brought a new emphasis on learning science by doing science in ways that reflect the actual practice of science. One particularly unfortunate turn of events in this reform movement was the separation of the process of doing science from the ideas driving those processes (Fensham, 1992). Hence, teachers often assumed that the physical activity of investigation—so-called hands-on science instruction—was sufficient for learning science at this level. Moreover, this view became aligned with the assumption that children can independently discover principles and laws of science from simple exploration of the physical world.

This view, which still dominates elementary science instruction today, is far narrower than what theory and research suggest is necessary for learning science. Drawing on four different perspectives—philosophy of science, cognitive psychology, curriculum theory, and sociocultural theory—in this chapter, we describe the design of a novel, text-based tool for supporting the development of scientific knowledge and reasoning in inquiry-based science instruction. These are the perspectives that have guided the development of a particular orientation to teaching science known as Guided In-

31

quiry supporting Multiple Literacies.[1] GIsML instruction assumes that learning science via inquiry involves the interplay of firsthand and second-hand investigations (Magnusson & Palincsar, 1995). Firsthand investigations involve direct exploration of the physical world, and secondhand investigations involve exploration of what others have done and learned in exploring the physical world in a firsthand way. Secondhand investigations are typically text based and, in the research and development that has occurred relative to the GIsML orientation, are centered around the use of a novel and innovative form of expository text that includes features that are common to the notebooks of actual scientists (Palincsar & Magnusson, 2001). In this chapter, we describe the key ideas drawn from each theoretical/philosophical perspective that informs the design of notebook texts used in secondhand investigations. Furthermore, we link these principles to the design features of notebook texts, which we illustrate with excerpts from notebook texts.

THEORETICAL/PHILOSOPHICAL PERSPECTIVES

Philosophy of Science

Traditional perspectives regarding the work of scientists depict the development of scientific knowledge as a matter of diligence and skill on the part of scientists who know where and how to uncover the secrets of nature. Contemporary views, however, represent knowledge production as a process of invention in which the scientific community ultimately determines what is "discovered." This perspective can be thought of as a cultural view. That is, the activity (thought and action) of scientists is informed by values and beliefs that dictate what is of sufficient interest to the community that merits further study. Furthermore, this activity is guided by norms and conventions regarding how investigations are to be conducted, how knowledge claims will be generated from those investigations, and the evaluation procedures by which knowledge claims will be accepted by the community. Thus, scientific practice in this view is thought and activity patterned in particular ways through the social processes of a community drawn together by shared values and beliefs, experienced both interpersonally and through public artifacts shared by community members.

A philosopher of science whose work is particularly helpful in characterizing contemporary views of science is Pera (1994). Pera casts science as a game with three players: scientists investigating nature, nature, and the community of scientists that debates with the first according to the features

---

[1]For information about the program of research regarding this orientation, see http://www.umich.edu/~gisml/new/

of scientific dialectics.[2] In this dialectical model, nature responds to a "cross-examination" and scientific knowledge represents the community's agreement on nature's correct answer. Science in the dialectical model links rationality "not to certain *properties of theories* fixed by rules, but to the *quality of the arguments* which support the theories ... objects and facts are constructions, not carbon copies, images, or icons of reality" (Pera, 1994, p. 144).[3] It is in this sense that scientific practice invents rather than discovers nature. The community context in contemporary views also means that "data are theory-laden, that there is no logic of discovery leading from data to cognitive claims, that there is no clear distinction between observational and theoretical concepts, that theories cannot be reduced to their empirical basis, that they are underdetermined by it, and finally that there is no universal method" (Pera, 1994, p. 132).

This view of science suggests that the discovery learning assumptions of "hands-on" instruction are problematic. If students are to learn through investigation in which they genuinely explore physical phenomena—guided by their own inclinations and powers of reasoning—concepts of science are only likely to emerge if the students' work is guided by the values, beliefs, norms, and conventions that guide scientific knowledge production. Several national standards documents reflect this perspective. For example, the American Association for the Advancement of Science (1989, 1993) includes a section on the "habits of mind" to be cultivated in the course of science instruction, and the National Research Council (1996) proposes unifying concepts and processes that are integral to teaching science as inquiry. However, it is not necessarily recognized that such outcomes are more accurately thought of as emerging from an enculturation process in which dispositions to think and act in particular ways are pressed for and reinforced. Conversation plays a critical role in such a process, leading one to conceptualize instruction as providing students with opportunities to "try on" scientific activity and discourse and support them, over time, in developing facility with such activity and discourse (cf. Gee, 1996; Latour, 1987; Lemke, 1990). Moreover, because the activity and discourse that students experience in the course of scientific inquiry are distinctly different from everyday activity and conversation and from routine classroom work (Cobb & Yackel, 1996; Driver, Asoko, Leach, Mortimer, & Scott, 1994), students need guidance and support as they learn to think and act in different ways.

---

[2]As in the language peculiar to an occupational group as well as "a method of argument or exposition that systematically weighs contradictory facts or ideas with a view to the resolution of their real or apparent contradictions" (Muns, 1976). Pera (1994) defines rhetoric as the "*practice* of persuasive argumentation," whereas dialectics refers to "the *logic* of such a practice or act" (p. viii).

[3]Note the similarity of this statement to the radical constructivist position articulated by von Glasersfeld (1989): whether or not there is an objective reality, we cannot come to know it; we can only know our construction of it.

Curriculum Theory

Contemporary views of science began to emerge during the middle of the last century and influenced curriculum development efforts of the 1960s (Fensham, 1992). In particular, Schwab (1962), a biologist turned curriculum theorist, identified the need for the public to have a different view of science from the rhetoric of conclusions that he thought characterized most science teaching. Schwab (1962) was particularly troubled that "the current and temporary constructions of scientific knowledge are conveyed as empirical, literal, and irrevocable truths" (p. 24). Schwab (1962) advocated for a representation of science as a product of fluid enquiry: "a mode of investigation which rests on conceptual innovation, proceeds through uncertainty and failure, and eventuates in knowledge which is contingent, dubitable, and hard to come by" (p. 5). Schwab represented this view of learning science as "enquiry into enquiry," which would produce quite different understandings. In Schwab's words:

> If ... the curriculum illustrates with care and clarity the role of idealizations and conceptions in the construct of scientific knowledge and exhibits the growth of knowledge which takes place through the replacement of one body of conceptions by others, the student would see the ground for change and revision, and for the deviations of common-sense objects from the ideal objects of science.
>
> [The student] would see, too, that the authority consists, not in possession of information, but in possession of competence in enquiry. Change in what authority says would no longer appear as a sign of confusion or mere change in fashion but as a sign of the progress of enquiry. The student could understand that to be true does not necessarily mean to be fixed and eternal; that what is said in one set of terms may give way to something else, not because the first was false or has become unfashionable but because it was limited. [The student] could understand that a new formulation may arise and be more desirable because it encompasses more, in more intimate interconnection, than did its predecessors. (p. 48)

Thus, instead of the nonproblematic nature of investigation that seems to be suggested by hands-on instruction in the elementary school, Schwab (1962) argued for investigative contexts that provide opportunities for students to understand the uncertainties and difficulties associated with knowledge production and, in particular, "to provide a tangible experience of some of the problems dealt with and of the difficulty of acquiring data" (p. 53). Schwab (1962) advocated for contexts that feature "phenomena which give rise to problems, the circumstances surrounding the acquisition of data for solving these problems, and the difficulties of working with and among these circumstances" (p. 54), pointing out that such a context no longer tells the student "what to do and what to expect" (p. 55).

In addition, Schwab (1962) argued that teachers need to make explicit the alternative answers arrived at by students and to set them in juxtaposition, asking questions that help students learn "that there is room for alternative interpretations of data; that many questions have no 'right' answer but only *most probable* [italics added] answers or *more and less defensible* [italics added] answers; that the aim of criticism and defense of alternative answers is not to 'win the argument' but to find the most defensible solution to the problem" (p. 70).

Schwab (1962) also specifically wrote about the use of text in inquiry-based instruction. Schwab advocated for the use of actual scientific papers, citing the employment of such materials in science courses for entering undergraduates at several universities and with 10th- through 12th-grade students. However, recognizing that original papers may not be appropriate for a variety of reasons, Schwab (1962) also discussed the employment of "translated" versions of original papers in which "simpler words and explanatory phrases can replace the more difficult items ... and ... they can be recast in a contemporary idiom readily accessible to the student" (p. 81). In further discussion of the use of text, Schwab presented additional ideas for thinking about the meaningful use of "traditional" text in conjunction with original papers. In cases in which the content of original papers required background knowledge that may not be present for students, Schwab suggested the use of brief, traditional text to introduce the student to the area of inquiry and specific technical terms used by scientists in the papers. In other cases, Schwab imagined a single paper or set of papers in the role of introducing students to the "first" problems and solutions in a field. Such papers would provide specific detail about the inquiries of scientists whose work had been foundational to a field of study.

Schwab's (1962) intent in describing the use of original papers or versions of them translated for specific student use was to advocate for students having access to examples of actual inquiry. As Schwab (1962) puts it

> Each individual paper poses the problem of discovering its basic parts (problem, data, interpretation, and so on). Each poses the further problem of discerning the relationship among these parts: why the data sought were the appropriate data for the problem; why the data actually acquired depart from the data sought; what principles justify the interpretation of the data.
>
> The individual paper poses problems of evaluation, as well. Are the actual data as appropriate as the reporting scientist considers them to be? What additional assumptions, beyond those noted by the author, are involved in his interpretation? (pp. 73–74)

These views suggest a much more complex perspective of the content of science instruction. Instead of immutable truths, students are to understand that scientific knowledge is the product of the interpretation of selected facts that are dependent upon the principles employed in the inquiry, which themselves are tested in the process of inquiring (see Schwab, 1962, p. 14). Thus, the products of science must be understood as contingent upon the nature of the context in which they arose.

Cognitive Psychology

Cognitive psychology has contributed significantly to our understanding of individual processes of learning. Central principles of human learning, distilled from decades of research informed by cognitive theories, include the importance of prior knowledge, the role of metacognition, and the development of rich conceptual frameworks as the mark of expert knowledge (Bransford, Brown, & Cocking, 1999). For the purposes of this chapter, we focus on the ways in which these ideas have similar application in learning science via inquiry or comprehending informational text.

In both text comprehension (cf. Chan, Burtis, Scardamalia, & Bereiter, 1992; and Chi, de Leeuw, Chiu, & LaVancher, 1994; Goldman, Saul & Coté, 1995) and science inquiry learning (Clement, 1993; Magnusson & Palincsar, 1995; Schwab, 1962), children construct meaning by integrating new information with prior knowledge and by building representations or mental models of the referential situation. In both text comprehension and science learning, the capacity to build these mental models is assisted by the learner's awareness and use of both general discourse structures and domain-specific knowledge structures. Comprehension is enhanced to the extent that the reader is aware of and makes use of text genre and structure (Goldman & Rakestraw, 2000; Richgels, McGee, Lomax, & Sheard, 1987). Inquiry-based activity similarly engages participants in learning the structure of discourse that best communicates a scientific argument (cf. Kuhn, 1993; Lemke, 1990; van Zee, 1997).

Finally, skilled comprehenders engage in metacognitive activity to the extent that they maintain an awareness of the success with which they are constructing meaning, and have a repertoire of strategies to enlist if they encounter impediments to their understanding. Inquiry requires a similar disposition on the part of the learner: a mindfulness about the purpose of the inquiry, attentiveness to the relationship between the question that is guiding the inquiry and the investigation itself, and the ability to monitor the progress of the inquiry in terms of how well it is advancing one's understanding of the phenomenon under investigation.

These similarities suggest that the use of text in inquiry-based science instruction can support—rather than undermine—the type of thinking necessary for scientific inquiry. A critical issue, however, is that the text not undermine students' own authority for developing scientific knowledge from firsthand investigation. Moreover, there must be a reason to read about the ideas in the text, and students need support in making meaning of the ideas in relation their own prior knowledge and experience.

Sociocultural Theory

From a sociocultural perspective, learning is viewed as the transformation of participation (physical and intellectual) within a community (Lave, 1991; Rogoff, 1994). As Brown, Collins, and Duguid (1989) state, "situations might be said to *co-produce* [italics added] knowledge through activity" (p. 32), which means that knowledge is developed as a function of our thoughts and actions in particular contexts and that the nature of those contexts—that is, the community in which they are embedded—is instrumental to the nature of the knowledge that is produced. Schools are communities, and so are classrooms. The institution of school supplies a community context for learning but does not ensure a community focused on academic learning or a community that holds shared views about the knowledge construction process. In a traditional classroom, the bulk of activity consists of students being assigned, completing, and getting feedback relative to "academic tasks" (Doyle, 1986). The issue pertinent to this chapter is that such activity does not resemble the practice of any of the communities whose products are typically the targeted understandings of schooling. Thus, despite the community basis of schools, the nature of traditional learning environments does not provide the sort of intellectual context that can maximally support academic learning in particular disciplines. The development of learning environments more conducive to specific subject matter learning, such as science, requires different actions and tools.

One idea that we believe is key to creating a different environment is conceptualizing learning relative to the zone of proximal development (ZPD). This concept was proposed by Vygotsky (1978) to represent how the social world functions to promote cognitive development. A ZPD can be defined as an "interactive system" formed by working on a problem that one of the participants could not effectively solve alone (Vygotsky, 1968, p. 61) and that is enabled by the other. One "enters" a ZPD when one can successfully perform a task, with the assistance of materials or a more experienced other, that one could not successfully perform alone. One is no longer in a ZPD when successful performance is not possible, even with the assistance of materials or a more experienced other. When a ZPD is constructed with a more experienced individual (e.g., a teacher), that individual changes cognitively as he or she develops understanding of the perspective of the learner (and perhaps the problem and its solution as well). The learner in a ZPD also changes cognitively through the process of coming to learn how to solve the problem. As described by Newman, Griffin, and Cole (1989)

Children can participate in an activity that is more complex than they can understand, producing "performance before competence," to use Cazden's (1981) phrase. While in the ZPD of an activity, the children's actions get interpreted within the system being constructed with the teacher. Thus the child is exposed to the teacher's understanding without necessarily being directly taught. (pp. 63–64)

The activity in which the individuals engage to form a ZPD is culturally specific. As a result, the appropriation of tools assumes "adopting the belief system of the culture in which they are used" (Brown et al., 1989, p. 33). With regard to conceptual change in science, the establishment of desirable ZPDs should reflect the culture of science, that is, reflect the particular epistemological and ontological categories that mark the values and beliefs of the community of scientists whose field is the foundation for the targeted understandings (e.g., Mortimer, 1995). For example, Driver et al. (1994) point out that "the objects of science are not the phenomena of nature but constructs that are advanced by the scientific community to interpret nature" (p. 5). Moreover, the assumptions guiding our everyday knowledge building are quite different from those guiding scientific knowledge building. Explanations in science are expected to fit particular standards such as being consistently applied across contexts, coherent with respect to other explanations, and complete in their accounting of some aspect of the physical world (Smith, diSessa, & Roschelle, 1993, describing the view of Einstein, 1950). In addition, the norms guiding knowledge building within any one area of science include assumptions that are more content specific than these standards. For example, what counts as a viable explanation of a particular phenomenon will be dictated by the knowledge, experience, and beliefs regarding previous explanations that were ventured to explain the phenomenon of interest and that gained community support. Thus, development with respect to specific scientific knowledge requires attention to disciplinary-specific and topic-specific norms. Indeed, even scientists have been found to revert to commonsense notions and make inaccurate predictions when confronted with everyday problems—of the very nature that we typically use to engage elementary and middle school students—even though they could have used scientific knowledge in their area of expertise (e.g., chemists—Lewis & Linn, 1994; physicists—McDermott, 1984). Thus, to support the development of scientific knowledge, we must signal the standards by which knowledge is to be applied in sense-making and knowledge construction.

Some sociocultural theorists use the term *cognitive* change to "characterize a process involving a dialectical interaction between the social world and the changing individual" (Newman et al., 1989, p. 59). This type of change involves "the internalization and transformation of the social relations in which individuals are involved, including the cultural tools which mediate the interactions among people and between people and the physical world" (Newman et al., 1989, p. 60). We hold a similar view regarding conceptual change. We view *conceptual* change as a process that involves a dialectical interaction in which one individual, using psychological and material tools reflective of the activity of science (one aspect of the social world), supports another individual in using language and performing actions that represent appropriate ways of engaging the world from the perspective of the scientific community. The conceptual change that results from this type of interaction over time is the gradual development of knowledge that is marked by epistemological and ontological features consistent with that of practicing scientists.

Whereas this development may appear to result in radically different knowledge from the everyday ideas individuals hold, it should not be viewed as a change to different ideas because the initial conceptions remain and are useful in many nonscientific contexts. Instead, it should be viewed as the evolution of ideas within particular ontological and epistemological categories, which results in the development of parallel conceptions that can be expressed in a conceptual profile (Mortimer, 1995). In addition, whereas we depict this change as evolutionary rather than revolutionary, that is not to say that the change is easy, unproblematic, or occurs readily. Taking the perspective of constructing ZPDs assumes that the learning outcome is proximal to the initial knowledge of the learner; hence, development will occur in small steps. Furthermore, in the case of developing knowledge within a different ontological or epistemological category, difficult challenges may arise if individuals have few ideas or experiences to support knowledge construction. It is fair to describe this as a process of enculturation, and—as such—it will take time, errors will occur, and individual differences may mean that conceptual development will look different across individuals. In the next section, we describe a tool that we have designed—informed by the ideas presented previously—for the purpose of supporting teachers to enact science instruction in a fashion that is consistent with a sociocultural perspective.

DESCRIPTION OF NOTEBOOK TEXTS

As indicated previously, notebook texts are called such because they are modeled after the type of notebooks that actual scientists keep in recording their investigative activity and findings. They represent an innovative, multigenre text that is designed not only to support student development of scientific knowledge but also scientific reasoning. The notebook format makes this possible and shifts the role of text in instruction from a presentation of the products of science to representing the process of scientific activity and the construction of scientific knowledge. Creating these ourselves allows us to explicitly model aspects of scientific reasoning, not in the sense of being exemplary but in the sense of reflecting the values, beliefs, norms, and conventions of the scientific community.

Notebook texts present students with insights into the planning and conduct of scientific investigation as well as the process of determining outcomes from those investigations. They seek to "lay bare" the reasoning of a scientist and the influences on that reasoning, serving both to illustrate and model the type of cognitive activity in which the students are expected to engage in the course of their own investigations. They sometimes focus on everyday conceptions of learners that are alternative to targeted scientific knowledge, providing explicit opportunities for students to confront those ideas and see data that contradict them. They also illustrate the nonlinear path that is common to any complex reasoning by showing the scientist's reasoning through several investigations and modeling that sequences of investigation are often necessary to scientifically answer a question.

Norms and conventions of scientific activity that are featured include (a) engagement in systematic investigation to understand causes of physical phenomena, (b) the goal of making knowledge claims about the physical world from those investigations, (c) the need to publicly present one's findings to other scientists whose acceptance is necessary for the knowledge claims to be considered new scientific knowledge, (d) the role of scientists' perceptions of the precision of data collection in their acceptance of others' claims, and (e) the need to rule out competing hypotheses in developing explanations for the cause of relationships. In this way, notebook texts are a source, besides the teacher, for presenting and modeling norms and conventions of scientific investigation and knowledge building.

Our notebook texts are constructed as excerpts from the notebook of a fictitious scientist named Lesley Park who uses her entries to (a) identify the problem she is investigating, (b) think aloud about how she can accurately model particular phenomena for the purposes of investigation, (c) make decisions about how to effectively represent the data collected to support its analysis, (d) describe claims that she believes she can make from these data, (e) respond to the critical reactions of her colleagues as they weigh the evidence for her claims, and (f) revise her thinking in light of new data or alternative explanations. Although we don't use notebook entries of actual scientists, we sometimes feature data from actual scientific investigation of the past (e.g., Newton's study of light through prisms). Furthermore, the data that are featured as being collected by Lesley are actual or slightly modified data that we have collected.

Notebook texts typically include multiple ways of representing data including figures, tables, and graphs. For example, figures may contain observations of phenomena that students can interpret along with the scientist. Tables model the various ways in which data can be arrayed, and narratives accompanying the tables model the activity of interpreting these data. Finally, graphical displays of data in tables provide opportunities to discuss how graphs can reveal relationships in data that are not readily apparent in tables as well as a means to extend one's data such as through interpolation or extrapolation.

An additional feature of our notebook texts is the inclusion of notes from reference materials (properly cited to provide appropriate modeling of the use of published material) that our fictitious scientist sought to inform her thinking. These notes are typically followed by entries from Lesley describing her thinking about the newly acquired information and its application to the problem at hand. For example, in a notebook entry regarding static electricity, Lesley consults with a historian of science who refers her to a volume containing descriptions of Benjamin Franklin's (and others') experiments with static electricity. In this volume, Lesley encounters a chronology of what scientists since the sixth century B.C. have observed about static electricity. Lesley uses this reference material to help shape the focus and process of her investigation.

Notebook texts also contain entries that portray the ways in which scientists interact with one another and follow particular conventions. For example, in one text, Lesley notes that fellow scientists were not persuaded by her conclusions because her data were imprecise. They suggest the use of an instrument that will allow for more precise measurements, and she investigates again. This sort of activity makes it possible to feature the development of conceptual understanding across a text. In some cases, this means that ideas expressed at the outset of the text are built onto. In other cases, the ideas may be revised or discarded in response to the collection of additional data. In one case, Lesley draws an opposite conclusion from an early investigation describing a phenomenon. Thus, the notebook text provides a view of scientific knowledge production in action much like it may occur for students.

Finally, notebook texts are intentionally high-inference; that is, they do not make explicit all of the thinking and decision making behind what is written or represented in drawings. This partly occurs so that it resembles the actual notebook of a scientist's who would not likely spell out every step in the thinking process. It also functions to provide genuine reasons to discuss the text. The high-inference nature of a notebook text has the additional benefit of supporting the development of student comprehension monitoring abilities in ways that low-inference texts do not.

LINKING DESIGN FEATURES OF NOTEBOOK TEXTS TO THEORETICAL/PHILOSOPHICAL PERSPECTIVES

Whereas there is overlap among the ideas presented from these various perspectives, Table 2.1 shows particular ideas that we draw on from each perspective and how those ideas lead to design principles for the development of notebook texts.

TABLE 2.1

Perspective	Concept(s)	Design Principles
Philosophy of science	Scientific knowledge is produced by the scientific community's agreement on nature's correct answer to a problem as determined by the quality of the arguments that support it	Represent the development of scientific knowledge in terms of the quality of argument that can be constructed Represent the role of the community in determining whether an argument is acceptable
Curriculum Theory	Scientific knowledge is the product of the interpretation of selected facts that are dependent on the principles employed in the inquiry at the time and contingent on the nature of the context in which it arose Papers describing individual inquiries illustrate the problems/challenges of constructing scientific knowledge	Represent the challenges and uncertainties en route to the "discovery" process Represent scientific knowledge as changeable and contingent Show the process of developing knowledge not just the conclusions that resulted
Cognitive psychology	Prior knowledge is used to build mental models of a context to build new knowledge Metacognition is key to successful learning	Focus the content in ways that facilitate students drawing upon prior knowledge Model metacognition. Provide sufficient information about the process of developing scientific knowledge so that students can engage in metacognition regarding the inquiry
Sociocultural theory	ZPDs must be constructed for learning to occur Cultural values and beliefs and norms and conventions must be made explicit in the learning environment to enable the development of desired knowledge and skill	Make the text sufficiently challenging so that competent "performance" requires a more expert other Have the teacher's guide provide sufficient information to enable the teacher to construct multiple ZPDs with students and the text Make explicit the values, beliefs, norms, and conventions of the scientific community

Note. ZPD = zone of proximal development.

Specific Examples of Design Features

The previous description illustrates many of the features that Table 2.1 identified as stemming from particular philosophical or theoretical perspectives. In this section, we provide specific examples using actual excerpts from notebook texts.

Scientific Knowledge in Terms of Quality/Acceptability of Argument.   The following excerpt is from a six-page notebook text about flashlights. Lesley observes that a flashlight lights even when some batteries in it are reversed. She proceeds through a series of investigations trying to figure out how that can happen and comes up with the explanation shown in Figure 2.1. There are explicit messages here about the explanation needing to convince others and the scientist seeking more data to even convince herself.

Figure 2.2 compiles excerpts from across a notebook text about current electricity. In this case, Lesley used conversation with a colleague to support her in thinking through explanations of a phenomenon in which light bulbs with filaments of different size exhibit different brightness and do not both operate when placed in a circuit together. This text also illustrates that scientists construct models to represent their thinking and to develop broader ideas about how the physical world works.

Representing Scientific Knowledge in Development and as Changeable. The previous excerpt explicitly states the expectation that ideas will develop, but in other texts, claims made at one point are rejected in the face of new data. Such is the case for a notebook text about the behavior of light in interaction with different solid materials (excerpts shown in Fig. 2.3). The excerpts in this figure also show the heading that appears at the top of every notebook page, marking the text as a notebook and providing additional information about the timeframe over which Lesley engaged in her inquiry.

Claim:
- reversing the direction of a battery in a series "cancels" the energy of one other battery in the series

I was quite excited to present this claim to Kiko to see what she thought. Would she find my reasoning about the data convincing? I'm not sure that I feel confident yet. So, I will first test out my claim with even more batteries. When I am satisfied that the pattern holds, I'll share it with Kiko.

FIG. 2.1.   Excerpt from notebook text about flashlights.

Model and Foster Metacognition.   Figures 2.1 and 2.2 provide some examples of ways in which Lesley is depicted examining her own thinking in relation to her actions and developing understanding. The following set of excerpts (Fig. 2.4) from another version of our notebook text about the impact of differences in the filaments of two light bulbs provide further examples of ways in which we make Lesley's metacognitive awareness and monitoring explicit. Here we see Lesley questioning the validity of her

Right now, my model suggests that the current is different in each place where there is a different light bulb. But that is not what my data show. So, how can I change the model so that it fits the data? The model <u>should</u> show that what determines the amount of current in the <u>whole</u> circuit is the thinnest wire in the circuit.

. . .

I talked with Carla to see what additional ideas she might have to help me improve my model. Thinking about current made me think about the energy of flowing water, and the way we use that energy to move things. My thinking led Carla to think about water wheels, and she suggested that those could be added to the model, inside of the pipe in each place where I modeled the different types of light bulbs.

. . .

Well, Carla agreed that the water wheel helped the model fit the relationships that I was trying to understand. However, she also pointed out that there were other relationships in my data that the model did not explain. For example, each time I added a light bulb of the same type to a circuit, the amount of current decreased. She did not see anything in my model that could explain that relationship. In fact, she thought my model would predict that the amount of current would stay the same as long as the bulbs were all of the same size.

FIG. 2.2.   Excerpt from notebook text about current electricity.

| Scientist | Lesley Park | Date | 10/27/97 | Page 2 |

What I concluded from my data:
  • Light reflects off all solid objects, except if they are black.

• • •

| Scientist | Lesley Park | Date | 10/28/97 | Page 4 |

What I concluded from these data:
  • Light reflects off all solid materials.

FIG. 2.3.   Excerpt from notebook text about light interacting with solid materials.

These findings are consistent with my idea that a thicker filament would give off more light. But, is my explanation correct that it is because there is more material to light?

. . .

It makes sense to me that there is more current in a light bulb with a thicker filament. But I was surprised that the current is the same throughout the circuit. That means that the bulb affects current in the whole circuit!

. . .

I found the water wheel model very interesting. It was more helpful than either my log analogy or the water pipe model. With the water wheel model, I could even explain previous results. My conclusion that a certain amount of voltage is needed to light a bulb is like needing a certain amount of water to move the wheel.

FIG. 2.4.   Excerpt from another notebook text about light bulbs and current.

thinking, commenting on how a result was unexpected, and indicating that a new idea was preferred because it could account for more of her data. In concert with such illustrations, it is also the case that the data presented allow the students to engage in the same reasoning process, along with Lesley, to make sense of the data. Thus, students can first draw their own conclusions and then compare them with Lesley's. The notebook texts are formatted to support this type of student engagement; for example, by ending a page with data and beginning the next page with Lesley's conclusions (e.g., as shown in Fig. 2.3).

Make Explicit the Values, Beliefs, Norms, and Conventions of the Scientific Community.   Notebook excerpts presented previously show Lesley making statements that reveal aspects of the cultural values, beliefs, norms, and conventions of the scientific community. In addition, the notebook format itself is an exemplar showing the specification of questions, the registering of hypotheses and predictions, the representation of data in the form of tables, analyses using graphs, and so forth. However, in particular, we seek to represent the ways in which the community functions in evaluating the results of individual experimentation as illustrated in the excerpts in Fig. 2.5.

Make Challenging Enough for Students and Teachers to Form Multiple ZPDs.   Although notebook texts vary in their level of difficulty linguistically—because of differences in the level of abstractness of the concepts addressed—all notebook texts are conceptually challenging because of their high-inference nature. The excerpts shown indicate variability in sentence structure and length including long sentences that express complex ideas, which makes them cognitively demanding. The excerpts also show variation in the level of vocabulary necessary to comprehend the ideas in the text. The

When I showed my claims and evidence to other scientists, they were not convinced of my conclusions because my data were not exact. The other scientists were not confident in my judgments about how the amount of light reflected from an object compared to the amount of light that was transmitted through it.

One scientist suggested that I use a light meter to collect more data. She told me a light meter is an instrument that measures the brightness of light. With this tool, I can actually measure the amount of light at any place. Figure 2 shows a picture of a light meter. It measures light in units of candles. I plan to repeat my experiments with the same materials, but using a light meter.

FIG. 2.5.   Another excerpt from notebook text about light interacting with solid materials.

point of this is not to intentionally make the texts challenging for students: They are challenging because it is difficult to convey meaningful ideas relative to representing scientific inquiry and the nature of the concepts in the texts that are intended to support student development of scientific knowledge and reasoning. As a result, the texts are not intended to be read independently; they are intended to be read interactively. Teacher's guides that are prepared to support teachers in conducting effective instruction with notebook texts provide several different types of information. This information is believed to be critical to support teachers in constructing ZPDs with their students during the use of notebook texts. Figure 2.6 shows one page of a teacher's guide for a notebook text.

In the center of each page is a replica of the text that students read. The student text is surrounded by three different types of information. To the left under the heading "Scientific Information for the Teacher" is information about the scientific ideas in the text and author's notes explaining particular choices in the writing of the text. These notes provide supporting or clarifying information about the science in the text, and they identify an author's choices in the writing of the text that were made for pedagogical rather than scientific reasons. On the right side under the heading "Teacher Prompts for Instructional Conversation" are notes about questions to ask or tasks to pose to students to support comprehension of and learning from the text. The prompts are intended to be examples of questions that promote substantive conversation; furthermore, they are written to provide specific guidance for teaching with the featured text. However, there are more prompts on a page than needed to promote conversation and support knowledge building, so teachers are expected to make choices about what to ask, guided by the direction of the conversation. Finally, in the center on the bottom of the page, in a dark

Scientific Information for the Teacher

This phenomenon described in this paragraph - the brightening or dimming of light from a flashlight - could occur if the batteries in the flashlights were of different voltages. Batteries can have different amounts of voltage if they have been in use for different amounts of time. Batteries in a flashlight are arranged in series, and the voltage of batteries in series is the sum of the individual batteries. A light bulb's brightness is directly related to the amount of voltage in the circuit: the higher the voltage the brighter the light bulb. So, if a flashlight first had batteries whose voltage summed to 2.7, and then batteries were switched with ones whose voltage summed to 2.1, the bulb would not light as brightly.

The phenomenon of batteries being reversed and a flashlight still lighting is possible. Whether a flashlight will still light depends upon how many batteries are in the flashlight, how many are reversed, and what amount of voltage is needed to light the flashlight bulb. If a reversed battery has the same amount of voltage as a non-reversed battery, it has the effect of negating or canceling that voltage. Thus, if a flashlight only has two batteries and one is reversed, there is no voltage to light the bulb. If a flashlight with three batteries has one reversed, 1.5 volts is available to light the bulb, which means much dimmer light than three batteries providing 4.5 volts.

Flashlights are constructed so that there is an electrically conductive path of material to connect the critical contact points on the light bulb to the negative pole of the first battery in the series and the positive pole of the last battery in the series. In a flashlight with a plastic case, there needs to be a strip of metal that runs from the negative pole of the first battery in the series to the critical point on the side of the light bulb base. In a flashlight with a metal case, the case itself acts as a conducting path for electricity, so the bottom of the first battery in the series simply needs to be in contact with the case as does the side of the light bulb base. To prevent unintended conduction of electricity from a metal case, a non-conducting layer is added to the metal.

Regarding the light bulb, identifying information is often stamped in the metal of the bulb. The information shown in the figure identifies an actual bulb that is suitable for use in a flashlight.

The difference in observations with one battery reversed in each flashlight is due to the fact that the plastic flashlight operates with two batteries and the metal flashlight operates with three. The dim light of the metal flashlight is an important observation because it provides the first clue that reversing a battery, although it does not keep the light from lighting, does have an impact on the circuit because the brightness of the light was different.

Scientist: Lesley Park   Date: 7/30/01   Page: 1

Last Saturday at a party, I watched two children playing with flashlights. First they took their flashlights apart. Then they switched batteries with one another. Then they put the flashlights back together and turned them on and off. Sometimes after switching batteries, the light from the flashlight seemed brighter or dimmer than before. Sometimes there was no light at all!

I didn't think that switching batteries would make that much difference. I decided to watch more closely. I saw that the children did more than switch batteries. Sometimes they reversed the direction of a battery when they put it back in the flashlight. I didn't think a flashlight would work if any batteries were reversed. But the light bulb still lit when they did this. How could that be?

At the end of the evening, I asked the children's parents if I could borrow the flashlights. I brought them to my lab to study, and made the observations in Figure 1.

Figure 1. Flashlight structure and battery arrangement.

My first test was to see what happened when I reversed one battery in each flashlight.

- plastic flashlight – no light
- metal flashlight – dim light, much dimmer than either flashlight with no batteries reversed

Writing Prompt

Using what you already know about electricity and complete circuits, explain how you think a flashlight works.

Teacher Prompts for Instructional Conversation

For the First Two Paragraphs

"Let's identify all the observations that Lesley has made."
Display student responses.
Check for the two main observations - dimming of the light, no light at times.

For the two main observations cited in the paragraph, ask, "What are your ideas about why that might have happened?" *Display student responses.*

"Why do you think Lesley thought switching batteries would not make as much of a difference?"
"What do you think?"

"Does Lesley's observation that a flashlight still gave off light when batteries were reversed surprise you? Why or why not?

"What does the title of Figure 1 tell us about what Lesley studied?"
[*Have students engage in this practice whenever they encounter a figure.*]
The structure of the flashlights, how the batteries were arranged (which is related to her observation of the children switching batteries)

"What do we learn in Figure 1 about Lesley's observations of the flashlights?"
Be sure that students notice major differences such as the different number of batteries in each flashlight, that the light bulbs were not of different types, and the different material of each flashlight case.

Have students trace the circuit in each flashlight; i.e., the critical contact points on the light bulb and batteries, and the paths of conducting material in between them.

"What do you think about Lesley's observations with a reversed battery? Do you have any ideas to explain her results?"
The role of the first question is to determine whether or not the students are surprised at or disbelieve Lesley's results. They may not have any ideas at this time about how such results could occur, which is fine.

FIG. 2.6.   Page 3 of the Teacher's Guide for the notebook text regarding flashlights.

47

gray box with white lettering, is a writing prompt to stimulate individual student reflection on the content of the text. These are not intended for whole class conversation; rather, they are to create opportunities for students to document their individual thoughts in reaction to the text.

In addition to this information, teachers are provided with general information about the science concepts in the text and general pedagogical principles regarding working with notebook texts. This volume of information is just one indication that teaching with such a tool is complex. There may be much for the teacher to learn regarding the science content in the text, working interactively with students with challenging text, and determining how to effectively make decisions to support student thinking and conversation while using the text considering local conditions of the students' abilities, prior knowledge, and experience.

We have hypothesized that a week's summer institute is necessary to introduce teachers to the concepts of working with notebook texts and give them opportunities to practice and give feedback from teaching with notebook texts to small groups of students. We also think monthly meetings during the school year are important follow-up as teachers tailor use of such sophisticated tools to their local context. Previous studies have indicated that even when teachers successfully learn the procedures of conducting complex instruction, they may make poor choices in adapting them to their local context if they do not also understand the principles underlying the instruction (Vaughn, Hughes, & Schumm, 1998).

CONCLUSION

We have described the application of a diverse array of theoretical/philosophical perspectives in the design of novel texts—notebook texts—for use in guided-inquiry science instruction. Implicit in this development is the idea that tools, such as texts, have an important role to play in supporting the translation of research into practice. Our focus has been on the design of a tool that we argue is useful to supporting the translation of theory and research into the kinds of teaching practice that advance children's learning of science. Although not the focus of this chapter, it is important to note that our research has indicated that the use of notebook texts advances learning of both scientific content and reasoning in more significant ways than does learning from traditional texts (Palincsar & Magnusson, 2001).

Complementing experimental research regarding the effectiveness of these texts has been descriptive research inquiring into the substance and features of the instructional discourse that unfolds as teachers and students use these texts (Hapgood, Magnusson, & Palincsar, 2004; Palincsar & Magnusson, 2001). These studies have been integral to identifying the opportunities and challenges afforded by these texts as well as the features of effective teacher mediation in the use of these texts. The results of this research on practice have played a critical role in the revisions we make to the texts, to the guides that are prepared for teachers, and to the professional development designed to support teachers' effective use of these texts.

ACKNOWLEDGMENTS

This work has been funded, in part, through grants from the following programs: The McDonnell Foundation's Cognitive Studies in Educational Practice Program, The National Science Foundation's Instructional Materials Development Program, The Office of Educational Research, and Improvement Center for the Improvement of Early Reading Achievement (CIERA). Any opinions, findings, conclusions, or recommendations expressed herein are those of the authors and do not necessarily reflect the views of these organizations.

REFERENCES

American Association for the Advancement of Science. (1989). *Science for all Americans: A Project 2061 report on literacy goals in science, mathematics, and technology.* Washington, DC: Author.

American Association for the Advancement of Science. (1993). *Benchmarks for scientific literacy: Project 2061.* New York: Oxford University Press.

Bransford, J. D., Brown, A. L., & Cocking, R. R. (1999). How people learn: Brain, mind, experience, and school. Washington DC: National Academy Press.

Brown, J. S., Collins, A., & Duguid, P. (1989). Situated cognition and the culture of learning. *Educational Researcher, 18*(1), 32–42.

Cazden, C. B. (1981). Performance before competence: Assistance to child discourse in the zone of proximal development. *The Quarterly Newsletter of the Laboratory of Comparative Human Cognition, 3*(1), 5–8.

Chan, C. K. K., Burtis, P. J., Scardamalia, M., & Bereiter, C. (1992). Constructive activity in learning from text. *American Educational Research Journal, 29,* 97–118.

Chi, M. T. H., de Leeuw, N., Chiu, M. H., & LaVancher, C. (1994). Eliciting self explanations improves understanding. *Cognitive Science, 13,* 145–182.

Clement, J. (1993). Using bridging analogies and anchoring intuitions to deal with students' preconceptions in physics. *Journal of Research in Science Teaching, 30 ,* 1241–1257.

Cobb, P., & Yackel, E. (1996). Constructivism, emergent, and sociocultural perspectives in the context of developmental research. *Educational Psychologist, 31,* 175–190.

Doyle, W. (1986). Classroom organization and management. In M. C. Wittrock (Ed.), *Handbook of Research on Teaching* (pp. 392–431). New York: Macmillan.

Driver, R., Asoko, H., Leach, J., Mortimer, E., & Scott, P. (1994). Constructing scientific knowledge in the classroom. *Educational Researcher, 23*(7), 5–12.

Einstein, A. (1950). *Out of my later years.* New York: Philosophical Library.

Fensham, P. J. (1992). Science and Technology. In P. W. Jackson (Ed.), *Handbook of research on curriculum* (pp. 789–829). New York: Macmillan.

Gee, J. P. (1996). *Social linguistics and literacies: Ideology in discourses* (2nd ed.). London: Falmer.

Goldman, S. R., & Rakestraw, J. A. (2000). Structural aspects of constructing mean-
ing from text. In M. L. Kamil, P. B. Mosenthal, P. D. Pearson & R. Barr (Eds.),
Handbook of reading research (Vol. 3, pp. 311–335). Mahwah, NJ: Lawrence
Erlbaum Associates.

Goldman, S. R., Saul, E. U., & Coté, N. (1995). Paragraphing, reader, and task effects on discourse comprehension. *Discourse Processes, 20,* 273–305.

Hapgood, S., Magnusson, S. J., & Palincsar, A. S. (2004). Teacher, text, and experience mediating children's learning of scientific inquiry. *Journal of the Learning Sciences, 13*(4), 455–505.

Kuhn, D. (1993). Science as argument: Implications for teaching and learning scientific thinking. *Science Education, 77,* 319–338.

Latour, B. (1987). *Science in action.* Cambridge, MA: Harvard University Press.

Lave, J. (1991). Situating learning in communities of practice. In L. B. Resnick, J. M.
Levine, & S. D. Teasley (Eds.), *Perspectives on socially shared cognition* (pp. 63–82).
Washington, DC: American Psychological Association.

Lemke, J. (1990). *Talking science.* Norwood, NJ: Ablex.

Lewis, E. L., & Linn, M. C. (1994). Heat energy and temperature concepts of adoles-
cents, naïve adults, and experts: Implications for curricular improvements. *Journal of Research in Science Teaching, 31,* 657–677.

Magnusson, S. J., & Palincsar, A. S. (1995). The learning environment as a site of science education reform. *Theory into Practice, 34,* 43–50.

McDermott, L. C. (1984). Research on conceptual understanding in mechanics.
Physics Today, 37, 24.

Morris, W. (Ed.). (1976). *The American Heritage Dictionary of the English Language.*
Boston: Houghton Mifflin.

Mortimer, E. F. (1995). Conceptual change or conceptual profile change? *Science and
Education, 4,* 267–285.

National Research Council. (1996). *National science education standards.* Washington,
DC: National Academy Press.

Newman, D., Griffin, P., & Cole, M. (1989). *The construction zone: Working for cognitive
change in school.* Cambridge, England: Cambridge University Press.

Palincsar, A. S., & Magnusson, S. J. (2001). The interplay of first-hand and text-based
investigations to model and support the development of scientific knowledge and
reasoning. In S. Carver & D. Klahr (Eds.), *Cognition and instruction: Twenty five years
of progress* (pp. 151–194). Mahwah, NJ: Lawrence Erlbaum Associates.

Pera, M. (1994). *The discourses of science.* Chicago: University of Chicago Press.

Richgels, D. J., McGee, L. M., Lomax, R. G., & Sheard, C. (1987). Awareness of four
text structures: Effects in recall of expository text. *Reading Research Quarterly, 22,*
177–196.

Rogoff, B. (1994). Developing understanding of the idea of communities of learners. *Mind, Culture, and Activity, 1,* 209–229.

Schwab, J. J. (1962). The teaching of science as enquiry. In J. Schwab & P. Brandwein
(Eds.), *The teaching of science* (pp. 1–103). Cambridge, MA: Harvard University Press.

Smith, J. P., diSessa, A. A., & Roschelle, J. (1993). Misconceptions reconceived: A
constructivist analysis of knowledge in transition. *The Journal of the Learning Sciences, 3,* 115–163.

Van Zee, E. H. (1997). Reflective discourse: Developing shared understandings in a
physics classroom. *International Journal of Science Education, 19,* 209–228.

Vaughn, S., Hughes, M. T., & Schumm, J. S. (1998). A collaborative effort to enhance
reading and writing instruction in inclusive classrooms. *Learning Disability Quarterly, 21,* 57–74.

von Glasersfeld, E. (1989). Cognition, construction of knowledge, and teaching. *Synthese, 80*(1), 121–140.

Vygotsky, L. S. (1978). *Mind in society: The development of higher psychological processes* (M. Cole, V. John-Steiner, S. Scribner, & E. Souberman, Eds.). Cambridge, MA: Harvard University Press.

Scaling Research on Beginning Reading: Consensus and Conflict

Jack M. Fletcher and Barbara R. Foorman
University of Texas Health Science Center at Houston

Carolyn A. Denton and Sharon Vaughn
University of Texas at Austin

In a recent report on the role of scientific research in education from the National Research Council, Shavelson and Towne (2002) cited research on beginning reading as an example of how knowledge in an area of education accumulates to a point of consensus and implementation through policy. This area began with what Stanovich (2000) described as a "big idea" in science, namely, the recognition of the necessity of teaching children the "alphabetic principle" by a small group of international researchers, most notably at the Haskins Laboratories led by Alvin and Isabel Liberman (Brady & Shankweiler, 1991). The alphabetic principle, simply put, is the representation of the sounds of language in print through the alphabet. As a core component of learning to read, this principle suggests that written language is built on more natural human capabilities for oral language. In processing oral language, the brain takes advantage of its segmental nature, that is, that words are composed of units of sounds called *phonemes*, the smallest part of a word that makes a difference in its meaning. In learning to read, children must access the phonological representation of words and become aware of its segmental structure. However, developing an awareness of the phonological structure of speech is not a natural occurrence. Because the brain's capacity for processing speech is established very early in human development, the internal structure of speech is known by the young child only on an implicit level. To learn to read, children must make an explicit discovery of the phonological structure of language and apply it to print, which they do with varying degrees of success through interactions with adults (parents, teachers) who engage them in the process of learning to read (Liberman, 1997; Lukatela & Turvey, 1998).

From these initial observations in the 1960s and 1970s emerged studies of beginning readers and then struggling readers. The research on the normative development of reading expanded around the world, and research on struggling readers encompassed neurobiological factors (genetics, neuroimaging) and instruction. Over time, the knowledge base grew rapidly, expanding horizontally in terms of the sheer accumulation of knowledge within disciplines and topics, but also vertically as knowledge was integrated across disciplines and topics. This development of a knowledge base occurred at a time when there was national concern about the level of growth of reading skills in children, especially after publication of *A Nation at Risk: The Imperative for Educational Reform* (National Commission on Excellence in Education, 1983). Furthermore, the National Assessment of Education Progress (NAEP) documents not only a lack of overall growth over the past 20 years but also a lack of impact of schooling on the minority achievement gap in reading. It is common to cite NAEP reports that 38% of fourth graders fail to read at "basic" levels of proficiency but that this figure is over 60% in minority children.

Not surprisingly (and to their credit), policymakers have become very interested in the body of research on beginning reading, which has helped stimulate the accumulation of knowledge in other areas associated with learning to read such as comprehension. Several consensus reports have been commissioned on behalf of policymakers, including the seminal research review by Adams (1990), the National Research Council's *Preventing Reading Difficulties in Young Children* (Snow, Burns, & Griffin, 1998), the National Reading Panel (2000) report, and the report of the RAND Reading Study Group (Snow, 2002). In addition, there are numerous state and even local district reports on this research that have led to state reading initiatives, most notably in California and Texas. At a national level, major pieces of legislation have been enacted, first the Reading Excellence Act and then the Reading First legislation as part of the reauthorization of the Elementary and Secondary Education Act of 2001, otherwise known as the No Child Left Behind Act. The growing body of research in reading was a factor in the emphasis on scientifically based instruction seen not only in these major pieces of legislation but also in the creation of the Institute for Educational Sciences in the Department of Education and the ongoing reauthorization of the Individuals With Disabilities in Education Act (IDEA, 1997) that provides for special education services in public schools.

Despite the apparent consensus, this research on reading is proving difficult to scale. It is clear that without the involvement of policymakers who worked on the Reading Excellence Act and the Reading First component of the No Child Left Behind legislation, the research most likely would not see widespread implementation in schools. These difficulties reflect in part the lack of acceptance of scientific research by decision makers in schools, lack of accessibility of research to these decision makers, and the fact that many of the instructional tenets stemming from the research run counter to prevailing views of learning to read and how these views are implemented in classrooms (McCardle & Chhabra, 2004). Furthermore, the teachers responsible for implementing these scientifically based research reading interventions often complete their teacher education programs with little access to this knowledge and few opportunities to observe instruction using these practices.

We have been deeply involved in this research and in its scaling, especially through the Texas Reading Initiative. In the remainder of this chapter, we explore some of the issues involved in scaling this reading research, especially in Texas, but also in scaling reading research across the nation as in the Reading First legislation. With these experiences as a base, we identify factors that enhance and impede scaling and the lessons for other areas of educational research.

TAKING READING SCIENCE TO SCALE

Barriers

In examining the scaling of research on reading, there are four essential barriers: (a) epistemological disagreements, (b) investments in the current system, (c) lack of resources, and (d) limited research base on how to scale. We consider each of these in turn.

Epistemological Disagreements.   There are two levels at which epistemology enters into attempts to scale beginning reading. The first, and most significant, is the lack of impact of scientific research on decision makers in schools. In general, scientific research has little bearing on the sorts of decisions that educators make (Carnine, 2000). Research is seldom cited as a factor in decision making. Similarly, when research is cited, there is infrequently any effort to evaluate the quality of the research. Rather, the decision-making process in public education often reflects commercial considerations and the marketing ability of an individual or publisher. Fads are common, fueled by the large markets that exist for textbooks, curriculums, and professional development (Anderson, 2000). This problem is magnified because individuals who do research are often able to communicate their findings in peer-reviewed research journals but are less effective in communicating the results of the research to educational leaders or practicing teachers. There is often inadequate consideration of what it takes to implement a set of research findings into a classroom.

A broader set of concerns involves significant epistemological differences about the value of empirical research (Shavelson & Towne, 2002; Stanovich & Stanovich, 2003). In education, including members of the research community, philosophies that are not terribly conducive to the introduction of scientific research often prevail. Many researchers place an emphasis on descriptive, observational studies of students in classrooms or their teachers. In defending this type of research, individuals commonly invoke epistemologies that tend to reduce the role of research that addresses questions of causality using quantitative methods. Considerations such as reliability and generalization are often downplayed in favor of the richness of the individual experience and the complicated sociocultural context of schooling (St. Pierre, 2000). Although there is certainly value in this type of research, what is often missing is an emphasis on the reliability by which such assessments are made, their generalizability to broader contexts, and a persistent tendency to use this type of research to address questions involving causation for which it is not well suited (Vaughn & Dammann, 2001). Interactions between individuals committed to the use of quantitative research methods and questions involving causality and those committed to ethnographic and observational research that by its very nature addresses questions involving description and mechanism are often bitter, failing to reflect the common ground in science that should characterize both of these superficially warring epistemologies (Shavelson & Towne, 2002).

Investments in the Current System.   Related to the issue of warring epistemologies is the impetus for continuing the current approach to decision making as it presently exists, often relying on a "hit or miss" approach to educational decisions. Many individuals have investments in the current system, particularly if they have commercial interests in which they profit from a less than systematic approach to educational decision making. In addition, it is often a system without rigorous accountability. Decision makers change frequently as do prevailing trends in education. Within the current system, there is considerable impetus for traditional ways of doing things. One of the biggest dangers is having research-based practices become a fad and having it treated as part of this system. Under this scenario, every vendor provides products that are allegedly research-based when the actual research support is of very low quality. The problem is that many educators do not have the background needed to evaluate the quality of the evidence supporting a practice or product.

Financial Resources. Implementing reading research will require most educators to implement different approaches to reading instruction than they are currently using. It is clear that although some improvements can occur simply by enhancing the teacher's capacity for core reading instruction in the classroom, other resources will be needed in kindergarten, Grade 1, and Grade 2 to accelerate the development of every child. In this respect, the resources needed to provide professional development for classroom teachers are expensive and logistically difficulty to implement on such a large scale.

There is also a need to develop the capacity for providing interventions earlier in a child's development than is presently the case. In many schools, the only alternative to general classroom instruction is special education. Intervention through special education is difficult and often ineffective, partly because children are identified for reading difficulties after Grade 3 when remediation is more difficult (Lyon et al., 2001). Yet two of every five children in special education are identified because of reading difficulties (Donovan & Cross, 2002; President's Commission on Excellence in Special Education, 2002). Special education is oriented toward identifying disabilities partly to protect the rights of students with disabilities. The idea that in some students, disabilities could be prevented contrasts with this focus. Many disability advocates worry that a focus on early intervention will direct resources away from special education. Thus, the issue is not only increasing resources to implement the research but also considering the possibility of reallocating resources away from a system that has considerable inertia and legal realities.

Research Base on Scaling. It is well known that in the educational sciences, the research base on how to bring validated educational practice to scale is limited (Denton, Vaughn, & Fletcher, 2003). In this type of research, attempts would be made to implement educational research on a large-scale basis and study the process of implementation in a systematic way, focusing initially on a limited number of school sites and then scaling up to many sites. By studying this process, it may be possible to discern methods and procedures that will facilitate the implementation of other forms of educational research (Elmore, 1996). As yet there has been little emphasis on scaling as a topic in educational research. In fact, there is often a disconnect between the research that might occur in a laboratory or a school and its widespread implementation. There seems to be a middle step that is missing, which is research on what it would take to scale a particular intervention. In the absence of a research base on scaling, implementations of research are often diluted and implemented with poor integrity (Fuchs & Fuchs, 1998; Gersten, Vaughn, Deshler, & Schiller, 1997). Specific implementations frequently depend on the interest of a particular group of decision makers and do not fail to persist beyond the tenure of that group.

Solutions

In the past decade, a variety of solutions addressing these barriers have been proposed. Some solutions are relatively simple and consist mainly of blaming the problem on teacher preparation and higher education. Along this vein, it is common to note that the preparation of beginning teachers for teaching students to read is poorly aligned with the scientific base on effective reading instruction. Investigations of teacher preparation practices often decry the epistemological beliefs of the preparers as well as the scientific basis of the instructional approaches that are taught and implemented. Thus, scaling is often complicated not just by the need to instruct teachers in new practices but is also a matter of altering teacher preparation practices.

In response, there has been an emphasis on enhanced certification. A common question is why teachers are not as well prepared as those in other professional occupations such as physicians. These comments often fail to note that teachers are expected to teach based on completion of an undergraduate degree, whereas preparation for physicians is more extensive. Initiatives relating to enhanced teacher certification include incentives for teachers who receive extended preparation and who are able to pass advanced examinations. However, simply extending the duration of teacher preparation will not result in widespread implementation of practices based on scientific research unless the professors who educate these teachers accept and teach these practices. A larger and much more complex question is how to bring together those with conflicting epistemological beliefs while respecting the contributions of valid quantitative and qualitative research.

In response to resistance to change, more complex solutions have emerged. Most notable are the examples of federal policies cited previously, including the Reading Excellence Act and the reauthorization of the Elementary and Secondary Education Act, which includes Reading First. These federal policies share some common emphases including specific attention to the research base on literacy instruction. There is a focus on younger children including children in preschools and in kindergarten through Grade 3. There is also an emphasis on early identification, particularly the idea of assessing all children for reading difficulties so that teachers will know with whom more differentiated instruction is needed. These initiatives include attempts to more closely link researchers and educators. They require, for example, peer review of state applications for implementation of scientifically based literacy instruction as well as scientific advisory committees at a state level. There is a major emphasis on accountability for results, focusing on a state's ability to demonstrate improved student performance over a long period of time. There are also specific provisions for funding of statewide professional development efforts.

These approaches to policy at a national level were preceded by similar efforts in several states—most notably California and Texas. In the next section, we specifically discuss some of the issues involved in the development of the Texas Reading Initiative as an example of issues involved in scaling up research on reading.

TEXAS READING INITIATIVE

The Texas Reading Initiative began in 1996 under leadership of then Governor George W. Bush. It did not emerge from a vacuum but was built on a long history of reform initiatives revolving around joint emphases on accountability of results and local control. In 1984, Texas introduced a statewide accountability system under the leadership of then Governor Mark White, which emerged from a commission chaired by Ross Perot. One of the central tenets of this commission was the idea that states are responsible for accountability but that local schools are in the best position to determine how to achieve better results for children. Thus, a cardinal principle of the Texas Reading Initiative has been an emphasis on accountability and local control. There are relatively few instructional mandates, which would be difficult to implement through the Texas legislature.

Government–Business Collaboration

A key piece of this 20-year history of education reform has been government–business collaboration through the Governor's Business Council. The Governor's Business Council is a bipartisan group of business leaders in Texas that has worked closely on education issues beginning with the Perot commission. The Governor's Business Council has worked with both Democratic and Republican governors, with education always a central concern. It has supported the emphasis on accountability, but more important, has helped raise resources and public awareness of the importance of education. The development of the Texas Reading Initiative stemmed directly from this government–business collaboration, and members of the Governor's Business Council took prominent leadership positions in the Texas Reading Initiative from the beginning.

University Partners

As part of the development of the Texas Reading Initiative, the Texas Education Agency (TEA) developed partnerships with universities that included researchers in the area of reading. The Texas Education Agency initially supported the Vaughn Gross Center for Reading and Language Arts at the University of Texas at Austin, which was asked to provide professional development for classroom teachers on a statewide basis. The Texas Education Agency subsequently facilitated the development of partnerships with other university-based groups including the Center for Academic and Reading Skills and the Center for Improving the Readiness of Children for Learning and Education, both at the University of Texas Health Science Center in Houston and the Texas Institute for Measurement, Evaluation, and Statistics at the University of Houston. Each of these centers has had different but cooperative roles in the Texas Reading Initiative. At each of these centers were individuals with a long history of research on different aspects of reading and an interest in implementing the research in public schools.

Large Districts

Central to the development of the Texas Reading Initiative was the recruitment of large urban school districts. One of the largest school districts in the state, the Houston Independent School District, has about 220,000 students including over 200 elementary schools. The superintendent at the time, Rod Paige (subsequently Secretary of Education in the G. W. Bush administration), developed a district-wide reading initiative in 1996 that coincided with the development of the Texas Reading Initiative. This occurred with the involvement of researchers at the University of Texas Health Science Center in Houston but also involved major segments of the district's language arts community, the business community, and parents. A Department of Reading was created, and a systematic attempt was made to upgrade professional development for all teachers in the district. The principles of the Texas Reading Initiative were adopted and systematically applied across the district. Other districts were also recruited early in the process, most notably, the Fort Worth Independent School District. Outstanding examples of implementation of reading instruction were sought across the state and then illuminated as examples of how schools could effectively teach reading, particularly in economically disadvantaged populations. These efforts resulted in identification of flagship schools in the state that were notable for obtaining excellent outcomes despite significant obstacles. The schools were identified on a Web site, volunteered to serve as mentors to other schools, and were described in a publication (Denton, Foorman, & Mathes, 2003).

Common Elements

There are common threads in all these efforts. One was an emphasis on scientific research on reading. This research focused on prevention as opposed to failure. The Texas Reading Initiative represents an attempt to identify children who are at risk for reading difficulties through ongoing screening of all kindergarten, first graders, and second graders and the provision of aggressive interventions so that all children would be able to read by the third grade and maintain that level throughout their schooling. The second was the importance of assessment for screening, guiding differentiated instruction, and for measuring outcomes. The third was a simultaneous emphasis on professional development and enhanced curriculums. Finally, there was an emphasis on attempting to provide formal and unfocused evaluations of all the different components of the Texas Reading Initiative for their effectiveness. These evaluations were oriented toward simple demonstrations of efficacy and surveys of consumer responses.

The implementation of the Texas Reading Initiative has been difficult. It includes an attempt to provide professional development for every classroom teacher in kindergarten through Grade 3 in the state. The Vaughn Gross Center for Reading and Language Arts developed curriculum materials for this professional development and trained a large group of individuals to provide the extensive professional development each summer. Teachers were funded to participate in the summer workshops, resulting in the participation of about 40,000 teachers in kindergarten through Grade 3.

Besides this emphasis on professional development of teachers, the legislature passed statutes mandating that each child in Texas receive a screening and diagnostic assessment of their reading ability in kindergarten, Grade 1, and Grade 2. There were no mandates about what tests should be used, but the statutes simply required that each child be assessed by the teacher using instruments that were reliable, valid, and aligned with scientific research. The assessments were specifically outside the state's accountability system, but the results were to be reported to the Texas Education Agency to ensure that the assessments were actually done. The Center for Academic and Reading Skills developed an early literacy assessment, the Texas Primary Reading Inventory (TPRI). A Spanish counterpart, the Tejas Lee, was developed by the Texas Institute for Measurement, Education, and Statistics at the University of Houston and the Office of Bilingual Programs at the University of Texas at Austin. These inventories are used by about 95% of districts in the state, reflecting the technical support of these instruments by the state. The instruments are not mandated, and some districts use alternative assessments that are on a list provided by the Texas Commissioner of Education by virtue of meeting acceptable levels of reliability and validity. Implementation of these instruments is not supported by the Texas Education Agency (TEA). The state provides financial support for all assessments provided under this legislation.

Other components of the implementation include funding of accelerated reading instruction. These funds are to be used to provide reading intervention for students in kindergarten, Grade 1, and Grade 2 who do not demonstrate mastery of important reading concepts on the early reading assessments. More recently, there has been an emphasis on early literacy programs that focus on Head Start and preschool programs. Curriculums and professional development are being introduced through the Center for Improving the Readiness of Children for Learning and Education to help preschool teachers enhance the literacy development and oral language development of young children. Requirements for program evaluation have been included in all of these different components, largely through the Texas Institute for Measurement, Evaluation, and Statistics.

Initially, there was considerable tension between the Texas Reading Initiative and teacher preparation programs in institutes of higher education. Explicit attempts to include teacher educators have been made, but the relationships have been contentious. This reflects many of the factors we identified previously as barriers. The Vaughn Gross Center for Reading and Language Arts with the TEA developed an initiative called the "Higher Education Consortium," which represents a systematic attempt to interact with teacher preparation programs around the research base in reading. This has proven effective not only in reducing some of the barriers but also in providing important information to those responsible for preservice development of teachers.

PROBLEMS WITH SCALING

The Texas Reading Initiative is an ongoing process and certainly has not been without problems. The four major problems are (a) implementation depends on a train-the-trainer model, (b) linking of programs and evaluation may be inconsistent, (c) important people leave, and (d) critics are persistent and generate disinformation.

Train-the-Trainer Model

The implementations in the Texas Reading Initiative have depended heavily on models in which the university-based partner and Texas Education Agency developed materials. These materials are then used to train individuals who in turn will do the training at the local education agency level. The materials themselves tend to be generic. The problem with these models is that even when materials are well organized and adequately reflect the intent of the training, the information that is provided to teachers by the trainers can be diluted or implemented without adequate integrity to the material and without further assistance in the classroom. As such, the generic nature of the material is then magnified so that the impact is diluted. The solution to the weaknesses of the train-the-trainer model is to follow up with in-class interactions with teachers using coaches and application of research-based ideas to curriculum materials used in the classroom. This link to the classroom has been difficult to achieve.

Evaluation of Programs

A second problem is that the implementations of new reading programs, assessments, and professional development are often difficult to link directly to outcomes. In this respect, school districts often receive funds, but exactly how the funds are implemented is not evaluated as carefully as might be desired. In many cases, an older model sometimes prevails, supported by funds provided by a federal or state agency to a school as "entitlement" funding. In Texas, this process is hampered because of the emphasis on local control and the lack of legislative support for mandates from the Texas Education Agency. This emphasis can be used to support the need for flexibility even at the level of implementing program evaluations. At the same time, all programs do have evaluations that can be examined for efficacy partly because they occur in a state with an established accountability system.

Important People Leave

The Texas Reading Initiative had outstanding leadership from 1994 to 2000 that began at the level of the governor, included the governor's primary advisors, and expanded through the Governor's Business Council and the Texas Education Agency. However, with the presidential election, many of these individuals left the state and went with the President to Washington, DC. Although there has been continuity of the leadership through the legislature, Texas Education Agency, and different partners, dealing with turnover and other issues has been difficult. The presence of the research centers and support from the Texas Education Agency and Governor's Business Council helped maintain the impetus for the reading initiative.

Critics Generate Disinformation

Scaling research to practice through the Texas Reading Initiative has been hampered by the national visibility of the reading initiative and the persistent criticism of many of its fundamental tenets. These criticisms often come from individuals involved in teacher preparation or who adhere to alternative epistemologies in which all forms of inquiry are equally scientific and can address any question, causal or otherwise. Although constructive criticism is always positive, many of these efforts have generated disinformation that has made it difficult to achieve the type of consensus necessary to support research. These efforts include articles and materials that are easily available to teachers as well as papers in journals and books that are widely marketed to teachers and those engaged in teacher education (Allington, 2001; 2002; Coles, 1998; Taylor, 1998). The depictions in these documents of the context of policy-making in the area of literacy in Texas were generally incomplete and inaccurate, reflecting what are likely the personal viewpoints of the authors (see Rayner, Foorman, Perfetti, Pesetsky, & Seidenberg, 2002).

For Texas, the most serious misrepresentation is the depiction of the consensus building as a top-down process in which public and professional opinion was molded and solidified through a small but highly organized central group that conspired to inflict code-based instruction across the state (Allington, 2001, 2002; Coles, 1998; Ellis, 1998; Taylor, 1998). From our viewpoints, four essential pieces of the context have been ignored. The first is the role of parents in requesting more code-based (phonics) instruction for their children. These parents often have children with reading problems but aren't simply representatives of groups such as the International Dyslexia Society of Texas. Indeed, parent organizations such as the Texas Parent–Teachers Association (PTA) and various teacher groups supported the Texas Reading Initiative (e.g., Texas PTA, 2000). Resolutions concerning reading instruction from the Texas PTA were adopted at the 1995 convention and first appeared in the 1996 list of resolutions (M. Vuichich, personal communication, June 23, 2000). The problems that lead to the involvement of groups like the Texas PTA were that parents were attending meetings at schools and were told that code-based instruction is not necessary, not available, and so forth. Through these organizations, the outrage that parents felt has been clearly articulated directly to legislators who, in our experience in providing testimony, are compelled much more by these testimonials than by discussions of science. Both the International Dyslexia Society of Texas and the Texas PTA maintain lists of several thousand parents concerned about issues involving reading (M. Vuichich and J. Butler, personal communications, June 23, 2000). Are these parental concerns reasonable? Unfortunately, both the amount and quality of code-based instruction across the nation declined for reasons described by Pressley (1998) largely as a consequence of assertions about the role of code-based instruction in beginning reading that Pressley shows are not correct. This instruction is necessary but not sufficient for the development of proficient reading and has been difficult for many children to obtain (Pressley, 1998; Snow et al., 1998).

The second little-understood factor related to the implementation of the Texas Reading Initiative is the struggle in Texas to keep a balanced perspective on early reading instruction amid competing interests from multiple sources. Some of these sources included individuals involved in teacher preparation programs in higher education. Another group, never

identified by any of the critics, represented social conservatives and supporters of a curriculum proposal known as the Texas Alternative Document (TAD). The TAD was strongly supported by the social conservatives
in the state who traditionally push for explicit phonics instruction. Social
conservatives occupied 6 of the 15 slots on the State Board of Education
(SBOE) when the new state curriculum standards, the Texas Essential
Knowledge and Skills (TEKS), were adopted in 1997 (Johnson, 1997;
Manzo, 1997; Walt, 1997a, 1997b, 1997c, 1997d). The TAD was ostensibly
developed in response to early versions of the TEKS, which had little to
say about phonics instruction and did not, for example, require kindergarten children to know the names and sounds of letters (Lindsay, 1997).
The TAD was essentially a scope and sequence document—not a set of
standards. It would have mandated specific instruction in phonics—children would be expected to write over 50 phonograms before seeing print,
to learn even more phonics rules once print is introduced, and to read
highly decodable text beyond Grade 1. The TAD was the subject of significant advocacy in the state, resulting in acrimonious SBOE meetings and
legislative hearings (Ballard, 1997; D'Entremont, 1997; Garner, 1998;
Johnson, 1997, 1998; Manzo, 1997). It is to the credit of the governor,
Commissioner of Education, and SBOE chair that the TAD did not become the basis for the state curriculum standards because the support for
the TAD was quite intense (Johnson, 1998; Walt, 1997c). At one point, the
TAD came within one vote of SBOE approval (Walt, 1997d).

The third missing component is the failure to take into account the
policymaking context in Texas. Educational reform in Texas has been an
ongoing process since 1984, with the Perot Commission and its focus on accountability and class size (Winnick, 1997). Since that time, reform has been
a bipartisan initiative based on two key principles: local control and accountability. The philosophy is that schools in Texas can teach however
they want so long as they meet accountability standards. The decisions are
up to shared decision-making teams that exist at each school. Code can be
taught implicitly, explicitly, or through osmosis so long as the accountability goals are met. As Winnick (1997) stated

> If you want to propose approaches to reading instruction in Texas, these pol-
> icy positions [local control and accountability] are important. We welcome
> any of you who can convince a local community that you have an approach
> worth trying. Our ability to measure and publicize results makes Texas a pre-
> ferred venue for reading program evaluation. We are comfortable in trying
> different approaches, because we are able and willing to monitor and publi-
> cize results. This ability to shift decisions and responsibility for results to the
> community is the cornerstone of our accountability system. (p. 1)

These problems lead to the fourth area not addressed by critics—the
broad base of support behind the TEKS and the Texas Reading Initiative.

Over 400 individuals contributed to the TEKS (Lindsay, 1997). Many of these individuals, as well as representatives of larger groups (e.g., Texas PTA), testified before the SBOE in support of the TEKS (Lindsay, 1997). Over 18,000 faxes and letters were written in support of adoption of the TEKS (Lindsay, 1997; Walt, 1997d). Reading professionals with multiple perspectives contributed to and publicly endorsed the TEKS (Hill, 1997). It was hardly the top-down process depicted by critics of the Texas Reading Initiative.

Summary: What Works?

In the Texas Reading Initiative, several related factors have facilitated scaling. The most significant is the key role of leadership at the top, with the Texas Reading Initiative providing clear examples of how state government, business leaders, and the state education agency can partner with universities and other interested groups, introducing new ideas and policies around education. Second, this type of leadership does not occur in a vacuum. The demand for enhanced reading achievement has been present in the state for many years, particularly through advocates and stakeholders for children who are struggling to learn to read. For example, Texas is one of few states that has separate legislation pertaining to children with dyslexia, a severe reading disability that accounts for the majority of individuals who fail to develop adequate reading skills. This legislation has been around for many years and emerged because of great dissatisfaction with the ways children were identified and served through special education services. This bottom-up process has been instrumental in helping achieve the goals of the Texas Reading Initiative.

The third factor is the statewide accountability system. There is enormous pressure on the Texas Education Agency and on local education agencies to demonstrate that more children have succeeded through performance on the state accountability tests. The presence of an accountability system has provided incentives for many school districts to participate in the Texas Reading Initiative with hopes of improving school performance in ways that especially demonstrate that economically disadvantaged children are narrowing the achievement gap.

Fourth, Texas' accountability system has been essential in providing incentives for implementation of the reading initiative. Coupled with an emphasis on accountability is permission for choice. One of the myths about the Texas Reading Initiative is that it represents a series of policy mandates. To reiterate, Texas is a very strong local control state, and the legislature is historically reluctant to approve mandates of any form. The reading diagnostic test legislation is a perfect example of this emphasis on choice in which schools can choose an instrument that meets different criteria. In fact, schools can use any test they choose but must pick one on a list provided by the Texas Commissioner of Education and based on evaluations of reliability and validity (one of the only mandates in the law) to receive funding to support the assessment. At the same time, the Texas Education Agency provided leadership by partnering with a university center to develop an instrument that complies with the requirement of the legislation. In other areas, including text book adoption and professional development, local education agencies have latitude in exactly how they will comply with different parts of the legislation supporting the Texas Reading Initiative. Altogether, choice is better than lack of choice, and the Texas Reading Initiative is not based on mandates. Rather, the emphasis is on accountability for results and local control.

The fifth factor has been the consistent appeal to scientifically based research and the involvement of university-based researchers. Appealing to research and the evidence base has been important to many local education agencies and certainly to individuals at the state level. At the same time, this appeal has also attracted considerable criticism from individuals who have other interpretations of the research or who simply do not accept the research to be a basis for decision making in education. Systematic attempts to respond to the critics have been made, with mixed results.

Sixth, teacher preparation and certification have been emphasized. The Texas Reading Initiative has worked closely with the State Board for Educator Credentialing around credentials for "master teachers." Examinations were developed that permitted teachers to earn advanced credentials that in turn were associated with salary increases and bonuses. In addition, an intense focus on both preservice and in-service professional development in schools was provided. The focus on preservice education for teachers has been contentious, but changes are slowly being made.

Ultimately, train-the-trainer models, appeals to research, and even accountability are diluted in the area where scaling must occur. The impact of all these policies and initiatives can be diluted if they are not compelling to an individual teacher, and the classroom is where it counts! Here, the absence of a research base on how to impact classroom practice is apparent. It is ultimately teachers' behavior that scaling must impact, not their knowledge or beliefs. The capacity to impact teacher belief systems is important, but if the policies are not compelling, teachers will simply shut the door and do what they want. When teachers are permitted complete instructional latitude by language arts coordinators, principals, and district administrators, it becomes even more difficult to scale research-based practices. These efforts have been hampered by consistent misrepresentation of the goals, purposes, and results of the Texas Reading Initiative.

What constitutes consensus in science and its relationship to policy is not as rigid as many of the critics of the efforts to scale reading research seem to desire. There are many examples in science in which a consensus emerges, and decisions are made despite an incomplete knowledge base. There is controversy, but the consequences are risks that are viewed with such high concern that policies are put into place. For example, data on the adverse consequences of fat and cholesterol for health are far from complete, and accurate predictions on individual outcomes are difficult to make. Nonetheless, dietary regulation of fat intake is recommended for everyone. Similarly, automobile emissions are cut at great expense despite incomplete evidence of the health risks involved, much less complete evidence that such policies reduce health risks or improve the ozone layer. We submit that not learning to read in our society represents a clearly demonstrated risk and that there is enough of a consensus to systematically implement practices that will prevent reading failure (National Reading Panel, 2000; Pressley, 1998; Snow et al., 1998). In the Texas Reading Initiative, the fact that education science is used as a basis for decision making on such a large scale is an educational innovation.

The main lesson from the Texas Reading Initiative is the importance of persistence and commitment to the task of scaling scientifically based research. Scaling will be more successful with a variety of sources of support, particularly in the context of strong leadership from government and educational officials. However, such support is never sufficient. In Texas, the efforts of policymakers occurred in the context of a long history of educational reform and emerging interest in evidence-based practices. There was also considerable support from parents and educators through a bottom-up process in which pressure was exerted to enhance reading instruction in schools. It is clear that scaling will be more successful with a variety of sources of support, but too little is known about securing and maintaining this support and ultimately, about having a sustained effect on day-to-day practices in the schools. Future efforts must focus on research addressing the factors and variables related to success for scaling as a key to any long-term effort. Examining the knowledge base related to successful implementations in education and in other disciplines is critical.

OTHER EXAMPLES OF SCALING

Reading

It is interesting to examine two approaches that include significant attention to reading as examples of models that have been scaled and sustained on a significant basis. One of these is the Reading Recovery program (Clay, 1993) and the other is Success for All (Slavin, Madden, Dolan, & Wasik, 1996). The implementations of these programs share fundamental similarities despite the fact that their underlying reading philosophies are different. In both of these programs, schools and/or districts must make a significant financial commitment to the program and must agree to follow procedures designed by the developers to ensure high-fidelity implementation (see Reading Recovery Council of North America, 2001; Slavin & Madden, 1999). The programs also require that trainers from a central facility be responsible for professional development of teacher leaders or facilitators within the school district. These individuals must be specifically identified. They then provide training in a train-the-trainer model but also provide coaching and facilitation on the site to ensure high implementation at the school. Both programs also systematically collect data on implementation and student performance. The teachers, schools, and districts are held accountable by the organization for integrity of implementation. This is often gauged in relation to the performance on different outcome assessments.

Cooper (1998) studied factors related to scaling and sustainability of the Success for All program. Cooper reported that some of these factors occurred within the school. High-integrity implementation was related to teacher acceptance and commitment and to the quality of instructional leadership. When successful, the leadership provided a supportive culture for change, addressed program resistance, made a commitment to the structure of the program, and hired strong facilitators at each school. Cooper emphasized the importance of "buy in" by all the individuals at the school. In general, schools that were able to obtain and maintain a strong level of commitment had teachers who felt empowered and who took ownership and responsibility for school change. These progresses enhanced feelings of professionalism and self-determination at the schools (see Fuchs & Fuchs, 1998).

Gersten et al. (1997) reviewed literature related to sustainability of research-based practices. Gersten found that sustainable interventions are

1. Practical, concrete, and specific, accounting for the realities of modern schools.
2. Have a scope and purpose that is neither vague or narrow.
3. Provide extensive collegial support networks within the school and between the school and the implementer of change.
4. Provide the teachers with many different opportunities and modalities not only for implementing new procedures but also for receiving feedback from the implementers.
5. Emphasize professionalism of teachers by involving them in problem solving and emphasizing the connection between everyday classroom situations and research.
6. Make sure that teachers can see the results of their efforts in enhanced student outcomes.

In both Cooper (1998) and Gersten et al. (1997), there is an emphasis on the role of leadership. Teachers need to perceive that instructional practices are valued by the principal and by the district. When this happens, they will implement the practice with more integrity (Klingner, Vaughn, Hughes, & Arguelles, 1999). Problems emerge when leadership changes so that effective practices may not be maintained and are commonly disregarded. This may occur even when practices have demonstrable effectiveness, and the school shows considerable improvement.

Examples of Scaling Other Types of Practices

Another approach to understanding how to scale educational research involves an examination of other disciplines. There are some particularly impressive efforts from Public Health in which schools are assisted in providing interventions that address the prevention of cardiovascular disease through exercise and nutrition. What is different about these programs relative to education is that the research implementations derive from large-scale clinical trials. The budgets for these trials are much larger than those typically seen in education. In addition, there has been explicit focus on the development of a research base that explicitly addresses scaling as part of the clinical trials. In public health, this research base has led to the development of theories of scaling. For example, diffusion theory has been used to describe how organizations adopt practices that lead to sustainability of research-based interventions. In this theory, *diffusion* is used to refer to a multistage process in which both individuals and organizations accept or reject innovations (Brink et al., 1995).

This process includes four stages: dissemination, adoption, implementation, and institutionalization. *Dissemination* involves informing stakeholders about the research and persuading them to try it as in intervention. In *adoption,* the entity makes the decision to commit to a program, which is often defined simply as the purchase of program materials. The *implementation* process involves actually carrying out the program. In *institutionalization,* the intervention is integrated into the institutional culture through practice and policy. The program becomes an integral part of the organization and is incorporated into standard operations and its budget (Goodman, Steckler, Hoover, & Schwartz, 1993), and obviously, for institutionalization to occur, the program requires resources far beyond the research agency's funding.

Project "child and adolescent trial for cardiovascular health" (CATCH) is an intervention that provides for enhanced nutrition and exercise to prevent obesity and reduce risk for cardiovascular disease in students (Hoelscher et al., 2001; Kelder et al., 2002). This program has been implemented in 25% of the school districts in Texas. It has great support from the State Board of Education. It is a program that includes the physical education teachers and district personnel responsible for nutrition. The interventions were initially developed and implemented through large-scale clinical trials in which the program materials were shown to be effective in increasing student's exercise and awareness of nutritional issues, with effects on weight and cardiovascular fitness. Then, through systematic attempts to institutionalize the procedures, the researchers worked with individuals at district and state levels to try to persuade schools to adopt these initiatives. The degree to which these materials have been adopted in Texas attests to the viability of this particular process as well as the capability for sustaining it over a period of years.

There are some important differences between the implementation of programs like Project CATCH and the efforts to implement the research on reading development and instruction that has been the topic of this chapter. First, the research base that supported the value of the implementations at the level of large-scale interventions was stronger than what exists in reading research. In general, in research on reading, interventions tend to be on a relatively small scale, and scaling moves almost directly from relatively small-scale studies to statewide implementations. In contrast, the interventions in public health models have an intermediate phase in which they are subjected to large-scale clinical trials in which issues around scaling are addressed as part of the clinical trial. Thus, in interacting with policymakers, the public health results are more like those that emerge from a trial in medicine, involving large numbers of children, schools, and teachers. Second, the interventions in Project CATCH occur in an area in which there is not a long history of contentiousness. This contrasts to a century of persistent reading wars. In Project CATCH, the community itself was not divided. Researchers had a consensus, and internal bickering about the role of science and clashing epistemologies did not exist. In other respects, the process of successfully scaling programs like Reading Recovery and Success for All parallels those observed in Project CATCH (Denton et al., 2003).

OVERALL CONCLUSIONS

In summarizing these different factors influencing scaling, Denton et al. (2003) provided a five-phase model for scaling and sustaining educational interventions:

1. Development of the intervention.
2. Empirical evaluation of the intervention.
3. Tests of robustness and generalizability.
4. Scaling up and sustaining.
5. Networking.

Within the scaling phase, steps included (a) dissemination, (b) decision, (c) implementation, (d) transition, (e) confirmation, and (f) institutionalization.

A detailed description of the model is beyond the scope of this chapter. It builds on Fuchs and Fuchs (1998) and Gersten et al. (1997) and incorporates components of diffusion theory. The critical point is that this and any other model of scaling be empirically evaluated. In public health models, scaling is an explicit research focus and is incorporated into the evaluation research. Such models can then be evaluated and used to scale research in other areas.

Education research would also benefit from explicit, empirically based attempts not only to scale research-based practices but also the development and evaluation of models, theories, and frameworks used to scale the research. Otherwise, attempts to scale will be largely anecdotal, and the gap in research, policy, and implementation in schools will remain wide. Such research must be more than description and should include attempts to address mechanisms, which may indicate a need for qualitative components of the research. Understanding the experience of principals, teachers, and policymakers through interviews, focus groups, and other more experiential approaches will help identify processes that promote or impede scaling (Shavelson & Towne, 2002). Research remains the key not only to developing and evaluating effective interventions but also for scaling and implementing the findings of the research.

In examining successfully scaled research, one sees the power of top-down mandates, of manualized procedures and products, and of bottom-up influences such as parental concerns about specific groups of students and of teacher-empowerment movements. The potency and sustainability of teacher empowerment is apparent in the success of whole-language, literature-based, and guided-reading approaches like Reading Recovery. These approaches were developed in part in reaction to the influence of the basal reader on beginning reading instruction. Some academic leaders have successfully steered teacher empowerment toward reflection on practice: Gardner (1983) with the idea of multiple intelligences, Hirsch (1996) with the core knowledge curriculum, Levin (1988) with accelerated schools, and Sizer (1984) at the high school level with the Coalition of Essential Schools.

Procedures and products are often better received in schools with educators who deal with difficult realities related to poverty and second-language issues. Success for All (Slavin & Madden, 1999), for example, is a school reform model that has become institutionalized as the Title I program in many districts. It is implemented by an organization that provides curriculum, teacher professional development, facilitators, tutors, and support staff. Similar components have been integrated into the implementations of different basal reading programs across the country. However, the latter is also evidence in support of the role of parents and others pressuring schools to improve practice. Thus, the factors affecting scaling of interventions are truly multilevel: students, parents, communities, teachers, schools, districts, states, and nations. Scaling is most effective when top-down and bottom-up practices converge. The Texas Reading

Initiative is an example of the convergence. We hope that the promise of No Child Left Behind Act and Reading First will be actualized by a similar coalescence of top-down and bottom-up processes that are inherent to successful scaling of research in reading and other areas.

REFERENCES

Adams, M. J. (1990). *Beginning to read: Thinking and learning about print.* Cambridge, MA: MIT Press.

Allington, R. A. (2001). Crafting state educational policy: The slippery role of research and researchers. *Journal of Literacy Research, 31,* 457–482.

Allington, R. A. (2002). *Big brother and the national reading curriculum: How ideology trumped evidence.* New York: Heinemann.

Anderson, K. (2000, June 18). The reading wars: Understanding the debate over how best to teach children to read. *Los Angeles Times,* p. 5.

Ballard, D. (1997, July 8). Still a chance to get Texas education on right track. *Houston Chronicle,* p. 23.

Brady, S. A., & Shankweiler, D. P. (1991). *Phonological processes in literacy.* Hillsdale, NJ: Lawrence Erlbaum Associates.

Brink, S. G., Basen-Engquist, K. M., O'Hara-Thompkins, K. M., Parcel, G. S., Gottlieb, H. H., & Lovato, C. Y. (1995). Diffusion of an effective tobacco prevention program. Part I: Evaluation of the dissemination phase. *Health Education Research, 10,* 283–295.

Carnine, D. (2000). Why education experts resist effective practices. *Report of the Thomas B. Fordham Foundation.* Washington, DC: Thomas B. Fordham Foundation.

Clay, M. M. 1993. *Reading Recovery: A guidebook for teachers in training.* Portsmouth, NH: Heinemann.

Coles, G. (1998). *Reading lessons: The debate over literacy.* New York: Hill & Wang.

Cooper, R. (1998). *Socio-cultural and within-school factors that affect the quality of implementation of school-wide programs* (Tech. Rep. No. 28). Baltimore, MD: Johns Hopkins University, Center for Research on the Education of Students Placed At-Risk.

Denton, C. A., Foorman, B. R., & Mathes, P. M. (2003). Schools that "beat the odds": Implications for reading instruction. *Remedial and Special Education, 24,* 258–261.

Denton, C. A., Vaughn, S., & Fletcher, J. M. (2003). Bringing research to practice in reading intervention to scale. *Learning Disabilities Research and Practice, 18,* 201–211.

D'Entremont, C. (1997, June 10). Distrust of Texas teachers. *Houston Chronicle,* p. 35.

Donovan, M. S., & Cross, C. T. (2002). *Minority students in special and gifted education.* Washington, DC: National Academy Press.

Elementary and Secondary Education Act of 2001, Pub. L. No. 117-110, 115 Stat. 1425 (2002).

Ellis, L. (1998). We'll eat the elephant one bite at a time: The continuing battle for control of literacy education in Texas. In K. Goodman (Ed.), *In defense of good teaching: What teachers need to know about the reading wars* (pp. 87–105). York, ME: Stenhouse.

Elmore, R. F. (1996). Getting to scale with good educational practice. *Harvard Educational Review, 66,* 1–26.

Fuchs, D., & Fuchs, L. S. (1998). Researchers and teachers working together to adapt instruction for diverse learners. *Learning Disabilities Research and Practice, 13,* 126–137.

Gardner, H. (1983). *Frames of mind.* New York: Basic Books.

Garner, D. (1998, June 17). Why students can't read: The approach is all wrong. *Plano Star Courier,* pp. 6A, 7A.

Gersten, R., Vaughn, S., Deshler, D., & Schiller, E. (1997). What we know about using research findings: Implications for improving special education practice. *Journal of Learning Disabilities, 30,* 466–476.

Goodman, R. M., Steckler, A., Hoover, S., & Schwartz, R. (1993). A critique of contemporary community health promotion approaches: Based on a qualitative review of six programs in Maine. *American Journal of Health Promotion, 7,* 208–220.

Hill, M. H. (1997, June 9). Alternative would mean less control of schools. *Houston Chronicle,* p. 23.

Hirsch, E. D. (1996). The *schools we need and why we don't have them.* New York: Doubleday.

Hoelscher, D. M., Kelder, S. H., Murray, N., Cribb, P. W., Conroy, J., & Parcel, G. S. (2001). Dissemination and adoption of the child and adolescent trial for cardiovascular health (CATCH): A case study in Texas. *Journal of Public Health Management and Practice, 7,* 90–100.

IDEA. (1997). Individuals With Disabilities in Education Act. Retrieved October 21, 2005, from http://www4.law.cornell.edu

Johnson, R. C. (1997, April 23). Texas standards flags hold up check to center. *Education Week,* p. 13.

Johnson, R. C. (1998, February 4). Pace is relentless for Texas school board chairman. *Education Week,* p. 11.

Kelder, S. H., Osganian, S. K., Feldman, H. A., Webber, L. S., Parcel, G. S., Leupker, R. V., Wu, M. C., & Nader, P. R. (2002). Tracking of physical and physiological risk variables among ethnic subgroups from third to eighth grade: The child and adolescent trial for cardiovascular health cohort study. *Preventive Medicine, 34,* 324–333.

Klingner, J. K., Vaughn, S., Hughes, M. T., & Arguelles, M. E. (1999). Sustaining research-based practices in reading: A 3-year follow-up. *Remedial and Special Education, 20,* 263–274, 287.

Levin, H. M. (1988). *Accelerated schools for at-risk students.* New Brunswick, NJ: Center for Policy Research in Education.

Liberman, A. M. (1997). How theories of speech affect research in reading and writing. In B. A. Blachman (Ed.), *Foundations of reading acquisition and dyslexia: Implications for early interventions* (pp. 3–19). Mahwah, NJ: Lawrence Erlbaum Associates.

Lindsay, D. (1997, November 12). Double standards. *Education Week, 17,* 33.

Lukatela, G., & Turvey, M. T. (1998). Reading in two alphabets. *American Psychologist, 53,* 1057–1072.

Lyon, G. R., Fletcher, J. M., Shaywitz, S. E., Shaywitz, B. A., Torgesen, J. K., Wood, F. B., Schulte, A., & Olson, R. (2001). Rethinking learning disabilities. In C. E. Finn, Jr., R. A. J. Rotherham, & C. R. Hokanson, Jr. (Eds.), *Rethinking special education for a new century* (pp. 259–287). Washington, DC: Thomas B. Fordham Foundation and Progressive Policy Institute.

Manzo, K. K. (1997, June 18). Showdown on Texas curriculum standards cited. *Education Week,* p. 3.

McCardle, P., & Chhabra, V. (Eds.) (2004). *The voice of evidence in reading research.* Baltimore: Paul H. Brookes.

National Commission on Excellence in Education. (1983). *A nation at risk: The imperative for educational reform.* Washington, DC: U.S. Department of Education.

National Reading Panel. (2000). *Teaching children to read: An evidence-based assessment of the scientific research literature on reading and its implications for reading instruction.* Bethesda, MD: National Institute of Child Health and Human Development.

President's Commission on Excellence in Special Education. (2002). *A new era: Revitalizing special education for children and their families*. Retrieved September 21, 2004, from http://www.ed.gov/inits/commissionsboards

Pressley, M. (1998). *Reading instruction that works: The case for balanced teaching*. New York: Guilford.

Rayner, K., Foorman, B. R., Perfetti, C. A., Pesetsky, D., & Seidenberg, M. S. (2002). How should reading be taught? *Scientific American, 286*, 84–91.

Reading Recovery Council of North America 1998. (2001). *Standards and guidelines of the Reading Recovery Council of North America* (3rd ed.). Columbus, OH: Author.

Shavelson, R. J., & Towne, L. (2002). *Scientific research in education*. National Research Council. Washington, DC: National Academy Press.

Sizer, T. R. (1984). *Horace's compromise: The dilemma of the American high school*. Boston: Houghton Mifflin.

Slavin, R. E., & Madden, N. A. (1999). *Disseminating success for all: Lessons for policy and practice* (Tech. Rep. No. 30). Baltimore, MD: Johns Hopkins University, Center for Research on the Education of Students Placed At-Risk.

Slavin, R. E., Madden, N. A., Dolan, L. J., & Wasik, B. A. (1996). *Every child, every school: Success for all*. Thousand Oaks, CA: Corwin Press.

Snow, C. (2002). *Reading for understanding*. Santa Monica, CA: Rand Corporation.

Snow, C. E., Burns, S. M., & Griffin, P. (Eds.). (1998). *Preventing reading difficulties in young children*. Washington, DC: National Academy Press.

Stanovich, K. E. (2000). *Progress in understanding reading: Scientific foundations and new frontiers*. New York: Guilford.

Stanovich, P. J., & Stanovich, K. E. (2003). *Using research and reason in education: How teachers can use scientifically based research to make curricular decisions*. Washington, DC: National Institute for Literacy.

St. Pierre, E. A. (2000). The call for intelligibility in postmodern education research. *Educational Researcher, 29*, 25–28.

Taylor, D. (1998). *Beginning to read and the spin doctors of science: The political campaign to change America's mind about how children learn to read*. Urbana, IL: National Council of Teachers of English.

Texas Parent–Teachers Association. (2000). *Legislative resolutions*. Austin, TX: Author.

Vaughn, S., & Dammann, J. E. (2001). Science and sanity in special education. *Behavioral Disorders, 27*, 21–29.

Walt, K. (1997a, July 11). Bitterly divided board approves new academic standards. *Houston Chronicle*, p. 1.

Walt, K. (1997b, July 12). Board divided on academic standards/Conservatives request changes, but lack votes to block approval. *Houston Chronicle*, p. 29.

Walt, K. (1997c, July 10). Fight over education standards to climax/Final curriculum debate set for today in Austin. *Houston Chronicle*, p. 29.

Walt, K. (1997d, May 9). Group nearly derails educational revisions. *Houston Chronicle*, p. 37.

Winnick, D. (1997, May). *Data, not dogma*. Paper presented at the conference on Critical balances: Early reading for lifelong literacy, Houston, TX.

4

Learning to Do Educational Research[1]

Robert C. Calfee
University of California, Riverside

Roxanne Greitz Miller
Chapman University

Kim Norman
California State University, Fullerton

Kathy Wilson and Guy Trainin
University of Nebraska, Lincoln

In this chapter, we present an account of selected research and development programs in the literacy arena conducted over the last decade under the direction of R. C. Calfee in collaboration with his coauthors. Three specific projects provide context and empirical findings for approaching the issue of translation of research into practice. Following are brief sketches of each project, laying out the framework and research strategy along with goals for practice. All three projects explore professional development strategies designed to promote fundamental change in teachers' knowledge, beliefs, and practices consistent with current sociocognitive learning theories. A concomitant concept has emerged during the work: the influence of organizational and contextual factors in generalizing the initiation and sustainability of the core concept. Following brief sketches of the three projects, we explore three themes emerging from our experiences in translating research into practice and then address the four questions posed by the editors.

[1]Support provided by Spencer 199900046, IERI 9979834.

THREE PROJECTS

READ-Plus

The umbrella project for this collection, READ-Plus, is a comprehensive and developmental literacy program incorporating four curriculum elements (decoding, vocabulary, narrative, exposition) within a constructivist instructional design also comprising four elements (connect, organize, reflect, extend); the early history of the project is recounted by Calfee and Patrick (1995). The project began in 1980 in response to the request by Graystone Elementary School in San Jose, California, for a review of their literacy program and suggestions for choosing a new basal series. R. C. Calfee and a team of Stanford graduate students met with the faculty during a summer workshop to discuss the implications of social-cognitive principles for practice, focusing on teacher knowledge and beliefs. Although the workshop had been requested by the teachers, the initial response was rather negative: "Too much theory! When will you tell us what to do? Why worry about memory and attention—we need to teach reading." The workshop was indeed rough around the edges; it was the team's first serious foray into a practical setting, and the materials were more suited to a doctoral seminar than a practitioner workshop. Our model of collaboration was that the Stanford team would present theory and research, and the Graystone team would provide the "so what" based on their extensive experience. The day was saved by two people: Jean Funderburg, the principal, and Doris Dillon, an outstanding kindergarten teacher. Funderburg offered low-key but persistent encouragement of the faculty following each session, and Dillon expressed enthusiasm for a framework that made sense of what she did in her classroom. By the end of the workshop, the teachers had committed to trying out the framework during the following school year. They would continue with the same basal series but prioritize some curriculum segments (e.g., stories with a solid narrative structure) and drop others (rote learning of vocabulary) while adopting an instructional strategy quite unlike the initiate–respond–evaluate (IRE) embedded in the Teacher's Manual (Cazden, 1988). The Stanford team developed *THE BOOK for the Reading Teacher* (Calfee & Associates, 1981) as a resource guide including sample lessons and assessments but in no way a replacement for the teachers manual.

The Graystone project affected major elements of curriculum, instruction, assessment, and organizational patterns over what became a multiyear collaboration. Evidence showed substantial improvements in student achievement on state indicators as well as on classroom-based assessments, particularly in the areas of writing and motivation. The impact on teachers was, from our perspective, the more important outcome. The project eventually came to an end as a school-wide endeavor; for 3 years in a row, Funderburg was informed by the district prior to the beginning of the school year that she would be returned to a classroom assignment and a new principal assigned and then at the last hour asked to remain as principal. After the third such experience, she took an extended leave to enter Stanford's doctoral program. Individual teachers, despite shifts in grade and school assignments, appeared to undergo fundamental changes, some of which we describe following.

Support from the Stanford team was largely voluntary and incidental. The project had little grant support, but as the years progressed, the model, which was eventually christened READ-Plus, emerged as a platform for conducting a variety of in situ investigations of literacy acquisition with external funding. When implemented as a school-wide strategy, the READ-Plus agenda entailed substantial changes in philosophy and practice. For practical reasons, we moved programmatically to explore two extensions, "Word Work" and "Reading and Writing About Science," described following. Limiting the agenda to specific curriculum components and selected grades proved more palatable, especially for schools serving large proportions of students with special needs and overwhelmed with a plethora of disconnected projects. The focal elements in these two projects—Decoding-Spelling and Exposition—were especially challenging for teachers, so it made sense to focus our research activities on these elements. To be sure, this approach brought some difficulties. READ-Plus transformed a school's contextual environment in significant ways, easing the way for experimentation across the board. A more limited agenda can foster a "band-aid" perspective—during certain times during the day and week, teacher and class engage in "something different," but otherwise it is business as usual; some teachers participate in the "special" program with little organizational impact. The focal strategy entails benefits and costs.

WordWork

The decoding/spelling component of Read-Plus, WordWork, provides kindergarten through second-grade teachers an elaborated framework for effective instruction in phonemic awareness and phonics (Calfee, 1998). Blocks of 2 weeks with short lessons spiral through a small number of highly productive letter–sound correspondences from the Anglo-Saxon layer of English, the primary source of the spelling patterns that students encounter in the primary grades. This focus on selected correspondences contrasts with current practice in which hundreds of objectives fill the phonics curriculum with weird patterns like "weird." The WordWork rationale emphasizes a streamlined and efficient phonics curriculum affording students rapid access to a variety of texts and expression in readable writing. The curriculum is supported by CORE (connect, organize, reflect, extend), the READ-Plus instructional model (Chambliss & Calfee, 1998; Miller & Calfee, 2004) we describe following. Lesson blocks incorporate the tenets of social cognition; students work in small groups actively exploring sounds and letters.

Phonemic awareness appears early in WordWork, but in ways that differ sharply with current practice. A single lesson block focuses on articulation, the production of sounds in the oral cavity. Based on the motor theory of speech perception (Calfee & Norman, 1999), students study the features of consonant production such as the contrast between popping and hissy sounds (plosives and fricatives for linguists). Organizing the consonants into categories or "chunks" provides a technical vocabulary for students (and the teacher) to think and talk about letters, sounds, and words across a range of new and unfamiliar words.

After establishing a small repertoire of consonants, the teacher immediately leads students to the phonics stage in which they connect the consonant sounds with symbols (letters). The strategy emphasizes the functional role of vowels; students learn to "make words" using vowels as "glue letters." The word *tap* can be built when "you touch your tongue to the roof of your mouth, then glue in the 'aaaa' sound and blow through your lips." WordWork emphasizes the *metaphonic* principle; students discuss why they spell a word in a particular way. For example, a student may explain that "'tape' needs the final-e as a 'buddy,' so that 'a' can 'say its name.'" Reflective talk based on an explicit technical vocabulary undergirds conceptual understanding of English orthography. Metaphonic talk is active, explicit, and social; conducted in teacher-guided, small-group settings, supported by "hands-on" devices such as letter tiles, allowing students to learn from peers, consistent with Vygotskian principles.

Reading and Writing About Science (RWS)

The RWS project centers around the Vocabulary and Exposition elements from READ-Plus. The curriculum integrates reading and writing instruction within the content area of science to improve students' reading comprehension and expository writing skills in the upper elementary and middle school grades (Grades 4–6). A significant undercurrent is the development of academic language encompassing all forms of spoken and written language (Heath, 1983). The RWS curriculum highlights the Read-Write Cycle, a variation of the CORE framework (Calfee & Miller, in press; Chambliss & Calfee, 1998). The Cycle reflects the essential connections between reading comprehension and writing performance for the expository genre.

Three principles are foundational for the RWS project. First, integration of reading and writing in instruction is key to improving students' reading comprehension and writing skills (Nelson & Calfee, 1998; Sperling & Freedman, 2002; Tierney & Shanahan, 1991). Second, all students, but particularly those who struggle with writing, benefit from explicit instruction in cognitive and sociocognitive strategies in reading, writing, and problem solving (Carr & Ogle, 1987; Lapp, Flood, & Hoffman, 1996; Prain & Hand, 1996). Third, incorporating research-based techniques into classroom practice depends more on teachers than on programs (Robinson, 1998). Hence, the emphasis is on instructional strategies that are *efficient,* not requiring additional enormous amounts of time to implement in the classroom; *effective,* incorporating methods that can be applied to a broad range of texts, grade levels, and subject areas; and *adaptable,* allowing the teacher to employ the strategies across a broad range of student achievement levels and interests.

In this chapter, we lay out three themes that capture our experiences during these research activities and then respond to the four questions presented by the editors. The themes are designed to provide coherence to the responses, so the reader will encounter some intentional redundancy.

THREE THEMES

Scientists learn methods for conducting research, and then they perform investigations using these techniques. This image of the scientific enterprise is promulgated from the early grades onward, including college and in some instances, even graduate study. Our position departs from this image to suggest that learning is an essential element in the research process, especially when the aim is to connect basic investigations with practical application. The three themes address this connection: (a) research as complex learning, (b) research valid for applied outcomes, and (c) research on the application of research to practice. The themes will not proceed in a linear sequence. Rather, they attempt to capture the interactive nature of educational research. The three projects sketched previously illustrate the concepts.

Research as a Complex Learning Task

The first theme centers on the view of scientific research as a learning task: a form of complex problem solving, a human enterprise, an ongoing effort to understand our existence. Science relies on shared beliefs and values to be sure, but these are scarcely fixed for all time. Rather, scientists are distinguished by the capacity to advance knowledge through concepts, methods, and interpretive techniques that undergo continual change both incremental and fundamental (Kuhn, 1970; Phillips, 2000). Critical analysis is an important part of the scientific process; can conceptual and empirical results stand up against systematic challenges (Kincaid, 1996; Stanovich, 2003)? Generalizability is a critical consideration. Newtonian principles operate within certain boundary conditions but are not universal. This constraint does not lessen the value of the Newtonian principles, but illustrates the importance of establishing the limits of generalizability.

In educational research, the goals are to understand and influence significant social practices that are inherently complicated, dynamic, and changeable. Social policy (and hence, politics) is part of the equation. The situation may resemble arenas such as environment and transportation but seems more intense where children are involved. A technique or program is advanced as a remedy to an educational need, with accompanying conceptual and empirical support. For policymakers and practitioners, the obvious response is "go with it!" For the researcher, the obvious question is, "When and where will it work?"

The generalizability of educational research is obviously challenged by differences among people and contexts, but time and space also matter. Valid designs must account for these variations: people and contexts—the teacher in New York City confronts a setting quite unlike her counterpart in the Four Corners region: time—student learning takes place over lengthy spans as does student development. The same can be said about teachers. Historical trends also matter; consider the educational terrains from 1950 through 2025: space—a facet found in research designs idiosyncratically if at all. Organizational layers are part of this dimension: classroom, school, district, region, state, and nation (Bryk & Raudenbush, 1992). Geography offers another lens, both physical and social: from amber waves of grain and purple mountain majesties to inner city ghettos and rural outposts. Whether a principle or program—the effectiveness of direct instruction or the benefits of whole language—data-based claims must respond to critics who ask for evidence that scientific findings apply to "us in the here and now."

The point is not that education is infinitely complex but that pinning down the critical constancies in the midst of substantial diversities should be taken seriously (Calfee & Nelson-Barber, 1991). What seems to work in one setting may disappear in another context, hence, the common complaint that research findings may support almost any side of any issue. For example, does class size matter? The answer is clearly "It depends." This answer does not waffle; the research challenge is to pin down the dependencies. For a variety of reasons, educational research has been relatively unsuccessful in dealing with generalizability; even the popular meta-analytic strategies designed to identify dependencies leave much to be desired. The situation is similar in fields such as medicine and engineering despite their more exalted position (e.g., Marshall, 2003; Sanders, 2003). The public tends to overlook or forgive "failures" such as hormone replacement therapy or the freeway failures during the Loma Prieta earthquake. When a doctor experiments to help a patient experiencing a complex syndrome or an architect wrestles with a persistent roof leak, the public does not conclude that research in medicine and engineering is worthless. Rather, they recognize (albeit with understandable frustration) that practical application of research is a learning experience dependent on research findings, practitioner expertise, and collaboration among practitioners and researchers.

Research That Is Up to the Demands of Practice

The second theme centers primarily around issues related to the quality of educational investigations. To meet the considerable challenges of practical applications, educational research must meet high standards of scientific inquiry. This topic has garnered considerable attention in the past several years including the superb National Review Council (NRC) review by Shavelson and Towne (2002; also Natriello, 2004; Shavelson, Phillips, Towne, & Feuer, 2003), along with legislative mandates spelling out appropriate methodologies for establishing valid knowledge (Eisenhart & Towne, 2003).

Our first point under this theme is the importance of establishing a conceptual framework as a foundation; sound design, methodology, and analysis are more likely when based on a coherent framework (Chambliss & Calfee, 2002). To be sure, education does not possess the theoretical underpinnings found in some other professional arenas. More to the point, although "conceptual framework" frequently appears in discussions of research strategy, it is difficult to find explicit mention in methods textbooks. Indeed, the usual strategy remains the null-hypothesis approach from a half century ago.

A second point about quality centers on methodological adequacy. Generally speaking, multiple methods that triangulate on the problem would appear to be preferred. Debate since the 1970s has centered around "the one right method," often replacing reasoned argument with rhetoric (Phillips, 2000). Experienced researchers are often classified as either quantitative or qualitative, which then serves as the model for doctoral students when they approach the dissertation. Methodological pendulum swings have been substantial in recent decades. Half a century ago, the prevailing model for educational research relied on experimental designs using quantitative outcomes; the target treatment was compared with a control using pretests and posttests to assess the statistical trustworthiness of the findings. The shortcomings of this design are numerous. Sir R. A. Fisher (1935), the originator of experimental design, opens his first volume by conceptualizing a practical problem in agriculture with a four-factor design as the basis for adequate control, a technical requirement for validity that is largely absent from today's discussions (but cf. Anderson, 2001).

The 1970s saw a major shift from the previous paradigm. Funding priorities from the National Institute of Education began to emphasize qualitative methods. Such methods had always been part of the palette along with descriptive and correlational studies and case studies. More recently, policymakers have returned to the experimental-control "gold standard," which is promoted as the foundation for cause–effect attributions (Reyna, in press). This claim is questioned by many philosophers of science, partly because experimental-control designs seldom suffice for such attributions and because other methods are generally required to inform and support causal claims (Kincaid, 1996). As Pearson (in press) notes, randomized field experiments in medicine and elsewhere depend on substantial background research, both fundamental and applied.

A third point that has emerged from our experiences centers around generalizability methods originally developed by Cronbach, Gleser, Nanda, and Rajaratnam (1972) to extend the concept of test reliability. Cronbach (1957, 1975) also reflected on generalizability as a unifying methodology for the "two disciplines of psychology." The idea was to view investigations as "tests" subject to the same requirements of reliability and validity. In essence, generalizability places on the researcher the task of identifying the facets that influence a phenomenon, both directly and through interactions. To be sure, some investigators eschew generalizability, suggesting that their findings cannot or should not be extended to other situations. Such claims of uniqueness seem to us more appropriate to art than to science, both having value in their own right.

The point is that whether advocating quantitative or qualitative approaches, experimental or descriptive techniques, all those involved in the research enterprise—investigators, practitioners, and policymakers—can benefit by reflecting on the generalizability concept. Indeed, method should well be considered a design facet for purposes of establishing trustworthiness. Research that is valid for practical applications is ideally grounded in a coherent conceptual framework and is multifaceted both with regard to designs and methods. Our investigations have aimed toward this ideal through multiple, overlapping, and intertwined approaches more than "grand experiments."

Pragmatics in Applying Research to Practice

The third theme centers around the possibilities and problems of applying "what we know," realizing that knowledge is always imperfect. Given a research base of the highest quality, engineering is required to fit the results to new and different settings. Primary among the challenges to this task in education is the disconnect between the worlds of research and practice, which is arguably greater in this field than other professional domains (Slavin, 2002).

Our experiences suggest that at least two phenomena are at work here. First are the ongoing debates about the roles and responsibilities of educational researchers. The camps include (a) those who see themselves as pure scientists whose job is to search for "true" knowledge; (b) others who take a descriptive approach, documenting the successes and writings of the clients; and (c) social engineers whose aims are pragmatic. Each perspective possesses functionality, but substantial energy goes into arguments about the relative merits of searching for the truth (cf. Anderson, 2002; Metz & Page, 2002, for a significant exchange). Whatever the merits of the various arguments, for practitioners, the result is a cacophony that discourages trust in any general pronouncements. From the beginning, then, efforts at applications appear fragmented on one side and skeptical on the other.

The second phenomenon arises from the "decoupling" typical of the school systems in the United States. In general, efforts to impose standard operating procedures at any level resemble herding cats. Once the classroom door closes, the teacher steers the ship of students with considerable autonomy. The managerial tools and incentives available to principals are limited except for programs that take shape as rigid scripts, with patrols enforcing the rules—a tactic that raises other problems. The more remote a mandate from the classroom, the less the response resembles the intended outcome. The national infatuation with Standards illustrates the point. In California, challenging academic standards were developed several years ago for the basic curriculum domains. At the same time, a standardized multiple-choice test with no basis in the standards was imposed to establish accountability. Today, when California educators emphasize teaching to the standards, they mean preparing students for multiple-choice items associated with one or more standards objectives.

The bottom line is that the educational system lacks stable points of leverage for program development, evaluation, and application. Under the best of circumstances, a district superintendent or a board of education, convinced of the merits of a particular program for whatever reason, directs implementation in one or more schools. Earnest discussion with principals reassures the program developer or researcher that the project is on track, teachers buy in, and all seems well. Even under these conditions, the activities and outcomes at the school, classroom, and student level, if anyone bothers to observe, can vary substantially from the original conception: sometimes at the surface level but more often in the deep structure. That is, all participants may do what they think they are supposed to do, but without understanding of the fundamental concepts, all of the pieces may be there, but they lack the skeletal structure.

For researchers, this state of affairs is a real problem in the sense of unwanted complications; to be sure, scholars interested in organizational issues make a living from such situations. Our experience suggests that this latter perspective may offer ways to address the matter. That is, researchers who decide to move toward application need to also study the implementation process. They can either develop expertise in the relevant domains or explore collaboration with other disciplines, a strategy posing challenges of its own. At one time, the federal laboratory and center system (Vinoskis, 2001) seemed poised to support this strategy, but legislative support for the system has been erratic at best.

FOUR QUESTIONS

In this section of the chapter, we attempt to address four questions incorporating illustrations from the three projects, weaving in the themes along the way. The questions suppose that as researchers, (a) we aim to translate research into practice and (b) we actually know how to accomplish this task. Since the early 1980s, our team has indeed been interested in translation and believe that we have learned important lessons during these efforts. Whether we are actually prepared for this task is open to question, of course, especially when it comes to the task of scaling up. We were not prepared for this task by graduate work; and for academic researchers, engagement in practice can be hazardous for their publication records given the difficulty of such tasks and the time and energy needed to move from A to B.

The projects we discuss in this chapter were initially based in more than two decades of fundamental investigations grounded in the social-cognitive revolution of the 1960s and supported by a positive funding environment. In the early 1980s, the time seemed right for extending basic research to more complex settings, beyond what Glaser (1978) once characterized as "hot house" situations. The aim was not to expand a program, a popular idea in the 1960s (e.g., the First-Grade Reading studies; Bond & Dykstra, 1967), but to learn. How did the fundamental concepts and techniques play out over time and space, over contexts and groups? READ-Plus emerged as a research platform, an opportunity to extend the scientific agenda. For this reason, the task clearly fell within our province as researchers.

More recently, federal agencies have advanced the notion that researchers should act entrepreneurially to scale up their ideas and activities. Such a request is quite intriguing and can entice educational researchers to become advocates for their ideas and efforts. Without claiming to have completely avoided such temptations, we now approach the four questions from the stance that our aim is to advance a research agenda, which means grappling with the thematic issues raised earlier.

Question 1: Problems in Translating Theory and Research Into Practice

We first unpack three essential elements in this question: theory, research, and practice. Theory can be viewed from three stances. First is the academic perspective in which conceptual analysis provides an essential foundation for virtually all scholarship. A second emphasizes the underpinnings that connect research with practice. The third appears in complaints from practitioners that "All 'they' talk about is theory; just tell us what to do."

Research encompasses several constituents: empirical findings, methodologies, interpretations, and application. Schools must select research-based reading programs. A publisher may conduct rigorous evaluations to demonstrate positive learning outcomes, a relatively rare event. Other parties may employ the program in pursuit of other questions, and supporters can certainly use the data to advantage. Districts, schools, and teachers may also conduct investigations through local review of programs, pilot testing of materials, and occasional long-term evaluations; our experience is that such studies are discounted in favor of external, decontextualized reports. Local research may appear in anecdotal form in practitioner outlets, but less often in peer-reviewed journals.

Finally, practice takes different shapes. It can refer to a developer's success in demonstrating the successful application of laboratory findings in school settings over an extended time. Given adequate resources and administrative support, most programs can manage this level of translation with positive outcomes, especially when the indicators are defined by the program and results are short-run (Goldberg, 2003). A different translation occurs when practitioners adopt ideas and techniques, using as part of their argument their review of research evidence. Players in this scenario can include teachers, school administrators, or policymakers; examples range from whole-language activists to phonics advocates.

Four learnings have emerged from our work in this complex arena. We do not characterize the following items as problems in the sense of unwanted difficulties hindering our efforts but rather as opportunities for extending the scope of our research.

Instruction as Learning Rather Than Activity. The first point reflects the emphasis in our work on concepts rather than activities as the basis for improving literacy instruction. Activity is captured in the IRE sequence; the teacher manages a time-filling routine that proceeds regardless of the outcome. A middle school incident illustrates the activity concept. Students have written geometry proofs on the board, and the teacher moves along evaluating each sketch. A student inquires, "Every 'given' has to be there, right? I think that C needs to be there as the center of the circle." The teacher responds, "That's right." He modifies the proof and moves on with the activity. A conceptual response would have stopped the process: Why is C important? What happens to proof validity?, And why did the student ask the question? However, the clock was running.

The aim in each READ-Plus program is a shared understanding by teachers (and administrators) of fundamental ideas about language, literacy, and learning, which then provide the basis for adapting curriculum sequences and applying instructional strategies. In countries where education is viewed as a profession, the idea that knowledge is the basis for action provides a more friendly environment for this approach. To be sure, when the cognitive leap takes place for an individual practitioner, the result is a permanent change. At the outset, however, this mismatch between prevailing practice and the program foundations can lead to puzzlement and tension. Workshop evaluations complain frequently about "too much theory" and requests to "tell me what to do."

An incident in the early READ-Plus workshop illustrates the point. At the end of each session, teachers were asked to react to the morning's activities. As noted earlier, our team was new to the workshop business, and the focus on learning research probably seemed strange to the teachers. At the end of the second session, one teacher was bold enough to say, with some passion, "I don't understand most of what you're talking about—memory and meta-something and 'chunking.' And I don't see how any of this stuff is going to help me teach reading this fall! But I'm staying, because we made a commitment—just wanted to let you know...." Several heads nodded agreement; the event was critical in surfacing both reactions and emotions. The opening discussion the following day continued with questions about bridging ideas and practices. Our team possessed expertise of one sort, but we clearly were in need of the "wisdom of practice." The workshop was transformed by this event, which opened the opportunity to talk about literacy not as a basic skill but as a tool kit for problem solving and communication, the basis for the bridge that supported implementation during the following school year.

A central issue here is the assessment of student learning. For researchers, assessments are an integral part of program design; for administrators, assessments are tests; and for teachers, assessments are less clear-cut. In the translation to practice, two challenges emerge from our experience. First is the reliance in practice on surface-level indicators. The lesson—an event lasting an hour or less—is the centerpiece. If students complete the lesson activity, then learning has happened. Understanding and transfer seldom enter the picture. The second centers around the conception of individual differences. A common assumption in practice is that students vary in their potential, which leads to organization of the classroom into instructional groups, each associated with particular pedagogical practices and expectations. READ-Plus programs emphasize the commonality in human potential, more attuned to Brunerian/Bloomian notions that all students can attain significant achievements given appropriate instructional settings, time, and resources (Bloom, 1981; Bruner, 1966).

We assume that the same principles apply for adults, including teachers. Implementation of educational concepts and practices depends on learning outcomes. As we argue in our response to Question 3, success depends on time to internalize the concepts—time for practice with feedback in social settings that allow reflective interactions. That leads to the second topic in this section.

Sustaining Engagement.   A significant challenge, echoed by many colleagues, is the task of sustained engagement with and by districts and schools. Both prepositions are important. *With* refers to leadership changes needed to support agreements. *By* recognizes the tumultuous bureaucratic seas in which administrators operate. Educational reforms entail 3 to 5 years for implementation, evaluation, and institutionalization. Changes take different shapes at different levels of the hierarchy. Some READ-Plus concepts can be applied with positive effects at the classroom level in a matter of days or weeks. Expertise and automaticity take more time, requiring school-level support and collaboration. School-wide implementation typically takes years of stable leadership; a new principal with a new agenda can change the context overnight. District-level policies and actions have emerged in our experience as perhaps the most significant factor for sustaining program development and implementation—and the integrity of associated research endeavors. The cabinet—associate superintendents and coordinators—plays a critical role. They determine principal placements, allocation of resources, and establishment of priorities. Superintendents and boards may come and go, but cabinets remain. Sustained engagement is also complicated by the inefficiency of research teams including our own efforts (Calfee & Patrick, 1995). Schools have short attention spans for understandable reasons. Universities do not prepare researchers for the pragmatics of program implementation, and our team has learned on the job.

The Nature of Evidence.   The third problem centers around a cultural divide in views of the meaning and value of evidence. On one hand, data about student learning have limited impact on how schools operate, even in this age of accountability. Yearly reports of standardized test performance capture attention for a fleeting moment. Reactions fall into two categories. First is the "in your face" trend: Did scores go up or down? Gains are attributed to recent actions; declines call for something new. Second is relative rank: Schools with low scores are populated by students from poor families, a situation beyond the control of schools. The evidentiary base on which schools operate is sparse, most often externally mandated, multiple-choice tests and spring tests that arrive too late for action in the fall.

Other views of evidence build on a balance between externally mandated and internally generated sources of information, recognizing the several contrasts that distinguish these sources (Cole, 1988): authenticity of assessments, frequency of information gathering, availability of results, and linkage to curriculum, among others. Creation of longitudinal databases that portray trends is largely ignored in both external and internal assessment programs. Education is about learning, and one might think that as a matter of course, educators would look at students' progress through the years. Testing companies typically deliver the results in yearly chunks, however, leaving it to districts, schools, and teachers to link achievements across the years.

A final point about evidentiary matters is the scarcity of local evidence about significant factors influencing student learning. Teachers matter, but they are seldom identified; the value-added method offers an approach along these lines but is by no means a commonplace. Innovative programs are introduced to make a change, but systematic local evaluation of these programs is relatively rare, nor is local evidence necessarily used in making local decisions. A collaborative research-based innovation is conducted between a researcher and a local district. Results are positive, long-lasting, and appear to transfer to a broad range of academic outcomes. The researcher is enthused, and the results are published. However, whether the innovation is retained is likely to depend not on the evidence but rather the vagaries of the local context. Politics and procedures are more likely to carry the day than scientific evidence. Researchers are tolerated but generally play a negligible role in decisions.

Resources for Research and Evaluation. A fourth barrier springs from the limited resources available for educational research and evaluation. The low importance placed on educational research is reflected in funding levels both locally and externally. Federal investments are a fraction of a percent of the educational enterprise. States and districts conduct mandated assessments but rarely go beyond required reports. Outside research activities must pay their own way, often including released time for teacher attendance at workshops. As Slavin (2002) points out, districts increasingly request bonuses for participation in experimental studies. The costs for preliminary pilot studies in limited and voluntary settings may be relatively inexpensive, but the researcher who aims to translate using large-scale studies will confront serious financial challenges. We might imagine a coordinated strategy involving researchers, districts, along with state and federal governments in which the design and collection of data became a collaborative enterprise. Some efforts can be found along these lines (the First-Grade Reading Studies attempted this approach; Bond & Dykstra, 1967), but the starting and ending points typically rest on data that are already available from bureaucratic mandates, which may not inform scientific questions.

Question 2: Ways to Overcome the Problems

The challenges we described previously are genuinely daunting, and one can understand why educational researchers might choose to conduct their basic work and let someone else worry about application. After all, the academy does not necessarily recognize the value of practical application in the field of education and may even disparage such efforts. The key may be to transform application activities into genuine research. In the following, we discuss two strategies that we think hold promise from this perspective.

Embedding and Scaling. The first strategy centers around the idea of embedding theory and research in practice rather than conducting research as an external and largely decontextualized activity to be passed on to implementers and practitioners at the end of the project. In proposing this idea, we are not suggesting that researcher and practitioner become one and the same. Backgrounds and roles differ significantly, and appropriately so. The design experiment concept offers a useful approach for accomplishing this goal (Collins, 1992; Calfee, Norman, Trainin, & Wilson, 2001). This term has assumed several shapes in recent years; the features we emphasize are (a) clear conceptualization of the educational problem and an explicit design for exploring the problem, (b) professional collaboration with practitioner partners in the operationalization and implementation of the investigation, and (c) ongoing reviews of activities and outcomes and continuous adaptation of the initial design based on the reviews.

One result from this approach has been our discovery of the value of both scaling up and scaling down. An early experience from scaling up is described in Calfee and Patrick (1995) when READ-Plus attempted in the early 1980s to move from the original middle-class site in San Jose to a collection of downtown schools serving large proportions of students from poor homes for many of whom English was a second language. The issue was not whether the program might benefit these students, but how it could survive in the chaotic organizational contexts typical of such schools. The effort came at the behest of the district administration, but that did not help with on-site implementation. The bottom line is that, although this effort at scaling up was not successful, the team learned a great deal about the influence of organizational context.

The importance of scaling down is a more recent learning. Once a particular activity has been implemented across a significant number of schools and districts, it often makes sense for the researcher to step back for a thorough review in a limited number of settings to better understand process and product, success and failure, and possibilities and limitations. In offering this advice, we assume that the researcher retains his or her role as researcher, which may conflict with entrepreneurial pressures. The aim is not program refinement but a deeper understanding of the concepts.

For instance, in Year 3 of the WordWork project, the research team decided to downscale, working with six teachers who volunteered for intensive exploration of the program. Teachers and researchers met for a full day each month to discuss "nuggets and lumps" encountered during implementation of WordWork during the previous weeks. Teachers provided data at each meeting on the progress of focal students along with details of their experience with program concepts and procedures. The mantra guiding the meetings was straightforward: By year's end, every student would meet district reading standards. Each meeting included a critical question springing from weekly classroom observations/interactions by the research team. Because the teachers had a year or more of experience with the team, they understood the place of critical review, and each discussion quickly took a life of its own, as teachers contributed their own questions and reflections. They developed remarkable adeptness at playing with ideas and offering suggestions but also challenging long-held beliefs. For example, the procedure for merging articulation with word building ran counter to teachers' previous experience with phoneme awareness ("Which word begins with the /b/ sound, *pat* or *bat*?") and phonics patterns ("Today we will work with '-*at*' words"). The engineering of popping/hissy sounds and glue letters was a continuing challenge for the research team. As the year moved ahead, enhancements of this program component came not from theory but from reflection on practical experiences.

The teacher meetings also covered more general matters that proved critical for program implementation. Especially significant were classroom management and grouping arrangements. The more experienced teachers had relied on ability grouping for decades; the idea of heterogeneous groups flew in the face of established beliefs and practices. The metaphonic concept at the core of WordWork requires student interactions that are difficult to sustain when students at the early stages of learning are placed together; none of the students can contribute to the discussion. A significant breakthrough came when one reluctant participant finally agreed to experiment with a mixed-ability group. Her subsequent report on the outcome reflected a genuine aha that altered her thinking and led to observable changes in her classroom practice; it also affected the entire group. The scientific import of this anecdote (by no means the only instance from this category) was not to inform the program design but to identify critical elements affecting program implementation. Establishing the effectiveness of a treatment for a traumatic disease like Alzheimer's is an important research goal. Equally important for doctors and patients is uncovering the pragmatics for implementing the treatment, which is likely to require scaled-down research—but research nonetheless.

As the year progressed, the research team documented increased depth of understanding as teachers discussed what worked and what didn't within the WordWork framework. The exchanges were grounded in shared terminology and perspective and in a focus on evidence-based student learning. Indeed, students made substantially greater progress on district indicators than similar students in previous years. By year's end, the teachers were able to demonstrate that virtually all their students had indeed met district standards. As a research activity, the exercise was an important demonstration, but it also generated significant refinements and understandings in the basic framework. These outcomes came about through the scaled-down strategy.

The RWS project also downscaled during its 3rd year. The five teacher participants during this phase exemplified deepening of understanding. Particularly interesting was a ripple effect that occurred during the year. As teachers gained greater confidence with the theoretical concepts, they were more effective at interacting with one another and sharing ideas with peers and the principal. The result was greater school-wide interest in RWS strategies along with a heightened awareness by district teachers and the administration about the relation of critical literacy to support for content area curricula. As it turned out, California's budget crisis took center stage at this point, ending the project.

Multilevel Connections. The second strategy calls for engaging practitioners across organizational levels as participants in the design experiment process. Embedding at the level of the classroom teacher, which we illustrated previously, is critically important. However, to understand contextual interactions requires going beyond self-selected volunteers to wrestling with the hierarchy. Most difficult in this regard is the district, especially in a time of intense accountability to external mandates; next is the school, given that leadership is subject to continual change; easiest is the teacher, assuming that access can be established.

A fundamental tension in the READ-Plus model, characteristic of most sociocognitive models, centers around the concept of professional teaching communities, which flies in the face of the hierarchical organization of American schools. At one point in the evolution of the model, we revived the concept of the "inquiring school" (Schaefer, 1967) in which we proposed that full-fledged literacy might provide the basis for genuine and equitable interactions among the various levels of the hierarchy. Both teachers and administrators often comment that "they didn't have time to think about what they are doing." Equally important, from our perspective, different levels of the system employ different concepts and technical language to describe their work. For the district, the curriculum consists of the textbook adoptions; for the teacher, it means moving through the daily lessons, picking up pieces along the way. For a district, assessment refers to standardized tests; for the teacher, it is a first grader's ability to make his or her way through a sentence during round-robin reading. The elementary school principal faces the challenge of bridging these gaps.

A practical illustration of the mismatch is found in the teacher's role in selecting curriculum programs. Contractual agreements allow teachers a voice in textbook adoption. Anecdotes at school board meetings can have significant impact. However, the discourse is informal and experiential, with little reference to scientific evidence, published or local. The result is that the district cabinet often manages the actual decision.

In the WordWork study, for instance, 3rd-year teachers presented their work, including student outcomes, to a meeting of district and school administrators, which led to a public commitment by the district to a 3-year implementation of the program. On reflection, it is not clear that the presentation and the commitment were on the same page conceptually, but a year later, the district decided to implement a new basal adoption, in response to a state mandate, ending the earlier commitment. As researchers, we are still not sure how to interpret these findings. On one hand, for teachers and students, the achievement outcomes were impressive. However, as a study of scaling up, what would be the best way to move from these results to formulating the next study in the sequence in which the problem also encompasses the investigation of scaling up? Large-scale field experiments typically overlook local variations like those we just described. The assumption is that randomness will average out variations. We argue that understanding the nature of such variations is an important scientific goal in its own right.

Question 3: Success of Strategies

Success can be defined in various ways: (a) How many classrooms are presently using research-based Program X?, (b) Given that test scores have improved, who is benefiting—success for whom?, (c) What is the staying power of Program X at the classroom, school, and district levels?, and (d) What has been learned from the various programmatic activities that contributes to basic and practical understanding? Question 3 may also intend to direct attention to the strategies identified in the previous section: (a) embedding research throughout the process, and (b) connecting research activities across organizational levels.

A generalization stance means attending to a range of facets—people and organizations, learning outcomes, and time. Focusing for the moment on students, systematic, long-term follow-up encompassing a range of educational outcomes is difficult, especially in the absence of district engagement and especially for children from low-income homes. These students, the center of much of our effort, are prone to mobility, often moving within a district but sometimes within and across states; mobility can have a quite different meaning for English language learners. Nonetheless, we have persisted in pursuing students for 3 to 5 years using both standardized and project-based outcomes. Tracking such outcomes is challenging and does not fit neatly into the typical field-based experiment paradigm, which tends to emphasize quantity more than quality. Nonetheless, determining the success of a program—both the outcomes for students and the quality of the research endeavor—entails serious efforts to obtain such data.

A similar remark holds for adults. The National Reading Panel report (Langenberg, 1999) found little acceptable research on teachers and did not even mention administrators. We have pursued the hypothesis that substantial and long-term impact of any literacy program will depend on how it affects teachers—over the years, we have added administrators to this facet. Our experiences have documented a variety of remarkable multiyear transformations at the teacher and school level. As noted previously, all the school-level programs were eventually undone by district actions. Many teachers sustained the program concepts at classroom level, but teacher collaboration disappeared. Our conclusion is that it is possible to produce enduring changes in teacher knowledge and classroom practice that transcend particular programs, assignments, and contexts. However, moving from the classroom to the school level is essential, in our judgment, to provide students with the cross-grade consistency that is helpful for all children but essential for those most in need of academic support.

In the following, we present three snapshots that illustrate different perspectives for defining and evaluating the notion of success, bringing into play along the way the four points raised in chapter 1 (this volume).

A Principal With Vision. In *Teach Our Children Well*, Calfee and Patrick (1995) describe a 5-year READ-Plus project at a school serving a distressed neighborhood near Stanford University. Whether gauged by standardized measures of achievement, student and parent enthusiasm, reactions by the teachers, or attention to the program by the district, this project reflects the kind of bright-line event featured in practitioner journals like *Educational Leadership*. It was distinctive in several ways: (a) the largely unfunded activity was a collaborative endeavor, fostered by strong support from a remarkable principal who created conditions that led to the engagement of the entire school faculty; (b) the project continued to thrive well beyond any level of assistance from the original READ-Plus team; (c) the benefits for students continued when they moved on to middle school, and (d) the benefits for individual teachers continued when the principal was abruptly shifted to a different assignment.

The project demonstrated the effectiveness of a professional development program to dramatically enhance the performance of students from impoverished backgrounds. Over time, student performance as measured by standardized measures actually surpassed other district schools from more privileged backgrounds and not by changing the school's demographics. The children were still "from the 'hood.'" Equally important, from our perspective, was the sense of student efficacy evident in classroom activities and in discussions with individual students. Such reports are not unique to our program to be sure, but they can be evanescent and fleeting.

Eventually the project failed when the principal was reassigned. With the arrival of a new principal, connections were broken, teachers closed their classroom doors, and opportunities for collaboration came to an end. Not exactly a new story, and what did we as researchers learn? From this instance in the mid-1980s, the answer was the initiation of a research question that we have yet to fully formulate but that underlies subsequent investigations under the WordWork and RWS banners: In what ways can professional development activities incorporate elements that support continuing school-level collaboration among teachers under prevailing conditions including changes in school and district contexts?

We continue to wrestle with how to conceptualize this question. Our initial ideas built on Schaefer's (1967) concept of *The Inquiring School: Literacy for the Year 2000* (Calfee, 1992). However, rather than basing inquiry on social science methods, our notion was to use literacy as the foundation; teachers with a shared vision of literacy as the capacity to solve problems and communicate already possessed the tools for school-wide collaboration! Perhaps so, but political savvy is needed as well as knowledge and skill—in the United States, unlike countries where the school is led by a head teacher, teachers do not perceive themselves as possessing professional authority. This chapter is not the place to explore the matter, but the challenge is how to reconstitute professional status in a conservative system that for decades has relied on the factory model. As things now stand, reform depends on remarkable leadership outside the classroom.

WordWork as a Targeted Activity. Unlike READ-Plus, which sought to transform all aspects of literacy instruction for the entire elementary school, WordWork focused on a delimited practice within a segment of the curriculum and for a subset of teachers. Development of the project was driven by practical as well as scientific considerations: phonics instruction was becoming a state emphasis; research support was available in this arena; and primary teachers told us that they needed more assistance in applying the READ-Plus concepts in the decoding-spelling area, an understandable request given the limited background available from current preparation programs (Calfee & Scott-Hendrick, 2004). Conceptually, our goal was to explore the metaphonic principle, the idea that acquisition of English orthography by young students would be enhanced by an emphasis on understanding rather than reliance on rote practice.

Accordingly, we proceeded to amplify the decoding-spelling segment of READ-Plus as a research platform. The focus was on classroom practice—curriculum, instruction, and assessment. The clients were primary grade teachers, lessening the pressures attendant to school-wide change. The curriculum was limited to phonics; to be sure, in the primary grades for schools serving high proportions of students from disadvantaged backgrounds, phonics can dominate the school day. The conceptualization centered around effectiveness and efficiency—reaching all students while ensuring adequate time for parallel growth in vocabulary and comprehension. School-wide change was not part of the agenda, although the program emphasized collaboration among the primary-grade team.

At one level, the experiment was a success. Teachers who participated in the WordWork project deepened their understanding of fundamental concepts and became more effectual in applying their evolving knowledge and beliefs to practice. Significant changes were observed in classroom discourse during WordWork lessons, a marked departure from teacher-dominated talk (e.g., the IRE discourse structure) toward greater opportunities for students to interact with one another as well as the teacher in exploring orthographic concepts. In discussing spelling–sound relations, students performed as "little linguists" as they explained the functions of consonants and vowels.

These transformations were scaffolded by significant professional development activities. Teachers observed one another's instruction and reflected on transcriptions of classroom discourse talk from WordWork lessons. These activities led them to insights about discourse patterns and the effect of teacher questions on student engagement and understanding. Traditional teacher–student roles—what gets said by whom—shifted when students had time to explore spelling patterns and reflect on their findings. In this context, time had two meanings: A big objective like "the short-A glue letter" would be the phonics focus for 2 weeks rather than only a single lesson, and during this time frame would also be part of the background agenda throughout the entire day, not just the 15 to 20 min of the official phonics lesson.

Equally important, transformations in teachers' beliefs about teaching and learning led to expectations for elaborated student responses including explanations of their thinking. For example, in one of the monthly seminars, a teacher explained that she could "see the students thinking—WordWork teaches the kids thought processes, just like it is teaching the teachers to think." Another teacher added that he now required students to "do the work, to manipulate letters and sounds and reason out why they go together like they do." He remarked that too often the teachers do the students' work.

These reflections are important in revealing the shift from activity to learning observed in most WordWork classrooms. This shift seemed to persist over time, well beyond the project's tenure. The most obvious indicator was in "teacher talk"; teachers took less time and shaped their questions to evoke broader cognitive responses. When asked to explain what was going on, their intended focus was on finding out how students were thinking about a particular objective.

At several school sites, primary-grade teachers moved toward the creation of a Primary Team, joining kindergarten through second grade as a developmental group, a model employed in other countries but unusual in the United States. WordWork is designed as a spiral curriculum in which students move through the same orthographic concepts during the first 3 years of schooling. The spiral makes sense for young children and also promotes teacher collaboration. This model goes against the grain of current practice in which teacher manuals differentiate among grades; kindergarten is for readiness, first grade is the time for learning to read, and by second grade, the emphasis shifts to spelling.

Over several replications at different school sites, several WordWork teachers (their label) became recognized for their skill and knowledge in the area of early reading instruction. They presented at state and national conventions, served as district resources, and were notable for their professionalism in personal conversations. Classroom visitors were impressed, but as school and district change agents, their impact was limited. Success in this mix of outcomes can take many forms, but for the research agenda, scaling down was critical for investigating the process of teacher development.

RWS—Locating the Target. In the RWS project, the primary elements taken from READ-Plus came from the areas of vocabulary and expository text during the later elementary and middle school grades, with the intention of integrating language and literacy learning in the area of science. For readers familiar with the U.S. school system, the challenge of locating the target in this mix is apparent. Teachers in these settings tend to compartmentalize instruction, driven by instructional schedules akin to those in high schools. Even in the early elementary years, the concept of integrated, interdisciplinary instruction can be subverted by the textbook system and the daily schedule. "How are we going to have time to do 'this' *too*?" was often the first response from teachers asked to consider the project. A strategy designed to integrate elements on the daily menu was viewed as one more thing to do.

Once over this hurdle and with some consistent administrative support, an appreciation that integrating reading and writing in the content areas could actually save instructional time eventually became apparent to many teachers, sometimes by the end of the first curriculum unit. For most participating teachers, concepts of text analysis, rhetorical structure, graphic organizers, vocabulary development, and expository writing were genuinely new. The initial workshop sessions on theory were, as usual, a challenge. The rubber hit the road during full-day meetings held prior to each unit to review and discuss specific components. During these sessions, teachers worked through lesson plans, assessment materials, curriculum mandates (how to cover the textbook), and ancillary resources from the library and Internet.

In later phases, RWS scaled down the formal agenda for these sessions, encouraging teachers to become more active participants in curricular adaptations. Although teacher collaboration was an important facet of the program design, the reality was that interactions were largely limited to project meetings. Unlike WordWork in which primary grade teachers were eager to compare notes, the RWS experience suggests that upper elementary teachers are less likely to seek out occasions for collaboration—perhaps reflecting the enormous burden they bear as teachers of everything.

Administrators at the school and district levels found the project interesting, but this constellation of curriculum topics was not high on their priorities. In California, reading and math are the centerpiece for state testing and school accountability. Writing is tested at selected grades, and science is part of the mix, but neither receive much weight in the current school accountability index. Context matters.

In summary, instructional strategies falling under the general READ-Plus umbrella have proven effective for students, especially those who arrive at school lacking fluency in academic language. Professional development strategies, where these can be implemented for a sustained amount of time, appear to lead to fundamental changes for teachers. However, context is a critical factor. Efforts to deal with organizational issues at the school and district level—through sustained engagement, attention to evidence of instructional practice and student learning, and efforts to promote local support for research and evaluation—have been far less effective in our experience. Research on large-scale implementation may require small-scale investigations.

Question 4: Lessons for the Field

So, back to the title: What have we learned from our experiences about the relation/translation of educational research into the realm of practice? Our answer must necessarily be contextualized within the contemporary arenas of policy and practice. We couch the lessons against the three themes presented earlier.

Three Themes Redux.   If one is to accept current congressional and administrative promulgations, educational research is actually quite simple: follow legislated methodological mandates. Our experience suggests otherwise, hence the theme of research as complex learning. We think that a careful reading of the record of educational research during the past half century supports this conclusion. Research is clearly complex, whether in physics, biology, medicine, engineering, or education. The challenge is greater in those fields, such as the latter three, that emphasize practical application of fundamental findings.

At the core of any research effort are three elements: conceptualization, methodology, and the empirical base. In education, the conceptual base has substantial potential but is scattershot to say the least. Education is a political endeavor, and so the emphases can vary widely; environment and ecology pose similar challenges. Should education be conceived as the acquisition of prescribed skill and knowledge or the development of the educated individual capable of contributing to a democratic society?

Methodology follows on conceptualization. Demonstrating the statistical superiority of particular programs for the attainment of specific outcomes calls for one set of methodologies; understanding the underlying processes of learning calls for a different set of methodologies. Joining these two endeavors, which seems desirable, calls for combined methodologies.

The evidentiary base for education has for several decades been catalogued in the Educational Resources Information Center, with relatively permissive criteria for entering documents. More recently, policymakers have determined that the empirical base in education—the database for researchers and decision makers—should be proscribed, limited to particular problems and methodologies. Our experience suggests that such proscriptions may not be in the best interests of researchers or practitioners or the public. Empirical resources presently far exceed our reach in most areas. The quality is mixed, to be sure. However, the lesson would seem fairly straightforward: More is probably known about improving practice and enhancing student outcomes than is presently realized in practice—conceptually, methodologically, and empirically.

A second theme focused on the issue of research that can be applied to practice. The body of research on how humans learn that has accumulated during the past several decades is impressive beyond belief (Bransford, Brown, & Cocking, 1999). Application stands forth as the challenge—what should be applied, for whom, and with what resources. Decisions about valued outcomes are central to approaching this matter. R. Tyler (personal communication, June, 1991) once commented that "education comprises the means by which a society passes on its values from generation to generation." The starting assumption for our work rests on the notion that American education should promote the capacity of every individual to play a significant role in a democratic society, which entails independence, lifelong learning, and consideration of others. Another assumption centers on scientific validity, the rigor of conception, design, methods, and interpretations of contributions to the research base, with particular attention to generalizability. The lesson we take away here relates in part to the engineering task we mention next, but also to the need for adequate support for applied and basic educational science.

The third theme centered around the practicalities of application—the engineering task. This theme accents the contrast between academic and practitioner environments in education. In other domains—engineering and medicine come to mind—the connections appear more workable; in education, the chasm seems greater. Federal policy can exacerbate the problem when it endorses particular problems and methods and directs practitioners to follow external mandates. Such policies finesse the engineering task.

Despite the plethora of meta-analytic reviews available in a variety of domains, including reading, the translation of findings into practical advice seems rather limited. As an example, a recent review of the impact of direct-instruction programs in the primary grades suggested limited transfer to reading comprehension in the elementary grades (Kemper & MacIver, 2002; also Wenglinsky, 2003). It seems unlikely that most teachers and administrators will have read the review. More often, a program is presented to school districts as research based with a sprinkling of citations. Local research and evaluation of program effectiveness become critical at this point. More likely are the newspaper reports in which a district or school uses a jump in reading scores to justify a particular program. To be sure, local expertise is generally sparse, except in large districts. Collaboration with academic partners might help, but resources for research and evaluation are also sparse, and the participants live in different worlds. Except for occasional large-scale projects, the typical paradigm is the request by a district or school for a local campus to "find a grad student" who can conduct an evaluation, perhaps as a dissertation project. In the spring of 2003, the National Research Council called for a state-based strategic research partnership, but the half-billion-dollar cost seems unlikely in today's fiscal environment ("National Academy Calls," 2003).

The lesson from our experience is that exploring the effectiveness of ideas and practices—the local engineering—requires more than assistance from novices. It requires a system that combines sustained efforts from universities with the field of practice. At the University of California Riverside, agricultural research is a major activity, including studies of "turf grass," the playing field serving golfers in Palm Springs and thereabouts. Research on turf grass spans the spectrum from laboratory studies to field work, investigations that follow a new strain from genetic construction to putting surface in which the various players speak a common language and share common values (cf. Kohler, 2002, for a discussion of experimental field stations).

Our explorations of ideas and practices for improving the educational opportunities for youngsters at risk for school failure resonate with the experimental educational station concept—a system in which all parties establish common ground. Realizing such a visionary goal will call for resolution of three tasks raised at the outset—sustained engagement, agreement on valid evidence as a basis for action, and local involvement in systematic research and evaluation. These are important targets and warrant continued pursuit—by researchers interested in fundamental issues of learning science and by colleagues entrusted with implementation of effective policies and practices at the local level in schools and classrooms.

REFERENCES

Anderson, G. L. (2002). Reflecting on research for doctoral students in education. *Educational Researcher, 31*(7), 22–25.

Anderson, N. H. (2001). *Empirical direction in design and analysis*. Mahwah, NJ: Lawrence Erlbaum Associates.

Bloom, B. S. (1981). *All our children learning.* New York: McGraw-Hill.

Bond, G. L., & Dykstra, R. (1967). The cooperative research program in first-grade reading instruction. *Reading Research Quarterly, 2*(4).

Bransford, J. D., Brown, A. L., & Cocking, R. R. (Eds.). (1999). *How people learn: Brain, mind, experience, and school.* Washington, DC: National Academy Press.

Bruner, J. S. (1966). *Toward a theory of instruction.* Cambridge, MA: The Belkanp Press of Harvard University.

Bryk, A. S., & Raudenbush, S. W. (1992). *Hierarchical linear models.* Newbury Park, CA: Sage.

Calfee, R. C. (1992). The inquiring school: Literacy for the year 2000. In C. Collins & J. N. Mangieri (Eds.), *Teaching thinking: An agenda for the twenty-first century* (pp. 147–166). Hillsdale, NJ: Lawrence Erlbaum Associates.

Calfee, R. C. (1998). Phonics and phonemes: Learning to decode and spell in a literature-based program. In J. L. Metsala & L. C. Ehri (Eds.), *Word recognition in beginning literacy* (pp. 315–340). Mahwah, NJ: Lawrence Erlbaum Associates.

Calfee, R. C., & Associates. (1981). *THE BOOK for the reading teacher: Components of reading instruction. A generic manual for reading teachers.* Unpublished manuscript, Stanford University School of Education.

Calfee, R. C., & Nelson-Barber, S. (1991). Diversity and constancy in human thinking: Critical literacy as amplifier of intellect and experience. In E. Hiebert (Ed.), *Literacy for a diverse society: Perspectives, programs, and policies* (pp. 44–57). New York: Teachers College Press.

Calfee, R. C., & Norman, K. A. (1999). Psychological perspectives on the early reading wars: The case of phonological awareness. *Teachers College Record, 100,* 242–274.

Calfee, R. C, Norman, K. A., Trainin, G., & Wilson, K. (2001). Conducting a design experiment for improving early literacy, or, what we learned in school last year. In C. Roller (Ed.), *Learning to teach reading: Setting the research agenda* (pp. 166–179). Newark, DE: International Reading Association.

Calfee, R. C., & Patrick, C. (1995). *Teach our children well.* Stanford, CA: The Portable Stanford Series, Stanford Alumni Association.

Calfee, R. C., & Scott-Hendrick, L. (2004). The teacher of beginning reading. *Contemporary Perspectives on Early Childhood Education, 5,* 87–117.

Carr, E., & Ogle, D. (1987). K-W-L plus: A strategy for comprehension and summarization. *Journal of Reading, 30,* 626–631.

Cazden, C. B. (1988). *Classroom discourse: The language of teaching and learning.* Portsmouth, NH: Heinemann.

Chambliss, M. J., & Calfee, R. C. (2002). The design of empirical research. In J. Flood, J. M. Jensen, D. Lapp, & J. R. Squire (Eds.), *Handbook of research on teaching the English language arts* (2nd ed., pp. 152–170). Mahwah, NJ: Lawrence Erlbaum Associates.

Chambliss, M. J., & Calfee, R. C. (1998). *Textbooks for learning: Nurturing children's minds.* Oxford, England: Blackwell.

Cole, N. (1988). A realist's appraisal of the prospects for unifying instruction and assessment. In C. V. Bunderson (Ed.), *Assessment in the service of learning* (pp. 1–23). Princeton, NJ: Educational Testing Service.

Collins, A. (1992). Toward a design science of education. In E. Scanlon & T. O'Shea (Eds.), *New directions in educational technology* (pp. 37–53). New York: Springer-Verlag.

Cronbach, L. J. (1957). The two disciplines of scientific psychology. *American Psychologist, 12,* 671–684.

Cronbach, L. J. (1975). Beyond the two disciplines of scientific psychology. *American Psychologist, 30,* 116–127.

Cronbach, L. J., Gleser, G. C., Nanda, H., & Rajaratnam, N. (1972). *The dependability of behavioral measurements: Theory of generalizability for scores and profiles.* New York: Wiley.

Eisenhart, M., & Towne, L. (2003). Contestation and change in national policy on "scientifically based" research. *Educational Researcher, 32*(7), 31–38.

Fisher, R. A. (1935). *The design of experiments.* Edinburgh, Scotland: Oliver & Boyd.

Glaser, R. (1978). *Advances in instructional psychology.* Hillsdale, NJ: Lawrence Erlbaum Associates.

Goldberg, M (2003). Everything works. *Phi Delta Kappan, 85,* 304–306.

Heath, S. B. (1983). *Ways with words.* New York: Cambridge University Press.

Kemper, E. A, & McIver, M. A. (Eds.). (2002). Direct instruction reading programs: Examining effectiveness for at-risk students in urban settings. *Journal of Education for Students Placed at Risk, 7*(2).

Kincaid, H. (1996). *Philosophical foundations of the social sciences.* New York: Cambridge University Press.

Kohler, R. E. (2002). *Landslopes and labscopes: Exploring the lab field border in biology.* Chicago: University of Chicago Press.

Kuhn, T. S. (1970). *The structure of scientific revolutions* (2nd ed.). Chicago: University of Chicago Press.

Langenberg, D. N. (1999). *Report of the National Reading Panel.* Washington, DC: NICHD.

Lapp, D., Flood, J., & Hoffman, R. P. (1996). Using concept mapping as an effective strategy in content area instruction. In D. Lapp, J. Flood, & N. Farnan (Eds.), *Content area reading and learning* (2nd ed., pp. 291–306). Boston: Allyn & Bacon.

Marshall, E. (2003). In critical condition. *Science, 300,* 1225–1226.

Metz, M. H., & Page, R. N. (2002). The uses of practitioner research and status issues in educational research: Reply to Gary Anderson. *Educational Researcher, 31*(7), 26–27.

Miller, R. G., & Calfee, R. C. (2004). Building a better reading/writing assessment: Bridging cognitive theory, instruction, and assessment. *English Leadership Quarterly, 26,* 6–13.

National Academy calls for $500 million strategic education research partnerships. (2003, April). *Science, 300,* 231.

Natriello, G. (2004). Scientific research in education. *Teachers College Record,* http://www.tcrecord.org, ID 11165.

Nelson, N. N., & Calfee, R. C. (Eds.) (1998). *The reading-writing connection: The yearbook of the National Society for the Study of Education.* Chicago: University of Chicago Press.

Pearson, P. D. (in press). The reading wars: The politics of reading research and policy—1988 through 2003. In B. C. Johnson & W. L. Boyd (Eds.), *Politics of Education Yearbook, Special Issue on Educational Policy.*

Phillips, D. C. (2000). *The expanded social scientist's bestiary: A guide to fabled threats to and defenses of, naturalistic social science.* New York: Rowman and Littlefield Publishers.

Prain, V., & Hand, B. (1996). Writing for learning in secondary science: Rethinking practices. *Teacher and Teacher Education, 12,* 609–626.

Reyna, V. F. (2004). The No Child Left Behind Act and scientific research. In J. S. Carlson & J. R. Levin (Eds.), *Scientifcally based education research and federal funding agencies: The case of the No Child Left Behind Act* (pp. 3–25). Greenwich, Ct: Information Age Publishers.

Robinson, V. M. K. (1998). Methodology and the research-practice gap. *Educational Researcher, 27,* 17–26.

Sanders, L. (2003, March 16) Medicine's progress, one setback at a time. *New York Times Magazine,* pp. 29–31.

Schaefer, R. J. (1967) *The school as a center of inquiry.* New York: Harper and Row.

Shavelson, R. J., Phillips, D. C., Towne, L., & Feuer, M. J. (2003). On the science of education design studies. *Educational Researcher, 32,* 25–28.

Shavelson, R. J., & Towne, L. (Eds.). (2002). *Scientific research in education.* Washington, DC: National Academy Press.

Slavin, R. E. (2002). Evidence-based education policies: Transforming educational research and practice. *Educational Researcher, 31*(7), 15–21.

Sperling, M., & Freedman, S. W. (2002). Research on writing. In V. Richardson (Ed.), *Handbook of research on teaching* (4th ed., pp. 370–389). Washington: American Educational Research Association.

Stanovich, K. E. (2003). Understanding the styles of science in the study of reading scientific-studies of reading, *Scientific Studies Research,* 7, 105–126.

Tierney, R. J., & Shanahan, T. (1991). Research on the reading-writing relationship: Interactions, transactions, and outcomes. In R. Barr, M. L. Kamil, P. B. Mosenthal, & P. D. Pearson (Eds.), *Handbook of reading research Vol. 2* (pp. 246–280). Mahwah, NJ: Lawrence Erlbaum Associates.

Vinoskis, M. (2001). *Revitalizing federal education research and development.* Ann Arbor, MI: University of Michigan Press.

Wenglinsky, H. (2003). Using large-scale research to gauge the impact of instructional practices on student reading comprehension: An exploratory study. *Educational Policy Analysis Archives, 11*(19), 2–15.

II

TRANSLATION THEORY AND RESEARCH INTO PRACTICE IN LARGE-SCALE REFORM

Commentary

Mark A. Constas and Robert J. Sternberg

The challenges associated with attempts to translate theory and research into practice grow significantly, in both magnitude and complexity, as the number and type of participating schools increase. Engagement with large-scale educational reform introduces a range of resource concerns, policy issues, and infrastructure issues. Dealing with concerns and issues of this kind, the authors in this second part of the volume describe challenges and successes related to their attempts to translate theory and research into practice for large-scale reform efforts. By applying research-based knowledge from the field of human development, the authors of chapter 7 (this volume) in this part, by Comer and Joyner, show how theories and findings about early-childhood development may inform educational practice. Their work with the School Development Project illustrates how a systematic approach to dealing with resistance to change can help create better, more durable connections between research and educational practice. Building on well-established body of knowledge that demonstrates the importance of child care in early child development, the authors of chapter 8 (this volume), Zigler and Finn-Stevenson, demonstrate the value of nonacademic services. The work Zigler and Finn-Stevenson have done with School of the 21st Century uses research from human development and insights on change processes to translate theory and research into practice. As an organizational analysis of integrated practice, Zigler and Finn-Stevenson show how viable, productive programmatic connections may be made between child-care provisions and basic school functions. In the chapter by Slavin (chap. 5, this volume), he describes the ways in which key elements of Success for All have been directly derived from a disciplined program of research on cooperative learning. Slavin also demonstrates the practical importance of creating a well-specified model of implementation. In the chapter by Finnan and Levin (chap. 6, this volume), the authors show how theory and research from several disciplinary perspectives may be combined to help support the educational development of both disadvantaged and gifted students. By applying research and theories of intelligence, social justice, and school culture to help advance disadvantaged students, Finnan and Levin challenge the stereotypical lines of demarcation drawn between disadvantaged and gifted student populations.

Authors in this second part of the book have based their observations on the experience of working with thousands of schools. As a collection of chapters focused on the challenges of trying to translate theory and research into educational practice on a large scale, the analyses provided by Comer and Joyner, Zigler and Finn-Stevenson, Finnan and Levin, and Slavin provide the reader with important insights and offer sound practical advice on how to translate theory and research into educational practice in large-scale reform efforts.

EDUCATION AS HUMAN DEVELOPMENT AND OVERCOMING OBSTACLES TO CHANGE

The School Development Project (SDP), pioneered by Comer nearly 40 years ago, has now been implemented in a large number of schools. The general aim of SDP is to improve human development and learning. Comer and Joyner (chap. 7, this volume) argue that one of the primary obstacles in translating theory and research into practice stems from a resistance to change. To address this problem, the SDP uses a selection of now well-proven, action-oriented approaches to build networks of parents, teachers, and administrators who help implement the model. Acknowledging the varied set of problems found in schools, the SDP assembles teams of psychiatrists, social workers, special-education teachers, and psychologists to help build and implement programs in school settings. The program's focus on human development urges one to move beyond the practice of habitual labeling (e.g., slow learners, underachievers) that has a limiting effect on human growth on development. What is perhaps most distinctive about the approach of SDP is the application of clinical skills to solve the seemingly recalcitrant problem of implementation. The analysis of children's developmental pathways stands as a clear example of how theoretical knowledge may be used to improve educational outcomes. With respect to organizational and structural solutions to the problem of how best to translate theory and research into practice, Comer and Joyner demonstrate the value of the "three guiding principles" on which the work of SDP is based. The focus on collaboration, "no fault" problem solving, and on a decision-making process based on consensus combine to support the goals of SDP. Viewing children through the lens of human development and seeing schools as complex environments, SDP has been able to translate theory and research from public health, the behavioral sciences, and management into effective practice. The application of a truly interdisciplinary framework and a deeply collaborative approach to support the development of children has produced remarkable successes across a variety of school settings.

CHILD DEVELOPMENT AND THE IMPACT OF NONACADEMIC SERVICES IN ACADEMIC SETTINGS

Zigler and Finn-Stevenson (chap. 8, this volume) describe the development and successful implementation of the School of the 21st Century (21C). Different than most educational-reform models, 21C focuses much of its programmatic effort on activities that would generally be regarded as supplementary or nonacademic. The accomplishments of 21C schools present a challenge to current policy initiatives that, according to Zigler and Finn-Stevenson, fail to recognize the importance of nonacademic contexts in which learning takes place. Although an emphasis on "time off" from academic activities will be viewed as counterproductive by many audiences, the studies of 21C suggest that students benefit from a more balanced approach to development. The provision and coordination of quality child care lie at the core of 21C. They are derived from research on child development that emphasizes both the paucity and the negative impact of inadequate child care. A distinctive feature of 21C is that the provision of child care is not conceptualized or delivered as a stand-alone service. In 21C schools, child care services are well integrated into the everyday operations of schooling.

Acknowledging the unorthodox nature of their reform effort, Zigler and Finn-Stevenson (chap. 8, this volume) connect their work to theories and research on change processes. Alterations to school use, staff relations, and parent–school interactions are just a sampling of the issues given consideration in the implementation of 21C. Viewing implementation as an ongoing process rather than as an isolated event, Zigler and Finn-Stevenson note the importance of factors (e.g., level of commitment, policies, community participation) that affect the success of 21C. The analysis of "challenges to widespread implementation" provides insights both about the pragmatics of implementation and about the complexities of designing studies that evaluate the effectiveness of 21C. With regard to the latter, the organic or ever-changing nature of programs presents difficulties related to the assessment of 21C. To address this problem, Zigler and Finn-Stevenson suggest theories of change be consulted as a way to systematically study the dynamic nature of programs.

FROM REMEDIATION TO ACCELERATION

Descriptive studies of schools that serve disadvantaged student populations have shown the negative effects of intellectually impoverished home and community environments within which many at-risk students live. Finnan and Levin (chap. 6, this volume) provide a description of how the Accelerated Schools Project (ASP) has effectively applied theory and research to address such problems. By integrating theories of intelligence with constructivism and organizational effectiveness, Finnan and Levin demonstrate how the conceptualization of ASP was derived from a combination of theoretical perspectives, philosophical positions, and practical concerns. Particularly notable is the fact that ASP has integrated a social justice framework that supports empowerment with a psychological perspective that fosters intellectual development. This is not a typical pairing of theoretical positions. The way in which ASP has combined elements from seemingly disparate theoretical strands demonstrates how theory and research from completely distinct but complementary disciplinary perspectives may be integrated. Recognizing the complexity of and resistance to change, ASP places analytic focus on beliefs, values, and assumptions that act to facilitate or inhibit the transformation of schools. A good deal of attention is paid to investigating and building consensus among teachers, administrators, and parents as a prerequisite to the decision to implement ASP. The absence of such consensus is viewed as a major internal obstacle to effective practice. Inverting or extending the notion of school culture that is often cited as a mediator of school effectiveness, Finnan and Levin also discuss the way in which the "culture of schooling," characteristic American education, interferes with attempts to establish sustainable programs of school improvement and interferes with efforts to translate theory and research into practice.

Noting the reciprocal effect of their work, Finnan and Levin (chap. 6, this volume) demonstrate how ASP was both derived from theory and has also spawned new theory. This reversal highlights the need for inductive models of knowledge production and raises questions about the limits of the common model of knowledge production and use that begins with theory and research and ends with practice. One of the most impressive features of ASP is the way in which it uses a selection of theoretical perspectives to construct and implement a wide range of programmatic offerings

SCHOOL-WIDE IMPLEMENTATION AND COMPREHENSIVE SUPPORT MECHANISMS

One of the common problems with prediction models is underspecification, the failure to include a comprehensive and well-defined set of variables on which predictions may be based. As an extension of this criticism, the same could be said of many school-reform models that fail to provide adequate or specific support to ensure success across the diverse populations and varied settings. The Success for All Model of school improvement offers a carefully designed, evidence-based response to the problem of programmatic underspecification. Building on a decade of research on cooperative learning, Slavin (chap. 5, this volume) demonstrates how research can be directly linked to a cluster of educational practices. As a balanced account of Success for All, Slavin describes both the successes and the shortcomings of cooperative learning as the theoretical platform on which educational practices were based. Slavin's work, and that of others who have studied cooperative learning, demonstrates the need for continual revision of theoretical frameworks and illustrates the need for a parallel program of research capable of refining guidelines for practice.

As a program that has amassed evidence of effectiveness, the achievements of Success For All can be at least partially attributed to the comprehensive nature of the intervention. Whereas many interventions appear as islands of concentrated program focus, Success for All is implemented in entire schools and provides a carefully selected and well-developed set of programmatic supports. The provision of tutors, support teams that work with teachers and families, and regular assessments that provide feedback are central to Success for All. These components of Success for All show how efforts to translate theory and research into practice must be accompanied by a broad range of supports that facilitate implementation. Demonstrating a strong and consistent connection between research and practice, Slavin (chap. 5, this volume) shows how central features of Success for All have been subject to rigorous empirical study. The consistent attempt to ground comprehensive, school-wide intervention strategies into carefully designed empirical studies is a distinctive feature of Success for All, a feature that ensures a close connection among research, theory, and practice.

5

Translating Research Into Widespread Practice: The Case of Success for All

Robert E. Slavin
Johns Hopkins University

The difficulty of translating research into practice in education is one of the most important problems in education reform. The problem is not so much that educators are resistant to change; on the contrary, certain kinds of innovation can be widely adopted, and educators are sure to cite research to support whatever innovation they advocate. Yet the connection between the findings of research and the practices of educators more resembles the faddism of art or fashion than the steady progress over time characteristic of medicine, agriculture, or technology (see Slavin, 1989). Educational innovations often appear and become widespread entirely in the absence of research. Research eventually appears on these innovations, but whether the research supports or fails to support the innovation, interest in it declines within a few years.

In 1987, my colleagues and I developed Success for All, a program that was designed in large part to try to break through the barrier between research and practice by building a well-specified, comprehensive approach to schoolwide practice in high-poverty elementary schools that would both be based on the best research available and would then be subjected to rigorous experimental evaluations. From the outset, the idea was to provide educators with every support they needed—student materials, teacher's manuals, training, follow-up, and school organization—to enable them to make daily, high-quality, thoughtful use of the findings of research. In this chapter, I describe the history of this attempt to translate research into practice, the obstacles encountered, and the findings of research and experience with the program.

SUCCESS FOR ALL: AN INTELLECTUAL HISTORY

The origins of Success for All reach back more than a decade before we began the first Success for All school in 1987. In particular, the development of Success for All was deeply rooted in experience with cooperative learning. Cooperative learning methods in which students work in small groups to help one another master academic content had begun to be researched by several investigators around the world in the mid-1970s (see Johnson & Johnson, 1998; Sharan & Sharan, 1992; Slavin, 1995; Slavin, Hurley, & Chamberlain, 2003). These methods became immensely popular in the 1980s; a national survey in the early 1990s found that 79% of third-grade teachers and 62% of seventh-grade teachers reported frequent use of cooperative learning (Puma, Jones, Rock, & Fernandez, 1993). In many ways, cooperative learning was a success story in translating research into practice. By 1995, I was able to identify 99 studies of at least 4-weeks' duration in elementary and secondary schools that evaluated effects of various cooperative learning methods on student achievement. Here, for once, was a popular educational innovation that really did have a strong research base, affecting millions of children.

Yet the success of cooperative learning as an example of research affecting practice was as much appearance as reality. By the early 1980s, it was clear from dozens of studies that there were conditions under which cooperative learning was or was not effective for achievement (see Slavin, 1983). When cooperative methods put children into small groups and gave them a clear goal that they could only achieve if all group members had mastered the academic material, then cooperative learning improved student achievement. If, on the other hand, it was possible for one student in a group to get an answer and give it to their groupmates or for one or two students to do the thinking part of a group task while others watched, cooperative learning did not work. A series of ingenious studies by Webb and her colleagues (see Webb & Palincsar, 1996) found that students who gave and received elaborated explanations gained from cooperative learning, whereas those who just received the answer (or no response) did not profit from the experience. Clearly, cooperative learning has to be set up in such a way as to ensure that students see the goal of the activity as explaining content to each other, not simply coming to a single right answer or completing a project together.

Although there was some disagreement about the specific conditions under which cooperative learning did or did not enhance achievement, by the mid-1980s, influential researchers in this field had generally agreed that some structure was necessary to ensure that students in cooperative groups were explaining content to each other, not just sitting together or doing activities with a single product. Yet in the world of practice, cooperative learning often bore little resemblance to the well-structured methods studied in the research. Studies of actual applications of cooperative learning found that most teachers were not using specific, named methods that had been researched and were not applying the principles derived from that research (Antil, Jenkins, Wayne, & Vadasy, 1998; Emmer & Gerwels, 2002; McManus & Gettinger, 1996). Instead, they were having students sit in groups and help each other as needed, or they were having groups do projects in which one student might do the thinking part of the task. I recall observing a math class in which small groups of second graders were making graphs showing how many pets each child in the group had. In each group, there was lively discussion about pets (and about what constitutes a "pet"). However, in every case, one child, typically either the best math student or the most assertive, actually held the pencil and drew the graphs. The others were discussing pets, not math. Later, the groups made a pretty version of their graphs and some of the students colored in the bars on the graph. Again, coloring is art, not math. In classrooms everywhere, cooperative learning became a way to keep students busy and productive looking in a setting in which students might gain some exposure to higher level content by observing their more capable peers, but group members seldom helped their groupmates master the academic material. Further, many teachers found it difficult to align cooperative learning processes with the books and curricula they were expected to teach, resulting either in a failure to use or to maintain cooperative learning over time or in implementation difficulties. For example, some teachers would teach outstanding cooperative learning lessons but would take so long on each of them that they could not cover the content for which they were responsible. Finally, many teachers had difficulty transferring cooperative methods from the workshop to classroom practice. Because cooperative learning workshops lend themselves so well to simulations and almost invariably use them, teachers usually leave their workshops with a strong, personal understanding of what cooperative learning is but still have trouble once they face the very different reality of their own classroom.

For all of these reasons, cooperative learning gained the dubious distinction of being massively misapplied. Today, cooperative learning continues to be featured in virtually every educational psychology text and teaching methods text, and there are questions about it on teacher certification tests. Yet appropriate use of cooperative learning is rare outside of comprehensive reform programs such as Success for All, which emphasize this strategy.

The cooperative learning experience greatly influenced the development of Success for All, which built directly on earlier attempts to solve the problem of ensuring quality implementation of research-based cooperative learning strategies. Beginning in 1980, we developed a comprehensive mathematics program, Team Assisted Instruction (TAI; Slavin, Madden, & Leavey, 1984) to confront the problems of implementation quality and curriculum integration in mathematics. In 1983, we developed Cooperative Integrated Reading and Composition (CIRC; Stevens, Madden, Slavin, & Farnish, 1987), which applied a similar solution to a comprehensive approach to reading and writing instruction in the upper elementary and middle grades. In 1985, these programs plus programs for social studies and science were integrated into a schoolwide cooperative learning strategy called the Cooperative Elementary School (Slavin, 1987a; Stevens & Slavin, 1995). In each of these cases, we found that we could obtain consistent, high-quality implementations of cooperative learning that could be sustained for many years by integrating cooperative strategies into specific curricula and providing extensive professional development, follow-up, and coaching. Several studies comparing CIRC (Stevens et al., 1987) and TAI (Slavin et al., 1984) to matched control classes found that these comprehensive models produced higher scores on standardized achievement assessments than traditional methods. With the Cooperative Elementary School, we learned how to incorporate school-level structures, such as on-site coaches and teacher's learning communities (Calderón, 1999), to further support quality implementation of cooperative learning.

Our experiences with TAI and CIRC in the 1980s convinced us that research-based practices could be successfully introduced in schools, could be maintained, and could produce enhanced achievement. They could adapt cooperative learning explicitly to a specific set of instructional materials and vice versa. Because they became the predominant approach to core academic content, they were taken seriously by the school and given professional development resources that generic, content-free cooperative learning rarely receives. Further, these methods could and did incorporate the findings of other research. For example, CIRC incorporated comprehension strategies (e.g., summarization, prediction, graphic organizers, story grammar) that are not inherently connected to cooperative learning (see Pressley & Woloshyn, 1995).

Development of Success for All

In 1986, our group at Johns Hopkins University was approached by the Baltimore City Public Schools and invited to develop a program capable of ensuring the success of all children in the city's most impoverished schools. Kalman Hettelman, a former State Secretary of Human Resources, engaged us in a series of discussions on behalf of the superintendent, Alice Pinderhughes, who was looking for major solutions to the widespread failure of inner-city youngsters. We eagerly embraced this challenge and used it as an opportunity to put into practice both everything we had learned in our own cooperative learning research and everything we could glean from the broader literature. We carefully reviewed research in each area we needed to address in our design. For example, we chose to use cross-grade performance grouping for reading, or Joplin Plan, based on a review of research on grouping strategies for elementary schools (Gutiérrez & Slavin, 1992; Slavin, 1987b). We based classroom management strategies primarily on the work of Evertson, Emmer, and Worsham (2000). We adapted a tutoring model for primary-aged students from Reading Recovery (Pinnell, DeFord, & Lyons, 1988; Pinnell, Lyons, DeFord, Bryk, & Seltzer, 1994). We built internal coaching mechanisms based on the research of Joyce (Joyce, Calhoun, & Hopkins, 1999; Joyce, Hersh, & McKibbin, 1983) and incorporated teacher's learning communities (Calderón, 1999). We carried out an extensive review of beginning reading strategies and came to the same conclusions reached by Adams (1990) a few years later that systematic, synthetic phonics should be the basis for early reading instruction. Drawing from a very different philosophical camp, we incorporated writing process models in which students work in groups to plan, draft, revise, edit, and publish compositions because of the strong research support for this strategy (Harris & Graham, 1996). Reviews of research on effective practices in preschool (Karweit, 1994a) and in kindergarten (Karweit, 1994b) have informed development in these areas. We adapted parent involvement strategies from the work of Epstein (1995) and curriculum-based assessment strategies from the work of Fuchs, Fuchs, Hamlett, and Stecker (1991). An emphasis on prevention and on mainstreaming derived from a review of research on mainstreaming and special education (Madden & Slavin, 1983). In each case, we focused on research that compared replicable strategies to matched or randomized control groups over periods of at least a school year and selected strategies that had repeatedly been found to be more effective than traditional methods.

The theory of action behind the design of Success for All was an assertion that research-based strategies could be incorporated into teachers' daily practices on a broad scale if and only if we provided well-developed student materials, teacher's manuals, assessments, training, follow-up, and implementation assessments as we had done in our TAI and CIRC experiments. Our cooperative learning experiences led us to believe that if we taught general principles of good practice and then asked teachers to work out how to apply them to their own materials and instruction, it would be difficult to obtain consistent high-quality implementations in the first place and even more difficult to maintain quality implementations over time.

Another key part of our implementation strategy was derived from our own experience, not from any formal research. This was a requirement for a school-wide vote, by secret ballot, of at least 80% of the staff in favor of program adoption. Our reasoning was twofold. First, with the extensive changes we were asking schools to undergo, we wanted to be sure that the teachers themselves understood and supported the program. Second, we knew that in the high-poverty schools in which we expected to work, we had a limited window of time to begin to show tangible benefits of our programs. We believed that we had to have a relatively rapid rollout of the main program elements so that teachers could see marked improvements in students' reading and behavior within a few months. Without a strong statement of teacher buy-in (or at least a temporary suspension of disbelief), we felt it was unlikely that such a rapid rollout could be accomplished.

The requirement of an 80% favorable vote has generally served us well. Most schools that take the vote get a positive outcome. In cases in which this is not true, the problem usually seems to be a lack of faith in the principal or a split among the staff, conditions we would want to avoid in any case.

The principal elements of the program we designed, and still implement today, are summarized in Table 5.1. Although our materials, training procedures, and other elements have been substantially revised over time, the basic structural elements I presented following (e.g., instructional methods, grouping, staffing, and school organization) have remained constant over 19 years.

RESEARCH ON SUCCESS FOR ALL

Early Research

The early research on Success for All used a consistent paradigm. In each case, children were pretested (usually on the Peabody Picture Vocabulary Test [Dunn & Dunn, 1997]) on entry to kindergarten or first grade and then followed over time with individually administered reading tests given to all children each spring. These were typically scales from the Woodcock Reading Mastery Test (Woodcock, 1998) and the Durrell Oral Reading Test (Durrell & Catterson, 1983).

From the first studies, it was clear that Success for All was making a substantial difference. Longitudinal studies of the first 5 schools in Baltimore found that these schools gained substantially more than matched controls, with effect sizes averaging around 50% of a standard deviation for students in general and more than a full standard deviation (effect size $= +1.00$) for students who began in the lowest 25% of their grades (Madden, Slavin, Karweit, Dolan, & Wasik, 1993; Slavin, Madden, Karweit, Dolan, & Wasik, 1992; Slavin, Madden, Dolan, & Wasik, 1996; Slavin, Karweit, Madden, Livermon, & Dolan, 1990). This paradigm was ultimately followed in schools in 11 dis-

TABLE 5.1

Major Elements of Success for All

Success for All is a school-wide program for students in preschool and kindergarten to Grade 6 that organizes resources to attempt to ensure that virtually every student will reach the third grade on time with adequate basic skills and build on this basis throughout the elementary grades and that no student will be allowed to "fall between the cracks." The main elements of the program are as follows:

A School-wide Curriculum: During reading periods, students are regrouped across age lines so that each reading class contains students all at one reading level. Use of tutors as reading teachers during reading time reduces the size of most reading classes to about 20. The reading program in kindergarten to Grade 1 emphasizes language and comprehension skills, phonics, sound blending, and use of shared stories that students read to one another in pairs. The shared stories combine teacher-read material with phonetically regular student material to teach decoding and comprehension in the context of meaningful, engaging stories.

In Grades 2 through 6, students use novels or basals but not workbooks. This program emphasizes cooperative learning and partner reading activities, comprehension strategies such as summarization and clarification built around, narrative and expository texts, writing, and direct instruction in reading comprehension skills. At all levels, students are required to read books of their own choice for 20 min at home each evening. Cooperative learning programs in writing/language arts are used in Grades 1 through 6.

Tutors: In Grades 1 through 3, specially trained certified teachers and para-professionals work one to one with any students who are failing to keep up with their classmates in reading. Tutorial instruction is closely coordinated with regular classroom instruction. It takes place 20 min daily during times other than reading periods.

Preschool and Kindergarten: The comprehensive, theme-based, pre-school and kindergarten programs in Success for All cover all domains of learning, with a particular focus on language and literacy.

Quarterly Assessments: Students in Grades 1 through 6 are assessed every quarter to determine whether they are making adequate progress in reading. This information is used to suggest alternate teaching strategies in the regular classroom, changes in reading group placement, provision of tutoring services, or other means of meeting students' needs.

Solutions Team: A Solutions Team works in each school to help support families in ensuring the success of their children focusing on parent education, parent involvement, attendance, and student behavior. This team is composed of existing or additional staff such as parent liaisons, social workers, counselors, and vice principals.

Facilitator: A program facilitator works with teachers to help them implement the reading program, manages the quarterly assessments, assists the Solutions Team, makes sure that all staff are communicating with each other, and helps the staff as a whole make certain that every child is making adequate progress.

tricts around the United States, and the results continued to strongly support the program's impact (see Dianda & Flaherty, 1995; Livingston & Flaherty, 1997; Nunnery et al., 1997). Figure 5.1 summarizes the impact from studies of various durations from 1 to 6 years. The figure shows that by the end of fifth grade, students in Success for All schools were performing about a full grade equivalent higher than matched control schools on individually administered tests. In addition to effects on achievement, studies have found substantial impacts on assignments to special education (Slavin, 1996) and other outcomes (Slavin & Madden, 2001).

The rapid growth of Success for All through the 1990s exposed Success for All to unusual attacks from political opponents, particularly Pogrow (2000) who had his own pullout program for Title I schools that he felt to have been slighted by the advent of comprehensive school reform. A series of articles and rebuttals in the *Phi Delta Kappan* and elsewhere (see Slavin & Madden, 2000) pointed out that the effects of Success for All were not miraculous and that the program did not maintain everywhere but did not call into question the repeated observation that Success for All students usually performed significantly better than other children on reading measures.

Later Research on Success for All

After the many studies establishing the basic effects of Success for All, research attention has shifted in different directions. One line of research has focused on effects for English language learners, evaluating both a Spanish

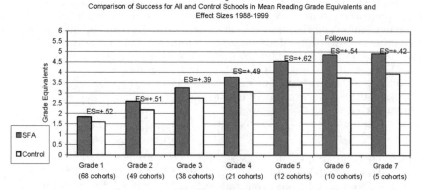

FIG. 5.1.   Comparison of Success for All (SFA) and control schools in mean reading grade equivalents and effect sizes (ES) 1988 to 1999. ES is the proportion of a standard deviation by which SFA students exceed controls. It includes approximately 6,000 children in SFA or control schools since first grade.

bilingual adaptation and an English language development adaptation (see Slavin & Madden, 1999; Slavin & Cheung, 2004). Both adaptations have been found to be effective. Research correlating quality and completeness of implementation with student outcomes has been a focus (Nunnery et al, 1997; Ross, Smith, Casey, & Slavin, 1995). A longitudinal follow-up of students who had been in the original Baltimore schools found that by eighth grade, these students were still performing significantly better on standardized reading measures than former control students and were substantially less likely to have been retained in grade or assigned to special education (Borman & Hewes, 2003).

Because of demands from policy audiences, some attention has shifted to studies that take data from routine state assessments. Formal studies in Texas (Hurley, Chamberlain, Slavin, & Madden, 2001), and California (Slavin, Madden, & Liang, 2002) have found substantially higher gains for Success for All students than for the state as a whole. Similar analyses have found the same patterns in nearly every state with more than 10 Success for All schools. Such comparisons are far less scientific than the longitudinal experiments, but they respond to a desire from policymakers and educators to know how the program performs on the assessments for which they are held accountable.

As research on comprehensive reform programs and on reading programs has taken on greater political and practical importance, a number of reviews of the research have appeared. The American Institutes of Research (Herman, 1999) rated comprehensive reform models and found Success for All to be one of two elementary programs with the strongest evidence of effectiveness. This conclusion was echoed in a report for the Thomas Fordham Foundation by Traub (1999). A meta-analysis by Borman, Hewes, Overman, and Brown (2003) identified 41 experimental–control comparisons done to evaluate Success for All, of which 25 were done by third parties. This was the largest number of such studies for any comprehensive reform model, and Borman et al. (2003) listed Success for All as one of three programs with the strongest evidence of effectiveness. Finally, Pearson and Stahl (2002) evaluated reading programs and gave Success for All the highest rating for evidence of effectiveness among all core reading programs.

Randomized Evaluation of Success for All

Despite the many rigorous experimental–control comparisons evaluating Success for All, these have all been matched experiments, which leaves open the possibility that selection bias or other unmeasured differences might account for some of the effects. To investigate this possibility, a randomized evaluation is currently under way in which 41 schools were randomly assigned to use Success for All either in kindergarten to Grade 2 or in Grades 3 to 5. The 2nd-year results found positive program effects on Woodcock reading measures (Woodcock, 1998) for the kindergarten through first-grade students (Borman et al., in press).

Enhancements to Success for All

Much additional research and development is under way to enhance the impacts and replicability of the Success for All literacy programs. This includes development and evaluation of video/DVD programs designed to model reading processes for teachers as well as students. Part of the idea of these video/DVD programs is to enable teachers to maintain program fidelity while moving away from excessive reliance on their teacher's manuals. A computer-assisted tutoring program is also in development. These are being evaluated in rigorous experiments. A randomized experiment involving 10 schools found significantly positive effects of the new video/DVD elements for first graders (Chambers, Cheung, Gifford, Madden, & Slavin, 2004). In addition, development and evaluation of a middle school program (Slavin, Daniels, & Madden, 2005), of new preschool and kindergarten programs, and of new approaches to English-language development and to transition from Spanish to English (Calderón et al., 2004) reading are under way.

Challenges for the Future

In its 19th year, Success for All is undergoing major changes to respond both to opportunities and to difficulties presented by the current education policy environment. Among the opportunities is an extraordinary shift in the newly reauthorized Institute for Education Sciences to support large-scale, randomized evaluations of practical, replicable interventions. This shift is opening new opportunities for high-quality research on Success for All in new contexts as well as research on new components and practices. The focus of the No Child Left Behind Act of 2001 on "scientifically based research" as a basis for practice has not yet been consequential in programs such as Reading First and Comprehensive School Reform, but this could change in the future, particularly as the newly funded What Works Clearinghouse begins a set of definitive, scientifically valid reviews of research on programs in many areas. These developments are helping Success for All return to its roots, as a vehicle for incorporation of new research knowledge into a replicable strategy, and as a program that carries out (or encourages third parties to carry out) high-quality research on programs with potential to improve outcomes for high-poverty students and schools.

One major challenge (and opportunity) facing Success for All is a dramatic shift nationally away from site-based management toward district coherence and consistency. Increasingly, districts are adopting a single program for all schools at a given level. This is problematic for Success for All, which has always emphasized an informed school-by-school decision process. However, we are experimenting with districtwide applications of Success for All and are finding very good results (see Slavin, 2003). In Hartford (CT), Lawrence (MA), Long Branch (NJ), Assumption Parish (LA), and other districts, whole-district implementations have helped districts make particularly impressive gains as district policies, staffing, and practices become aligned with the requirements and potential of Success for All. At the same time, Success for All can operate more effectively in clusters of schools with consistent and enlightened leadership. Subdistricts, such as New York's Chancellor's District (Phenix, Siegel, Zaltsman, & Fruchter, 2004) and feeder systems in several cities that are part of a program called Project GRAD, have also been very effective using similar strategies. A major focus in coming years will be on developing programs and supports to enhance our capacity to work with whole districts or subdistricts.

Success for All has demonstrated that well-structured, whole-school change is possible, sustainable, and effective. It provides one model for direct translation of research findings into wide-scale implementation. However, there is more development, research, and evaluation to be done on many aspects of the model, and it will surely change in response both to new research findings and to the external environment for reform.

REFERENCES

Adams, M. J. (1990). *Beginning to read: Thinking and learning about print*. Cambridge, MA: MIT Press.

Antil, L. R., Jenkins, J. R., Wayne, S. K., & Vadasy, P. F. (1998). Cooperative learning: Prevalence, conceptualizations, and the relation between research and practice. *American Educational Research Journal, 35,* 419–454.

Borman, G., & Hewes, G. (2003). Long-term effects and cost effectiveness of Success for All. *Educational Evaluation and Policy Analysis, 24,* 243–266.

Borman, G. D., Hewes, G. M., Overman, L. T., & Brown, S. (2003). Comprehensive school reform and achievement: A meta-analysis. *Review of Educational Research, 73,* 125–230.

Borman, G. D., Slavin, R. E., Cheung, A., Chamberlain, A., Madden, N., & Chambers, B. (in press). The National Randomized Field Trial of Success for All: Second-year outcomes. *American Educational Research Journal.*

Calderón, M. (1999). Teacher learning communities for cooperation in diverse settings. *Theory into Practice, 38,* 94–99.

Calderón, M., August, D., Slavin, R. E., Durán, D., Madden, N. A., & Cheung, A. (2004). *The evaluation of a bilingual transition program for Success for All*. Baltimore: Johns Hopkins University, Center for Research on the Education of Students Placed at Risk.

Chambers, B., Cheung, A., Gifford, R., Madden, N., & Slavin, R. E. (2004). *Achievement effects of embedded multimedia in a Success for All reading program*. Baltimore: Success for All Foundation.

Dianda, M., & Flaherty, J. (1995, April). *Effects of Success for All on the reading achieve-ment of first graders in California bilingual programs.* Paper presented at the annual meeting of the American Educational Research Association, San Francisco.

Dunn, L. M., & Dunn, L. M. (1997). *Peabody Picture Vocabulary Test—Third Edition.* Cir-cle Pines, MI: American Guidance System.

Durrell, D., & Catterson, J. (1983). *Durrell analysis of reading difficulty* (3rd ed.). San Antonio, TX: The Psychological Corporation.

Emmer, E. T., & Gerwels, M. C. (2002). Cooperative learning in elementary class-rooms: Teaching practices and lesson characteristics. *Elementary School Journal, 103,* 75–91.

Epstein, J. L. (1995). School/family/community partnerships: Caring for the chil-dren we share. *Phi Delta Kappan, 76,* 701–712.

Evertson, C. M., Emmer, E. T., & Worsham, M. E. (2000). *Classroom management for el-ementary teachers* (5th ed.). Boston: Allyn & Bacon.

Fuchs, L. S., Fuchs, D., Hamlett, C. L., & Stecker, P. M. (1991). Effects of curricu-lum-based measurement and consultation on teacher planning and student achievement in mathematics operations. *American Educational Research Journal, 28,* 617–641.

Gutiérrez, R., & Slavin, R. E. (1992). Achievement effects of the nongraded elemen-tary school. A best-evidence synthesis. *Review of Educational Research, 62,* 333–376.

Harris, K. R., & Graham, S. (1996). *Making the writing process work: Strategies for com-position and self-regulation.* Cambridge, MA: Brookline.

Herman, R. (1999). *An educator's guide to schoolwide reform.* Arlington, VA: Educational Research Service.

Hurley, E., Chamberlain, A., Slavin, R., & Madden, N. (2001). Effects of Success for All on TAAS reading: A Texas statewide evaluation. *Phi Delta Kappan, 82*(10), 750–756.

Johnson, D. W., & Johnson, R. T. (1998). *Learning together and alone: Cooperative, com-petitive, and individualistic learning* (5th ed.). Boston: Allyn & Bacon.

Joyce, B. R., Calhoun, E., & Hopkins, D. (1999). *The new structure of school improve-ment.* Buckingham, England: Open University Press.

Joyce, B. R., Hersh, R. H., & McKibbin, M. (1983). *The structure of school improvement.* New York: Longman.

Karweit, N. L. (1994a). Effects of preschool programs on early school success. In R. E. Slavin, N. L. Karweit, & B. A. Wasik (Eds.), *Preventing early school failure: Re-search on effective strategies.* Boston: Allyn & Bacon.

Karweit, N. L. (1994b). Issues in kindergarten organization and curriculum. In R. E. Slavin, N. L. Karweit, & B. A. Wasik (Eds.), *Preventing early school failure: Research on effective strategies.* Boston: Allyn & Bacon.

Livingston, M., & Flaherty, J. (1997). *Effects of Success for All on reading achievement in California schools.* Los Alamitos, CA: WestEd.

Madden, N. A. & Slavin, R. E. (1983). Mainstreaming students with mild academic handicaps: Academic and social outcomes. *Review of Educational Research, 53,* 519–569.

Madden, N. A., Slavin, R. E., Karweit, N. L., Dolan, L. J., & Wasik, B. A. (1993). Suc-cess for All: Longitudinal effects of a restructuring program for inner-city ele-mentary schools. *American Educational Research Journal, 30,* 123–148.

McManus, S. M., & Gettinger, M. (1996). Teacher and student evaluations of cooper-ative learning and observed interactive behaviors. *Journal of Educational Research, 90,* 13–22.

No Child Left Behind Act of 2001, Pub. L. No. 117-10, 115 Stat. 1425 (2002).

Nunnery, J., Ross, S., Smith, L., Slavin, R., Hunter, P., & Stubbs, J. (1997, March). *Effects of full and partial implementation of Success for All on student reading achievement in English and Spanish.* Paper presented at the annual meeting of the American Educational Research Association, Chicago.

Pearson, P. D., & Stahl, S. (2002). *Choosing a reading program: A consumer's guide.* (Tech. Rpt.). Berkeley, CA: University of California.

Phenix, D., Siegel, D., Zaltsman, A., & Fruchter, N. (2004). *Virtual district, real improvement: A retrospective evaluation of the Chancellor's District, 1996–2003.* New York: New York University.

Pinnell, G. S., DeFord, D. E., & Lyons, C. A. (1988). *Reading Recovery: Early intervention for at-risk first graders.* Arlington, VA: Educational Research Service.

Pinnell, G. S., Lyons, C. A., DeFord, D. E., Bryk, A. S., & Seltzer, M. (1994). Comparing instructional models for the literacy education of high risk first graders. *Reading Research Quarterly, 29,* 9–40.

Pogrow, S. (2000). The unsubstantiated "success" of Success for All: Implications for policy, practice, and the soul of our profession. *Phi Delta Kappan, 81,* 596–600.

Pressley, M., & Woloshyn, V. (1995). *Cognitive strategy instruction that really improves children's academic performance* (2nd ed.). Cambridge, MA: Brookline.

Puma, M. J., Jones, C. C., Rock, D., & Fernandez, R. (1993). *Prospects: The congressionally mandated study of educational growth and opportunity. Interim report.* Bethesda, MD: Abt Associates.

Ross, S., Smith, L., Casey, J., & Slavin, R. E. (1995). Increasing the academic success of disadvantaged children: An examination of alternative early intervention programs. *American Educational Research Journal, 32,* 773–800.

Sharan, Y., & Sharan, S. (1992). *Group investigation: Expanding cooperative learning.* New York: Teacher's College Press.

Slavin, R. E. (1983). When does cooperative learning increase student achievement? *Psychological Bulletin, 94,* 429–445.

Slavin, R. E. (1987a). Ability grouping and student achievement in elementary schools: A best-evidence synthesis. *Review of Educational Research, 57,* 347–350.

Slavin, R. E. (1987b). Cooperative learning and the cooperative school. *Educational Leadership, 45*(3), 7–13.

Slavin, R.E. (1989). PET and the pendulum: Faddism in education and how to stop it. *Phi Delta Kappan, 70,* 752–758.

Slavin, R. E. (1995). *Cooperative learning: Theory, research, and practice* (2nd ed.). Boston: Allyn & Bacon.

Slavin, R. E. (1996). Neverstreaming: Preventing learning disabilities. *Educational Leadership, 53*(5), 4–7.

Slavin, R. E. (2003). Evidence-based education policies: Transforming educational practice and research. *Educational Researcher, 31*(7), 15–21.

Slavin, R.E., & Cheung, A. (2004). *Effective reading programs for English language learners.* Manuscript submitted for publication.

Slavin, R. E., Daniels, C., & Madden, N. A. (2005). The Success for All middle school: Adding content to middle grades reform. *Middle School Journal, 36*(5), 4–8.

Slavin, R. E., Hurley, E. A., & Chamberlain, A. M. (2003). Cooperative learning and achievement: Theory and research. In W. M. Reynolds & G. E. Miller (Eds.), *Handbook of psychology* (Vol. 7, pp. 177–198). Hoboken, NJ: Wiley & Sons.

Slavin, R. E., & Madden, N. A. (1999). Effects of bilingual and English as a second language adaptations of Success for All on the reading achievement of students acquiring English. *Journal of Education for Students Placed at Risk, 4,* 393–416.

Slavin, R. E., & Madden, N. A. (2000). Research on achievement outcomes of Success for All: A summary and response to critics. *Phi Delta Kappan, 82,* 38–40, 59–66.

Slavin, R. E., & Madden, N. A. (2001). *One million children: Success for All.* Thousand Oaks, CA: Corwin.

Slavin, R. E., Madden, N. A., Dolan, L. J., & Wasik, B. A. (1996). *Every child, every school: Success for All.* Newbury Park, CA: Corwin.

Slavin, R. E., Madden, N. A., Karweit, N. L., Dolan, L., & Wasik, B. A. (1992). *Success for All: A relentless approach to prevention and early intervention in elementary schools.* Arlington, VA: Educational Research Service.

Slavin, R. E., Madden, N. A., Karweit, N. L., Livermon, B. J., & Dolan, L. (1990). Success for All: First-year outcomes of a comprehensive plan for reforming urban education. *American Educational Research Journal, 27,* 255–278.

Slavin, R. E., Madden, N. A., & Leavey, M. (1984). Effects of team assisted individualization on the mathematics achievement of academically handicapped and non-handicapped students. *Journal of Educational Psychology, 76,* 813–819.

Slavin, R. E., Madden, N. A., & Liang, C. (2002). *Effects of Success for All on SAT-9 reading: A California statewide evaluation.* Baltimore: Johns Hopkins University, Center for Research on the Education of Students Placed at Risk.

Stevens, R. J., Madden, N. A., Slavin, R. E., & Farnish, A. M. (1987). Cooperative Integrated Reading and Composition: Two field experiments. *Reading Research Quarterly, 22,* 433–454.

Stevens, R. J., & Slavin, R. E. (1995). Effects of a cooperative learning approach in reading and writing on handicapped and nonhandicapped students' achievement, attitudes, and metacognition in reading and writing. *Elementary School Journal, 95,* 241–262.

Traub, J. (1999). *Better by design? A consumer's guide to schoolwide reform.* Washington, DC: Thomas Fordham Foundation.

Webb, N. M., & Palincsar, A. S. (1996). Group processes in the classroom. In D. C. Berliner & R. C. Calfee (Eds.), *Handbook of educational psychology.* New York: Simon & Schuster.

Woodcock, R. (1998). *Woodcock Reading Mastery Test—Revised.* Circle Pines, MI: American Guidance Service.

Accelerated Schools and the Obstacles to School Reform

Christine Finnan
College of Charleston

Henry M. Levin
Teachers College Columbia

The Accelerated Schools Project (ASP) was established in 1986 to transform schools from remedial environments to accelerated ones based on academic enrichment and the educational treatment of all students as gifted and talented. This was a radical idea at that time, when it was believed that skill deficiencies of the "disadvantaged" must be repaired through low-level repetition and rote learning prior to undertaking more challenging and engaging tasks. By 2005, the ASP had reached over 1,000 schools in 41 states, Australia, and Hong Kong. Many accelerated schools had extended gifted and talented instruction to all classrooms, and the academic results were found to be very promising in independent evaluations by noted evaluation organizations (Bloom, Rock, Ham, Melton, & O'Brien, 2001).

The implementation of the ASP, like many other school reform models, has been beset with challenges. Our purpose in this chapter is to describe the conceptual underpinnings of ASP, the design of the project, and some of the obstacles that stand in the way of translating new ideas into everyday practices. In what follows, we first explain the origins of ASP and some of its features. Second, we develop a range of issues that make implementation a major challenge and strategies that were used to address them. Finally, we outline continuing sources of tension and recent changes in educational policy that undermine both the philosophy of accelerated schools and their practices.

RESEARCH INFLUENCES

By the early 1980s, the war on poverty of the middle 1960s had been largely forgotten. U.S. educational reform focused more heavily on competing educationally and economically with Japan, other Asian countries, and Europe rather than concerns with equity. Reports such as the influential *Nation at Risk: The Imperative for National Reform* (National Commission on Excellence in Education, 1983) were concerned with the alleged mediocrity of the entire system of U.S. education. The slogan that "a rising tide lifts all boats" became a rallying cry rather than singling out those boats most likely to founder. In this period, H. M. Levin was asked to look at the education of disadvantaged students in the United States in terms of their demography, educational practices, results, and consequences. The resulting reports have defined disadvantaged students as those who were unlikely to succeed educationally in existing schools (Levin, 1985, 1986). About one third of U.S. students met that definition, and the percentage was rising because of increasing child poverty rates, single-parent families, and immigration from less-developed regions of the world.

These reports (Levin, 1985, 1986) found that disadvantaged students began school with lower academic proficiencies and fewer experiences in the home and the community that auger academic success. The longer that they were in school, the farther they lagged the mainstream in academic results. It was obvious that a slow and less challenging form of instruction was at least partially responsible for this result. Thus began a search for forms of instruction that might accelerate the progress of these children so that they would enter the academic mainstream within a few years and succeed educationally.

We pursued three routes of investigation. "Exemplary programs" of the National Diffusion Network (NDN)[1] were found to be based on limited evaluation evidence and were characterized by statistically significant but small academic gains. Many of the initial sites for which the data had been collected were no longer in operation. The NDN seemed to be a far less productive source of direction than its good intentions had suggested.

A second route of investigation was a review of the research literature on the effectiveness of different types of interventions for "educationally at-risk students." A very substantial search of the Educational Resources In-

---

[1]The National Diffusion Network was established by the U.S. Department of Education to make innovative programs available to all schools across the country (Levinson, 1995).

formation Center database suggested that "statistical significance" was the standard criterion for declaring victory in this literature even though effect sizes were typically small with a few percentiles difference. For students in the 20th to 30th percentile, a gain of 2 to 3 percentiles may be statistically significant but not educationally significant.

The third information strategy was to visit schools with high concentrations of at-risk students. We found that classrooms in these schools were characterized by considerable repetition and memorization and lacked experiences that engaged students through enlisting imagination, previous experience, curiosity, and creativity (Levin, 1985, 1986). Teachers following these methods seemed uninspired and were preoccupied with keeping order in a situation that lacked intrinsic motivation for students. Only in the few gifted and talented classes did we observe students learning and using basic skills within a context of discussion, extensive writing, artistic endeavors, research projects, and collaboration. These classrooms seemed to be exciting places in which teachers and students were engaged in meaningful work.

We concluded that existing interventions from the research literature and the NDN were unlikely to have more than a very limited impact in improving achievement for at-risk students, and they tended to undermine other valued goals such as creativity, initiative, and facility in addressing real-world situations. Such practices were premised largely on the remedial assumption that students must be saddled with constant memorization and repetition of low-level skills before they could be engaged and provided with more challenging activities. Even the best of these interventions showed only slight improvements, inadequate to move students out of the educational repair shop of remedial and special education. If students were to reach the mainstream, we saw the solution as accelerated instruction much like that of the gifted and talented classrooms that would embed basic skills in meaningful tasks, drawing on the interest and experiences of the children.

The Research Base and Theories on Intelligence and Learning

The search for best practices in educating educationally at-risk students coincided with developments on intelligence that were challenging ideas on teaching and learning, especially for students considered gifted and talented. The work of Sternberg (1985, 1986) and Gardner (1983, 1999) questioned prevailing conceptions of intelligence by proposing broader, more contextualized theories.

Sternberg (1985, 1986) recognized that intelligence is manifested through abilities to analyze, synthesize, and apply knowledge. Sternberg (1985, 1986) posited that individuals have varying strength in these three areas. For example, some individuals possess high levels of analytic intelligence, excelling at dissecting and understanding the parts of a problem or a subject. Other people possess high levels of synthetic intelligence and thrive on novelty, finding creative ways to tackle tasks or address problems. Finally, other individuals possess practical intelligence and are accomplished at applying analytic or synthetic intelligence (Sternberg, 1991).

Gardner's theory of multiple intelligences (1983) also shaped ASP's conceptual and theoretical base through a recognition that students demonstrate strengths in many different ways. Gardner recognized that the Western concept of general intelligence, or g, was skewed toward linguistic and logical-mathematical intelligence, missing individuals' abilities and proclivities in other domains of knowledge (Gardner, 1983; Ramos-Ford & Gardner, 1991). In 1983, Gardner set out seven intelligences: linguistic, logical-mathematical, musical, bodily-kinesthetic, spatial, interpersonal, and intrapersonal intelligence (Gardner, 1983) as a more pluralistic approach to human intelligence; this was expanded in 1999 to include naturalist intelligence (Gardner, 1999).

Other compelling theories on learning that shaped the ASP, constructivism in particular, derive from the work of Dewey (1990) and other progressive educators. Constructivist theories of learning extend and expand on Dewey's beliefs about the importance of cultivating critical thinking and problem-solving skills and building on experience. Constructivist theory holds that it is the teacher's job to help learners internalize, reshape, and possibly transform understanding through acquisition, analysis, and synthesis of new knowledge (Brooks & Brooks, 1999). Unlike a more traditional transmission teaching approach, constructivist teachers assume students possess prior knowledge and interest in learning more about their world. This approach to teaching is also consistent with Vygotsky's (1978) theory that students learn best within their "zone of proximal development," the area between what children can do on their own and what they can do with the help of an adult or other children. Rather than transmitting information to students, a teacher provides the scaffolding needed to expand the zone.

THEORIES ON ORGANIZATIONAL EFFECTIVENESS AND DECISION MAKING

At the same time, considerable change was occurring in terms of how decisions are made in organizations. The traditional model of control through an authoritarian hierarchy in which the highest levels of management controlled decisions, and information was giving way to organizations with much greater worker participation in decisions at all levels (Carnoy & Levin, 1985). Although heavily inspired by the success of Japanese automobile manufacturers, the influence in the United States extended to many kinds of workplaces (Levine, 1996). The view was that highly motivated and well-informed workers could improve the operation and efficiency of organizations if provided with incentives and information, and these theories could be applied to schools (Levin, 1997).

THE ACCELERATED SCHOOLS SOLUTION

As we described earlier, the ASP grew out of deep concern for educationally at-risk students and the possibilities of more dynamic and participative forms of schooling that built on emerging work on intelligence, gifted and talented programs (e.g. Renzulli & Reis, 1985), and the pedagogies of Dewey (1990) and Freire (1970). The ASP also made a strong commitment to social justice, democracy, and equity consonant with the strong views of its founder (H. M. Levin) and was influenced by the work of others concerned with equity, oppression, and social justice (Bowles & Gintis, 1976; Carnoy & Levin, 1985; Freire, 1970; Kozol, 1991; McLaren, 1989).

The ASP Design

The ASP change strategy represents a philosophy and a process for transforming conventional schools into environments where powerful learning experiences are daily occurrences for all members of a school community. The philosophy of the ASP encompasses an overall goal (acceleration for all), three principles, a set of values, and a theory about learning that is summarized in the ASP terminology as powerful learning. The ASP process is constructed to embrace participatory organizational theory as a framework for guiding a systematic set of practices designed to "get from here to there"—from conventional schools to accelerated ones (Levin, 1998).

The Philosophy. Dewey's (1990) influence is evident throughout the ASP philosophy and practices of replacing memorization with enrichment, drill with engaging projects, and assessment of inert intelligence with what Sternberg (1997) called measures of successful intelligence. These influences are evident in ASP's three principles: unity of purpose, empowerment with responsibility, and building on strengths.

Unity of purpose refers to an active collaboration among parents, teachers, students, support staff, administrators, and the local community toward formulating and achieving a common set of goals and activities for the school. These shared goals and values become the focal point of everyone's efforts.

Empowerment coupled with responsibility refers to the ability of the participants of the school community in both the school and at home to make important educational decisions and to take responsibility for both implementing those decisions and for being accountable for outcomes. The purpose of this principle is to replace the stalemate among administrators, teachers, parents, support staff, and students in which the participants tend to blame each other as well as other factors "beyond their control" (e.g., the government) for the poor educational outcomes of students.

Building on strengths refers to utilizing all of the learning resources that students, parents, all school staff, and communities bring to the educational endeavor in which strengths extend to experiences, cultures, and curiosities as well as the many forms of intelligence. ASP communities actively look for and build on the strengths of all students, parents, teachers, support staff, administrators, the district and the local community as they implement the ASP process and develop powerful learning experiences.

Underlying the ASP principles and practices are a set of central values, beliefs, and attitudes that are embedded in the ASP process and school practices. When developed and shared, they help create the culture for ASP change. Equity, participation, communication, collaboration, community, reflection, experimentation, trust, risk taking, and the school as the center of expertise are among the central values that orient all actions of an ASP school.

Powerful Learning.   Especially central to building on student strengths is the concept of powerful learning, which integrates curriculum, instruction, and school and classroom organization rather than viewing each dimension as independent.[2] Powerful learning is based on the premise that the educational approach that we offer to gifted children works well for all children. Powerful learning enacts theories of multiple intelligence and builds on research on effective instruction for educationally at-risk students (Cohen, McLaughlin, & Talbert, 1993; Means, Chelemer, & Knapp, 1991; Newmann, Secada, & Wehlage, 1995) with practices normally identified with education of the gifted (Renzulli & Reis, 1985; Tomlinson, 1996). Accelerated schools create powerful learning situations that motivate students to grow and succeed. Students see meaning in their lessons and perceive connections between school activities and experiences outside of the school. They learn actively and in ways that build on their own strengths, develop their natural talents and gifts, and apply them in creative ways toward problem solving and decision making. These learning experiences require higher order thinking, complex reasoning, and relevant content. In such situations, children actively discover the curriculum objectives rather than passively going through textbooks and filling out worksheets. At the same time, this type of learning environment requires orga-

---

[2]Powerful learning also embraces five components of learning: authenticity, continuity, child focus, inclusion, and interaction. For details on these and other aspects of the powerful learning model, see the Accelerated Schools Web site at www.acceleratedschools.net.

nization and support, so adults are challenged to create a safe environment for learning that extends far beyond the classroom into every aspect of the school, home, and community.

The Process.   To function as ASP schools, school communities need to work toward a unity of purpose, to make responsible decisions, and to build on strengths. For these reasons, the ASP has developed a systematic process. The process involves taking stock of the "here and now" and forging a vision of what the school will become. Through this process, the entire school community becomes aware of its existing strengths and challenges and has a unified vision to strive toward. Once taking stock and the vision are complete, the school sets priorities, determining key areas of focus. At this point, a three-tier governance structure (working groups or cadres, a steering committee, and the School as a Whole) engage in an inquiry process focused on understanding and addressing school challenges. The inquiry process involves developing and testing hypotheses to explain why problem areas exist, identifying solutions, developing and enacting action plans, and evaluating outcomes of the interventions. Inquiry is the responsibility of cadres and is overseen by the steering committee. All important decisions are made through consensus by the School as a Whole. This process and governance structure reflects theories of organizational efficiency (Levin, 1997).

Accelerated Schools Training and Field Support

Schools across the United States are supported through a national center and a network of regional satellite centers. Training and field support is provided as close to the school site as possible, usually through the satellite centers. A school begins the process of becoming an ASP school by training a team consisting of an external coach (at least 25% time devoted to ASP at this school), the principal, and an internal facilitator (at least 25% time devoted to ASP at this school) to work together in transforming the school.

In addition to the more formal training requirements, coaches visit the school site on a weekly basis to build capacity and troubleshoot. All coaches are mentored by staff from regional centers with regular communications, monthly meetings, and mentorship visits to school sites. Through this model, we attempt to ensure that all schools have accessibility to trained coaches and facilitators who can provide the training, follow-up, and guidance at the school site that we have found necessary. There is also a National Conference for the ASP that draws participants, both nationally and internationally, for sharing experiences and ideas at workshops and through major presentations and informal discussions.

TRANSLATING THEORY AND RESEARCH INTO PRACTICE: INTERNAL OBSTACLES TO CHANGE

The ASP was designed to utilize both theoretical perspectives and research findings to create accelerated schools. The ASP change process was constructed by translating that knowledge base into a sequence of integrated activities based on a guiding set of values and principles. Despite such deliberate attempts to develop an informed and systematic approach with trained coaches and eager school community members, a variety of obstacles have arisen that have inhibited change. Some of these have been overcome, but others have not. Obstacles arise through the internal dynamics of schools and through external actions undertaken at the district, state, and national levels. Much of our attention has been devoted to internal transformation of schools and overcoming internal obstacles. ASP, like many other school reform models, has limited influence beyond the school site and is premised on a belief that lasting change requires profound modifications at the school level.

Obstacles to Transforming School Culture

Much of the literature (Cuban, 1990, 1992; Fullan & Hargreaves, 1996; Sarason, 1982, 1996; Tyack & Cuban, 1995; Tyack & Tobin, 1994; Tye, 2000) points to school culture as an intractable obstacle to reform. Considering the conservative nature of school culture, this finding is not surprising. The operation of the school depends on a shared, stable culture, and efforts to reform the school are an affront to that culture. At the heart of reforms is the quest to change culture. However, a deep understanding of school culture suggests that culture, in and of itself, is not necessarily an obstacle. How the reform builds on or opposes the existing culture determines whether the culture serves as an obstacle or a base for reform.

   To use school culture as a launchpad for implementing reform, we must acknowledge its hidden nature, the fact that it comprises key aspects of the school that we take for granted. Those who are part of a school culture are so fully immersed in it, and it is so much a part of their lives, that they do not question the cultural assumptions. Culture defines the school by building on traditions, habits, expectations, and images of what schools and classrooms should do and be. The school culture may be evident in our actions and surroundings, but more importantly, it resides within each individual in the school, shaping beliefs, values, and assumptions. To suggest that schools and classrooms should change implies that these beliefs, values, and assumptions, as well as existing traditions, habits, expectations, and images, are invalid and need to be immediately modified: a virtual impossibility. It also implies that each person in the school may need to change, another unpopular proposal (Evans, 1996). Few reforms acknowledge that they require such deep change to make a difference; even fewer take the time and have the structure to work from this base toward their intended outcomes.

The ASP purposefully works at the level of beliefs, values, and assumptions. Rather than imposing a rigid curriculum or instructional approach, it provides a set of tools and processes that are used by the school to transform its own culture. It is a reform model that seeks transformative rather than dogmatic or prescriptive change. Transformative change entails understanding and respecting the existing culture; providing a process for reflection, exploration, and inquiry; and modeling actions based on ASP's values, beliefs, and assumptions. Many other reforms ignore the existing beliefs, values, and assumptions and focus on more surface level change (Sarason, 1996). Efforts are directed toward changing structures or behaviors, but they do not delve into the assumptions underlying the existing structures or behaviors. For example, efforts to promote site-based management often lead to little more than what Fullan and Hargreaves (1996) describe as "contrived collegiality" because assumptions about the role of adults in the school have not changed. School reforms are directed toward several key components of school culture, and they meet obstacles if they do not recognize and work with the assumptions underlying these areas.

Assumptions About What Is Best for Students.   Many reforms are directed toward raising expectations for students. The standards movement, the recent No Child Left Behind Act of 2001 legislation, and all models approved for Comprehensive School Reform Demonstration funding are premised on holding high expectations for all students. These efforts meet obstacles when they ignore existing assumptions about students' academic and behavioral capabilities. Although few people admit holding low expectations for students, many believe that some students, particularly low-income students of color, cannot be expected to meet the same academic and behavioral standards as more affluent students. They drill students on basics, are quick to point out deficiencies in the home, and often provide very restrictive learning environments because they assume that students lack ability, self-control, and motivation (Hale, 1994; Knapp, 1995; Newmann, 1996; Page, 1999). These assumptions will change only through ongoing staff development, reflection, experimentation, and inquiry.

Assumptions Students Hold for Themselves and Their Future.   Few reforms are primarily directed toward changing students' expectations for themselves, but students actively participate in shaping school culture both individually and collectively. Too often students feel disconnected from school and society (Ogbu, 1987; Solomon, 1992), and they disengage because they feel that adults care little about them and their future. Once one student disengages, it is easy to bring others along (McQuillan, 1998). Without understanding students' assumptions and including them in reform efforts, even the best planned efforts are likely to fail (see McQuillan, 1998, for a vivid account of a failed reform). Student engagement is typically resisted by professions who believe in more constrained student roles.

Adult Roles and Behavior.   Many reforms, ASP included, are built on the assumption that it is best to involve all stakeholders in the decision-making process. These expectations cannot be met if the existing culture assumes that the administration's role is to keep order and make all important decisions (Christensen, 1996), that only ineffective teachers work in schools serving low-income students (Ayers, 1992), and that low-income parents do not care about their children's education. Unless the reform addresses these assumptions, efforts to involve stakeholders in decisions will never go beyond mechanical compliance.

Extant Educational Practices.   Nearly all school reform efforts seek to change educational practices across the school and within individual classrooms. Efforts directed at the school level involve how time is used; how classrooms, grade levels, and departments are grouped and organized; and how the curriculum is taught and aligned across grade levels and subject areas. Efforts to change current structures and practices run into obstacles if they do not account for conventional and widely held assumptions such as the following: that schools are organized primarily for maintaining order, that grouping and sorting students is an effective means of "differentiating" instruction, that stimulating instruction is best reserved for students identified as gifted and talented (relegating slower learners to a steady diet of drill and practice; Tomlinson, 1996), and that subjects are best taught in isolation (Sizer, 1992). When reforms are introduced to schools holding assumptions like these, their efforts are stifled by conflicts with existing school practices and teaching beliefs on what is best; teachers and administrators may try to break out of old habits but retreat quickly when efforts to change are not immediately successful.

Positive Value of Change.   School reform is about change, but change efforts are not always welcome. Despite their reputation for resisting change, school cultures are constantly changing (Finnan & Levin, 2000; Finnan & Swanson, 2000). Some changes occur through changing demographics, others through district and state initiatives. Schools do resist change though, especially when the existing culture is ignored or disparaged or when the school community members have no input in determining the direction of the change. Only if members of the school culture seek to be the initiators of change and are encouraged to build on existing strengths within themselves and their school culture will change be absorbed into the culture and remain a part of it.

Response of ASP to Obstacles in Changing School Culture

As described previously, ASP is a transformative reform model. It presents a philosophy about how schools should function and how students should learn, and it provides schools with a process for getting there. The fact that each school can be unique and build on its own strengths and directions enables school communities to build a transformed culture and new practices. The goal of ASP is not to create identical replicas of one model across the country but to embed ASP in existing school cultures. For that reason, each mature ASP school looks and feels different from others, even though they share a philosophy and use a common process to make decisions. Where conditions are right, ASP encounters few implementation obstacles because it builds on the existing base. Through experience and research ASP has identified and addressed conditions that must be in place for implementation to be effective.

First, the school community must be informed about and willing to embrace change through ASP. Schools need to engage in a "courtship" process in which they gain an understanding of ASP philosophy, its time and resource commitments, and its compatibility with the existing school culture (Finnan, 2000). They do so by reading materials, visiting Web sites, talking to ASP staff, and visiting other schools (Kushman & Chenoweth, 1996). Once this has occurred, the administration and at least 80% of the teaching staff, support staff and representative parents must agree to adopt the accelerated schools approach. Second, schools need strong, consistent coaching and support. ASP provides on-going training, extensive site based support, networking, and a coaching model that provides school-specific assistance. At training sessions and network meetings schools have a chance to meet together to discuss issues and concerns and to exchange ideas. During on-site visits, trained staff members work with the school to overcome obstacles. The coaches (both external and internal to the school) provide help on a weekly basis. Third, schools must have strong district support and stable leadership and staffing. These conditions, and ASP's efforts to cultivate them, will be discussed below under external obstacles to transformation.

Internal Obstacles Within Classrooms

Although most reform efforts are directed toward school change, it is the classroom culture that has the most profound influence on student learning. Classrooms exist within schools, but as L. Anderson (personal communication, June 23, 2001) describes, many schools are a set of classrooms brought together by a common parking lot. The nature of teaching has always been solitary. Teachers spend the bulk of their time as the only adult with a classroom of students; they can close the classroom door and create magic or mayhem, and other adults may never know. Even when schools buy into a project like ASP, it is not uncommon for a teacher who exemplifies the ASP philosophy and who is committed to powerful learning to teach in a classroom adjacent to a teacher with no interest or understanding of ASP or powerful learning. In a recent study of ASP schools in South Carolina and Georgia, Finnan, Schnepel, and Anderson (2003) found more variation in implementing powerful learning within schools than between schools. In these schools, it was clear that the commitments made at the school level are unevenly manifested in the classroom.

To make teachers realize that ASP requires change in classroom culture as much as school culture, we emphasize the importance of powerful learning occurring in all classrooms. The processes of taking stock and inquiry focus on classroom practice, and teachers apply the inquiry process as a self-reflection tool and as a teaching tool. Focus groups, book clubs, and peer support teams are also vehicles that ASP schools use to break down barriers among teachers by increasing communication and improving mentoring and support. Building on existing classroom culture is key to overcoming obstacles to changing classroom practice in ASP schools. We recognize that the autonomy enjoyed by teachers is sacrosanct, but that mutual support, communication, and decision making can alter practices.

PROBLEMS ENCOUNTERED TRANSLATING THEORY AND RESEARCH INTO PRACTICE: EXTERNAL OBSTACLES TO TRANSFORMATION

In addition to the internal obstacles to school reform, there are many external challenges. External barriers are distinguished from internal ones because they emanate from sources that are outside of the school. At the broadest level, obstacles exist within American culture in widely held values, beliefs, and assumptions about education. In addition, governmental entities at all levels may undermine ASP and other school reforms through practices and policies formulated for other purposes.

External Obstacles in American Culture

Beliefs, values, and assumptions about schools, generally, and about teaching and learning, specifically, exist not only within schools but also within the more general culture. In a previous work (Finnan & Levin, 2000), we made the distinction between school culture and the culture of schooling. The culture of schooling encompasses the beliefs, values, and assumptions related to schools and schooling shared by the general population. Although school cultures at particular sites may change, the culture of schooling is much more conservative and resistant to change. This insight explains many of the paradoxes in American education. For example, it clarifies the fact that there is a general assumption that schools are in terrible shape even though the majority of parents repeatedly report in Gallup polls that they are satisfied with their own children's schools (Tye, 2000). The culture of schooling, on one hand, perpetuates obsolete governance structures, supports curriculum decisions that lack research backing, and accepts inequity in educational opportunity. On the other hand, the culture of schooling reveres public education and holds it up as one of America's finest institutions, claiming that through education, all people have equal opportunity (Finnan & Swanson, 2000). Reform models have little control over the culture of schooling, and they are often buffeted between the conflicting assumptions that underlie it.

External Obstacles Imposed by Federal, State, and District Policies and Practices

External obstacles arise not so much from conscious decisions to oppose ASP and other school reforms but from inconsistent practices and policies formulated for other purposes that have the consequence of contradicting or undermining existing reforms. Discussions with other educational reform leaders and research on reform implementation (Datnow, 2000; Finnan & Meza, 2003; Tye, 2000) suggest that these problems are not unique to ASP. The disconnection between policies and mandates created outside of schools is evident in relation to how leaders are chosen and supported and how time is used. Efforts to standardize the curriculum, with the associated reliance on standardized testing, also serve as obstacles, as does the general instability of district offices.

Site Leadership. Usually the principal or site administrator at a school has been an active participant in the "buy-in" process and is a champion of the reform that is chosen. However, in some cases the principal is appointed independently of the reform. Or when a principal retires or is promoted, a replacement is chosen who may be inappropriate for leading the reform. School districts seem to choose principals for schools on the basis of criteria which are insensitive to the specific culture and aspirations of ongoing school reforms. In all too many cases, the assignment is based on more mechanical considerations. For example, many districts rotate principals among schools every few years or assign new principals primarily on the basis of gender, race, or tenure in the district rather than the leadership style and educational orientation of the principal (Tye, 2000). Thus, ASP schools have been assigned principals who had no interest in ASP or who had an authoritarian style of leadership precluding staff participation in decisions. Principals who are not sympathetic to ASP practices and goals tend to resist or undermine ASP school dynamics. Within a short period, we have seen staff committed to ASP leave the school in frustration, further destroying the underpinnings, and new personnel have been hired according to priorities set out by the new principal. In such a situation, ASP practices evaporate completely.

A similar story is found for coaches. The ASP model is premised on the development of leadership at the school site through a coaching model. The school coach along with the principal and teacher facilitators spearhead the effort, building on training that they receive from ASP centers. In some cases, the schools are able to choose their own coaches. In other cases, the districts choose them, often making no effort to match coaches to the unique ASP process and culture. Thus, some Accelerated Schools have been assigned coaching personnel who were made available because they lacked full-time assignments or who had not succeeded in other central office roles. Even when the coaches were appropriate, the duties of coaching have often been added without relief from preexisting obligations. This has placed many coaches under great stress, as they spread themselves over so many activities that the ASP coaching gets short shrift.

Time Availability. At its heart, the Accelerated School requires an internal transformation from standard operating procedures to active inquiry and problem solving and from remediation to academic acceleration. However, such change is not magic. It entails considerable human endeavor for the training, practice, debate, discourse, deliberations, decisions, implementation, and evaluation. All of these activities require time in which both the full school staff and separate working groups can interact to undertake change in a systematic and responsive way. Unfortunately, most school schedules are not arranged to provide the time required for serious planning, preparation, and implementation. Typically, school districts provide a total of 4 days or less for professional development each academic year and occasional "early release" days. Some small part of the week or month is also set aside for parental meetings and individual classroom preparations as well as obligatory faculty meetings. The school's schedule is devoted overwhelmingly to instruction and other duties. It is not possible to squeeze in serious study and deliberation of issues or even the introductory process of Accelerated Schools within such narrow time constraints. We believe that the ASP process requires at least 6 to 10 full days for intense professional development each academic year as well as a half day a week for other activities and time for continuous coaching and follow-up in class-rooms and for other school roles. Most schools provide only a small fraction of this time.

However, even with the overall limitation of time, school districts often commandeer a portion of this time to address district priorities. Thus, bilingual teachers at an ASP school may be asked to relegate their profes-sional development days to attending a presentation by a bilingual expert; or all schools may be required to send their staffs to an overall district as-sembly. All of these uses of time may be meritorious in some sense, but they compromise seriously the ability to develop the Accelerated School model and rarely involve any follow-up to assist teachers in applying what was learned. Both formal training and group interaction are compromised so that there is inadequate time to develop ASP governance and decision mak-ing and the practice of powerful learning. In this respect, districts are often at cross-purposes with the requirements of the very reforms that they have endorsed for individual schools.

Standards and Standardization. A major recent threat to ASP imple-mentation and success is that of standardization of curriculum and testing that has been promoted by school districts, states, and the federal govern-ment. The issue is not a matter of standards but whose standards and how they are assessed. Standards can be broad enough to provide guidelines for which subjects and skills should be covered, but the present approaches of states are far more prescriptive in what should be taught at each grade level and how it will be tested. All ASP schools set standards for their students and staff, but they are often standards that cannot be easily placed in a narrowly focused curriculum or measured by conventional, standardized tests. Pow-erful learning may require that students do research on specific topics, prepare for and engage in debate, write poetry, undertake community pro-jects, write and perform skits based on a book that they have read, initiate public opinion surveys, interpret the epidemiology of a health problem, and so on. All of these activities require standards for evaluating what has been learned, but these are not likely to be the same standards as those used by school districts and states to assess learning.

In contrast, the use of standardized testing restricted to specific subjects and forms of tests (e.g., multiple choice) evaluates schools on the basis of much narrower criteria than those suggested by powerful learning. There is great pressure on schools to obtain test score gains that meet federal regula-tions from the No Child Left Behind Act of 2001 or to meet state require-ments. Schools are often ranked on the test scores or test score gains, placing great pressure on them to narrow their efforts to the standardized requirements that may well be inconsistent with powerful learning. Thus, the external pressures of testing and standardization tend to undercut the emphasis on powerful learning and the ASP approach to educational development. They pressure schools into traditional memorization and rote learning approaches associated with remediation and the preparation of students for taking standardized tests. Attention to curriculum is also narrowed to that which will be tested (Pedulla et al., 2003).

District Instability.   The instability of school districts in establishing and maintaining direction is also a major stumbling block to sustaining ASP. At one point, a district will be very enthusiastic about the philosophy, activities, and results of ASP. However, changes in school boards, superintendents, and other key personnel will often take the district in different directions, replacing existing reforms with new ones on the basis of other predilections. The situation in Memphis, Tennessee is a case in point. This well-documented (Bodilly, 1998; Ross, Alberg, & Wang, 2001; Stringfield & Datnow, 1998) and promising effort to involve all schools in comprehensive school reform was abandoned overnight when the innovative superintendent left and was replaced by a local administrator with deep ties to the old order. Within months, few of the changes initiated remained (Finnan & Meza, 2003).

A major project on urban school reform studied 57 urban districts and found that the typical district launched more than 11 "significant" reforms between 1992 and 1995, an average of one new reform every 3 months (Hess, 1999, p. 95). In such an environment, the initial support and enthusiasm for a school engaged in ASP can be displaced by a new set of reforms, which may be short-lived in themselves as new waves of reform wash over and obliterate the older ones (Cuban, 1990). Even when ASP schools are allowed to continue their development, the new reforms are often imposed on them, diluting, conflicting with, and enervating ASP efforts.

Responding to External Obstacles.   It is difficult to overcome external obstacles because they are outside the control of schools and school reform models. Projects like ASP have neither the carrots nor the sticks needed to influence the culture of schooling or federal, state, or district policy and practice. ASP schools are problem-solving entities, so they attempt to address the external threats to their functioning. However, their power to do so is limited.

ASP has devoted considerable effort to addressing leadership issues in ASP schools. The ASP national center and several regional satellite centers offer principal academies designed to help principals develop facilitative leadership skills. These academies are especially useful for principals who are new to ASP schools. Unfortunately, many districts do not support further principal training so that new principals are not always permitted or encouraged to attend the academies. Individual schools may request that school representatives be involved in the selection of a new principal or coach, but such a request may be approved or not and may simply represent a charade in which school involvement is a "courtesy" that is not taken seriously.

ASP has also been involved in several initiatives designed to eliminate district-level obstacles. The most prominent was the ambitious partnerships between Memphis City Schools and a set of major comprehensive school reform models mentioned previously. In the mid-1990s, the Memphis City Schools joined with New American Schools[3] to bring comprehensive school reform models to all 164 schools in the district.[4] Many of the conditions needed to support reform existed, especially initially (e.g., a supportive superintendent, good support from the models, additional funding), but the initiative failed for many of the reasons listed previously. Although the superintendent was fully supportive, buy-in at the schools and support by other district administrators was inconsistent. Most important, the culture of schooling in Memphis never changed to accommodate school reform. When the superintendent left, all comprehensive school reform was quickly abandoned. Schools were told they could no longer participate in any comprehensive school reform initiative, and they accepted this order without protest. Soon, few remnants of ASP or any other reform movement remained in Memphis (Finnan & Meza, 2003).

The fact that school districts and states adopt reforms without conferring with individual schools in the midst of reform compromises the ability of individual ASP schools to influence district policy. School personnel try to point out the contradictions between new and previous reforms, but districts continue to jump from one reform to another, rarely considering the impact on existing reform efforts. On the premise that some of these threats can be neutralized, much of the energy of ASP schools must be expended in defensive maneuvers, always scanning the horizon for new external threats and expending time and other resources in seeking solutions, often without success.

Efforts to address obstacles related to time are primarily made at the school level. Schools seek funding for covering substitute teachers to provide additional release time for training and collaboration, or they attempt to reschedule the instructional week to free up time. However, even these attempts are often constrained by collective bargaining restrictions and the difficulties of finding outside grants. Schools also deal with standardization of curriculum and the demands of high-stakes testing. The pressures of compliance with standardization and testing practices demanded by states

---

[3]New American Schools was a partnership between many of the major comprehensive school reform models.

[4]For a more complete account of the Memphis experiment, see Finnan and Meza (2003).

and districts diverts teacher efforts to create powerful learning environments. In many cases, ASP schools must meet two sets of standards, their own and those of government authorities, a strain on school personnel and other resources (Pedulla et al., 2003).

ACCOMPLISHMENTS AND THE FUTURE

Despite these obstacles, we believe that the ASP has shown substantial success in at least three major ways: legitimating acceleration for at-risk students, developing a process to convert schools from remediation to acceleration, and producing educational results.

Legitimating Acceleration

A major accomplishment of ASP has been in changing assumptions in the culture of schooling regarding acceleration. Prior to initiating the ASP in 1986, we did a literature search on educational acceleration to study its application to disadvantaged or at-risk populations. Virtually all of the extant literature had referred to acceleration as a mechanism for reducing the time required for gifted students to complete educational requirements such as skipping through grades or courses. One exception was the work of Renzulli and Reis (1985) whose concept of school-wide enrichment bore similarities to what we had in mind, although they did not use the term *acceleration*.

As we established pilot schools and began to disseminate publications arguing for acceleration into the mainstream rather than remediation (e.g., Levin, 1987, 1988), this perspective began to appear in educational writings and presentations by others. The concept of educational acceleration began to be used commonly to refer to a strategy for all students, not just those who were deemed gifted and talented. For example, in 1990, the Educational Testing Service produced a widely cited monograph on National Assessment of Educational Progress results titled *Accelerating Academic Achievement, America's Challenge: A Summary of Findings From 20 Years of NAEP* (Mullis, Owen, & Phillips, 1990). In 1991, the Texas Education Agency, a state department of education, converted its division for services to disadvantaged and handicapped students into one dedicated to accelerated education employing the three principles of ASP. By 1994, a new strategy for seeking adequacy in school funding was premised on "How to Accelerate Educational Outcomes for the Disadvantaged" (Clune, 1994, p. 395). Additionally, by the latter 1990s, school districts were predicating their plans for at-risk students on acceleration rather than remediation (e.g., district-wide programs in Cleveland, Minneapolis, and Columbus), and states and the federal government under the No Child Left Behind Act of 2001 were using the acceleration metaphor to push for closing the achievement gap between minority and nonminority students. We believe that much of the change in terminology and direction was associated with the more than 1,000 Accelerated Schools that were launched in 41 states as well as the extensive discussion of these ideas associated with ASP in professional publications (e.g., Finnan, St. John, McCarthy, & Slovacek, 1996; Finnan & Swanson, 2000; Hopfenberg et al., 1993; Levin, 1987).

ASP Process

It is not enough to change the language and ostensible goals of educating at-risk students. Marshaling support and the possibility of change must also be buttressed by a process for achieving change and producing results. The ASP devoted considerable attention to the development and testing of processes that embody the principles, values, and goals of accelerated schools. Numerous changes were made in that process, as some attempts were disappointing and others succeeded. These were embodied in a set of integrated steps that became the focus of coaching, training, and evaluation and that were constantly updated for new knowledge (Finnan et al., 1996; Hopfenberg et al., 1993) with newsletters and guidance placed on the Web site www.acceleratedschools.net. The large numbers of accelerated schools also meant that educators could observe practices in other schools. Thus, the ideas behind ASP were shown to be replicable.

Educational Accomplishments

Finally, a large number of schools that were transformed into ASP schools were evaluated for educational outcomes. Independent evaluations of student learning witnessed significant achievement gains, even though performances on standardized tests are not the primary goal of accelerated schools. In a 3-year evaluation by one of the most prominent national evaluation organizations, 8 schools from eight different school districts in seven states were selected randomly from a pool of 100 schools to assess gains in third-grade achievement (adjusted for changes in student composition; Bloom et al., 2001). The evaluation model employed an interrupted time series of 3 years prior to the initiation of the ASP reform and 5 years following it, 8 years of data. Five years after the intervention, average reading and mathematics scores had increased by 7 to 9 percentage points, with larger increases for those schools with the lowest initial scores. These gains were comparable to those of the well-known Tennessee Class Size experiment (Finn & Achilles, 1999) in which class size was reduced from about 25 to 15 but with the ASP costing only a fraction of the cost of class-size reduction. Even these results tended to understate the achievement growth because about half of the students who were assessed had not attended the school for the full period of the intervention (Levin, 2002, pp. 14–15). In contrast, other studies of whole-school reform evaluated achievement gains only for the most stable students, those who had attended the schools continuously during the intervention. Further, the achievement gains were based on conventional tests rather than instruments more closely aligned with the goals of ASP schools.

A 1999 study of six Accelerated Schools in Memphis found gains in all five subject areas tested in contrast to a similar group of schools that had not undertaken reform. In reading, average student achievement had risen from the equivalent of the 30th percentile to almost the 70th percentile (Ross, Wang, Sanders, Wright, & Stringfield, 1999). Two independent studies comparing costs of reforms for at-risk students have found that the ASP had the lowest costs among the alternatives (Barnett, 1996; King, 1994). A range of other independent studies have also found a variety of measures of educational success (Accelerated Schools Project, 2001).

ASP and the Future

In the 17 years of development and implementation of ASP, we have learned many things. We have learned that learning theories can be applied effectively to school reform, although not always in a straightforward manner. Implementation requires building on the existing culture of schools and providing a process that embodies the values and principles but allows school communities to use these as a framework to create their own unique approaches to powerful learning and problem solving. Such schools build on the strengths of their students, staffs, and parent communities.

The most serious challenges are those that come from external sources, particularly from school districts, states, and the federal government. Especially threatening to ASP is the present thrust of states and the federal government under the No Child Left Behind Act of 2001 legislation to value educational results only in terms of annual progress on standardized achievement tests. In using the broader notions of intelligence of Sternberg (1985, 1986, 1997) and Gardner (1983, 1999) as guidelines for educational development, the ASP is committed to what it considers to be more comprehensive and valuable goals of human development than the standards and accountability strategy encourages. Unfortunately, the emerging system for evaluating school quality threatens to punish schools that depart from maximizing standardized tests. Although ASP has overcome most of the internal challenges to success, it is not clear that it can always prevail over the external forces of narrow testing standards; instability and inconsistency of district, state, and federal educational policies; and inadequate time resources and leadership. Still, accelerated schools are an exercise in optimism.

REFERENCES

Accelerated Schools Project. (2001). *Accelerated Schools Research and Evaluation Bulletin*. Retrieved January 5, 2005, from http://www.acceleratedschools.net/main_acc

Ayers, W. (1992). Work that is real: Why teachers should be empowered. In G. A. Hess (Ed.), *Empowering teachers and parents: School restructuring through the eyes of anthropologists* (pp. 13–28). Westport, CT: Bergin and Garvey.

Barnett, W. S. (1996). Economics of school reform: Three promising models. In H. F. Ladd (Ed.), *Holding schools accountable* (pp. 299–326). Washington, DC: Brookings Institute.

Bloom, H. S., Rock, J., Ham, S., Melton, L., & O'Brien, J. (with Doolittle, F., & Kagahiro, S.). (2001). *Evaluating the Accelerated Schools approach*. New York: Manpower Demonstration Research Corporation.

Bodilly, S. J. (1998). *Lessons from New American Schools' scale-up phase: Prospects for bringing designs to multiple schools*. Santa Monica, CA: RAND Corporation, MR–942–NAS.

Bowles, S., & Gintis, H. (1976). *Schooling in capitalist America*. New York: Basic Books.

Brooks, J. G., & Brooks, M. G. (1999). *The case for constructivist classrooms*. Alexandria, VA: Association for Supervision and Curriculum Development.

Carnoy, M., & Levin, H. L. (1985). *Schooling and work in the democratic state*. Stanford, CA: Stanford University Press.

Christensen, G. (1996). Toward a new leadership paradigm: Behaviors of accelerated school principals. In C. Finnan, E. St. John, J. McCarthy, & S. Slovacek (Eds.), *Accelerated schools in action: Lessons from the field* (pp. 185–207). Thousand Oaks, CA: Corwin Press.

Clune, W. H. (Ed.). (1994). Equity and adequacy in education: Issues for policy and finance [Special issue]. *Educational Policy, 8*(4).

Cohen, D. K., McLaughlin, M. W., & Talbert, J. E. (Eds.). (1993). *Teaching for understanding: Challenge for policy and practice*. San Francisco: Jossey-Bass.

Cuban, L. (1990). Reforming again, again, and again. *Educational Researcher, 19*(1), 3–13.

Cuban, L. (1992). What happens to reforms that last? The case of the junior high school. *American Educational Research Journal, 29*, 227–252.

Datnow, A. (2000). Power and politics in the adoption of school reform models. *Educational Evaluation and Policy Analysis, 22*, 357–374.

Dewey, J. (1990). *The school and society*. Chicago: University of Chicago Press.

Evans, R. (1996). *Human side of school change: Reform, resistance, and the real-life problems of innovation*. San Francisco: Jossey-Bass.

Finn, J. D., & Achilles, C. M. (1999). Tennessee's class size study: Findings, implications, misconceptions. *Educational Evaluation and Policy Analysis, 21*, 97–110.

Finnan, C. (2000, April). Implementing school reform models: Why is it so hard for some schools and easy for others? Paper presented at the annual meeting of the American Educational Research Association, New Orleans, LA. (ERIC Document Reproduction Service No. ED446356).

Finnan, C., & Levin, H. M. (2000). Changing school culture. In J. Elliott & H. Altrichter (Eds.), *Images of educational change* (pp. 87–98). Milton Keynes, England: Open University Press.

Finnan, C., & Meza, J. (2003). The Accelerated Schools Project: Can a leader change the culture and embed reform. In J. Murphy & A. Datnow (Eds.), *Leadership lessons from comprehensive school reforms* (pp. 83–108). Thousand Oaks, CA: Corwin Press.

Finnan, C., Schnepel, K. C., & Anderson, L. W. (2003). Powerful learning environments: The critical link between school and classroom cultures. *Journal of Education for Students Placed At Risk, 9*, 391–418.

Finnan, C., St. John, E., McCarthy, J., & Slovacek, S. (Eds.). (1996). *Accelerated schools in action: Lessons from the field*. Thousand Oaks, CA: Corwin Press.

Finnan, C., & Swanson, J. D. (2000). *Accelerating the learning of all students: Cultivating culture change in schools, classrooms, and individuals*. Boulder, CO: Westview.

Freire, P. (1970). *Pedagogy of the oppressed*. New York: Herder and Herder.

Fullan, M., & Hargreaves, A. (1996). *What's worth fighting for in your school*. New York: Teachers College Press.

Gardner, H. (1983). *Frames of mind: The theory of multiple intelligences*. New York: Basic Books.

Gardner, H. (1999). *Intelligence reframed: Multiple intelligences for the 21st century*. New York: Basic Books.

Hale, J. E. (1994). *Unbank the fire: Visions for the education of African American children*. Baltimore: Johns Hopkins University Press.

Hess, F. M. (1999). *Spinning wheels: The politics of urban school reform*. Washington, DC: Brookings Institute.

Hopfenberg, W., Levin, H. M., Chase, C., Christensen, S. G., Moore, M., Soler, P., Brunner, I., Keller, B., & Rodriquez, G. (1993). *The accelerated schools resource guide*. San Francisco: Jossey-Bass.

King, J. A. (1994). Meeting the educational needs of at-risk students: A cost analysis of three models. *Educational Evaluation and Policy Analysis, 16*, 1–19.

Knapp, M. S. (1995). Introduction: The teaching challenge in high-poverty classrooms. In M. S. Knapp, N. E. Adelman, C. Marder, H. McCollum, M. C. Needels, C. Padilla, P. M. Shields, B. J Turnbull, & A. A. Zucker (Eds.), *Teaching for meaning in high-poverty classrooms* (pp. 1–11). New York: Teachers College Press.

Kozol, J. (1991). *Savage inequities*. New York: Crown.

Kushman, J. W., & Chenoweth, T. G. (1996). Building shared meaning and commitment during the courtship phase. In C. Finnan, E. St. John, J. McCarthy, & S. Slovacek (Eds.), *Accelerated schools in action: Lessons from the field* (pp. 82–103). Thousand Oaks, CA: Corwin Press.

Levin, H. M. (1985). *The educationally disadvantaged: A national crisis*. Philadelphia: Public/Private Ventures.

Levin, H. M. (1986). *Educational reform for disadvantaged students: An emerging crisis*. Washington, DC: National Education Association.

Levin, H. M. (1987). Accelerated schools for disadvantaged students. *Educational Leadership, 44*(6), 19–21.

Levin, H. M. (1988). Accelerating elementary education for disadvantaged students. In Council of Chief State School Officers (Eds.), *School success for students at risk* (pp. 209–226). Orlando, FL: Harcourt Brace.

Levin, H. M. (1996). Accelerated schools: The background. In C. Finnan, E. P. St. John, J. McCarthy, & S. P. Slovacek (Eds.), *Accelerated schools in action: Lessons from the field* (pp. 3–23). Thousand Oaks, CA: Corwin Press.

Levin, H. M. (1997). Raising school productivity: An x-efficiency approach. *Economics of Education Review, 16*, (3) pp. 303–312.

Levin, H. M. (1998). Accelerated schools: A decade of evolution. In A. Hargreaves, A. Lieberman, M. Fullan, & D. Hopkins (Eds.), *International handbook of educational change* (pp. 807–830). Boston: Kluwer Academic.

Levin, H. M. (2002). *The cost effectiveness of whole school reforms* (Urban Diversity Series No. 114). New York: ERIC Clearinghouse on Urban Education, Teachers College, Columbia University.

Levine, D. (1996). Reinventing the workplace: How business and employee can both win. Washington, DC: Brookings Institute.

Levinson, L. (1995). *Educational programs that work: The catalogue of the National Diffusion Network* (21st ed.). Retrieved October 25, 2004, from http://www.ed.gov/pubs/EPTW/index.html

McLaren, P. (1989). *Life in schools.* New York: Longman.

McQuillan, P. J. (1998). *Educational opportunity in an urban American high school: A cultural analysis.* Albany: State University of New York Press.

Means, B., Chelemer, C., & Knapp, M. S. (1991). *Teaching advanced skills to at-risk students.* San Francisco: Jossey-Bass.

Mullis, I. V. S., Owen, E. H., & Phillips, G. W. (1990). *Accelerating academic achievement, America's challenge: A summary of findings from 20 years of NAEP.* Princeton, NJ: Educational Testing Service.

National Commission on Excellence in Education. (1983). *A nation at risk: The imperative for national reform.* Washington, DC: United States Department of Education.

Newmann, F. M., & Associates. (Eds.). (1996). Introduction: The school restructuring study. *In Authentic achievement: Restructuring schools for intellectual quality.* San Francisco: Jossey-Bass.

Newmann, F. M., Secada, W. G., & Wehlage, G. G. (1995). *A guide to authentic instruction and assessment: Vision, standards and scoring.* Madison: Wisconsin Center for Education Research.

No Child Left Behind Act of 2001, Pub. L. No. 117-10, 115 Stat. 1425 (2002).

Ogbu, J. U. (1987). Variability in minority school performance: A problem in search of an explanation. *Anthropology and Education Quarterly, 18,* 321–334.

Page, R. N. (1999). The uncertain value of school knowledge: Biology at Westridge High. *Teachers College Record, 100,* 554–601.

Pedulla, J. J., Abrams, L. M., Madaus, G. F., Russell, M. K., Ramos, M. A., & Miao, J. (2003). *Perceived effects of state-mandated testing programs on teaching and learning: Findings from a national survey of teachers.* Boston: National Board on Educational Testing and Public Policy, Boston College.

Ramos-Ford, V., & Gardner, H. (1991). Giftedness from a multiple intelligence perspective. In N. Colangelo & G. A. Davis (Eds.), *Handbook of gifted education* (pp. 55–64). Boston: Allyn & Bacon.

Renzulli, J. S., & Reis, S. M. (1985). *The schoolwide enrichment model.* Mansfield Center, CT: Creative Learning Press, Inc.

Ross, S. M., Alberg, M., & Wang, L. W. (2001). *The impacts of alternative school restructuring designs on at-risk learners: A longitudinal study.* Memphis, TN: Center for Research in Educational Policy, University of Memphis.

Ross, S. M., Wang, S. W., Sanders, W., Wright, S. P., & Stringfield, S. (1999). *Two- and three-year achievement results on the Tennessee Value-Added Assessment System for Restructuring Schools in Memphis.* Memphis, TN: Center for Research in Educational Policy, University of Memphis.

Sarason, S. (1982). *The culture of the school and the problem of change* (2nd ed.). Boston: Allyn & Bacon.

Sarason, S. (1996). *Revisiting "The culture of the school and the problem of change."* New York: Teachers College Press.

Sizer, T. (1984). *Horace's compromise: The dilemma of the American high school.* Boston: Houghton Mifflin.

Sizer, T. (1992). *Horace's school: Redesigning the American high school.* Boston: Houghton Mifflin.

Solomon, R. P. (1992). *Black resistance in high school: Forging a separatist culture*. Albany: State University of New York Press.

Sternberg, R. J. (1985). *Beyond IQ: A triarchic theory of human intelligence*. New York: Cambridge University Press.

Sternberg, R. J. (1986). *Intelligence applied: Understanding and increasing your intellectual skills*. San Diego, CA: Harcourt Brace.

Sternberg, R. J. (1991). Giftedness according to the triarchic theory of human intelligence. In N. Colangelo & G. A. Davis (Eds.), *Handbook of gifted education* (pp. 45–54).

Sternberg, R. J. (1997). *Successful intelligence*. New York: Plume.

Stringfield, S. C., & Datnow, A. (1998). Introduction: Scaling up school restructuring designs in urban schools. *Education and Urban Society, 30,* (3) 269–276.

Tomlinson, C. A. (1996). Good teaching for one and all: Does gifted education have an instructional identity? *Journal for the Education of the Gifted, 20,* 155–174.

Tyack, D., & Cuban, L. (1995). *Tinkering toward utopia: A century of public school reform*. Cambridge, MA: Harvard University Press.

Tyack, D., & Tobin, W. (1994). The grammar of schooling: Why has it been so hard to change? *American Educational Research Journal, 31,* 453–479.

Tye, B. B. (2000). *Hard truths: Uncovering the deep structures of schooling*. New York: Teachers College Press.

Vygotsky, L. S. (1978). *Mind in society: The development of higher psychological processes*. Cambridge, MA: Harvard University Press.

Translating Theory and Research Into Practice Through the Yale Child Study Center School Development Program

James P. Comer and Edward T. Joyner
Yale University

An enormous amount of financial and human resources has gone into the development of education theory and research over the years. Unfortunately, much of the useful knowledge gained has not been incorporated into practice at the classroom, school building, and district levels on a large scale. Our work suggests that the failure to use child and adolescent development and behavior as the foundation science for education theory, research, policymaking, and practice limits our understanding and generates conditions that obstruct reasonable utilization of what is known.

Activities throughout the education enterprise—classrooms, districts, schools and state departments of education, and other preparation and policy-making groups—are guided largely by a belief that the quality of academic learning is determined almost completely by one's genetic makeup. Despite long-standing behavioral and social science research emphasizing the importance of context and interaction, now buttressed by modern brain research, the genetic determination notion persists (Bransford, Brown, & Cocking, 2002; Epstein & Salinas, 2004; Hardiman, 2003; Healy, 2004; Henderson & Mapp, 2002; Shonkoff & Phillips, 2002). This has led to a largely linguistic and cognitive model of teaching and learning (Darling-Hammond, 2004; Haynes, Ben-Avie, & Ensign, 2003).

In this mechanistic model, the teacher is a transmitter of knowledge, and the student consumes at his or her capacity and will. Also, this model contributes to the notion that any intelligent person can teach. However, development and learning are inextricably linked and are greatly related to a variety of teacher competencies. A simple transfer of information model does not take into account the knowledge and competencies teachers need to support development and learning in classrooms and schools. Because these critical linkages and the need for particular competencies are not understood, many, if not most, in the education enterprise ignore the powerful influence of past developmental experiences of a child, the need to promote development in school, and the lack of preparation of individuals for service in schools to support learning and personal development.

Policies and practices throughout the education enterprise that are not informed by child development knowledge contribute to problem conditions and outcomes. Some of the most troublesome are as follows:

- Inadequate knowledge about child and adolescent development among teachers and administrators, particularly problematic among those that serve low-income students and students of color.
- A deficit rather than developmental perspective with respect to student potential.
- Failure by school districts to create structures and processes to determine whether their education programs promote development.
- District and building-level staff development that is rarely related to student developmental issues.
- Poorly informed policymakers.
- School unions that can be part of the solution to school reform or part of the problem.
- Frequent turnover of leadership and school staff also related to student underdevelopment and the lack of school readiness to support it.

These outcomes interfere with or prevent the use of best practices in schools. Affected schools cannot become communities that grow and develop in a way that can support student growth, development, and learning. They are characterized by minimal civility at best but often anger and conflict or apathy, uninspired teaching, and inadequate learning. The most severely affected are dysfunctional organizations that are harmful to all involved. The use of education theory and research are blocked here much in the way that nutrients from the blood stream are blocked by impermeable cell membranes. Outstanding leadership can sometimes promote improved effort and achievement, but the changes are lost with the loss of such leaders.

The troublesome contextual outcomes previously listed exist less often in high-academic-achieving schools and districts. Students in these districts are more often prepared for successful functioning in school through pre-school and school-age support for development they receive at home. Thus, even when their schools do not support development, they do not greatly limit the performance of students already prepared for reasonable success.

When schools are not successful, participants often coalesce as "common-cause" groups—teachers, professional support services, nonprofessional support, parents, administrators, unions, and others. Each group blames the other and sometimes each other within groups. Teachers often feel that they lack support of the administration and do not have the power to influence what goes on in the school. Many feel that their preservice preparation did not adequately prepare them to help students. Administrators often feel that they are in a power struggle. Parents feel they are closed out. These conditions create conflict, resistance, and often paralysis. Students that have not had adequate support for development are more vulnerable in such situations.

Yet most educators would like to be successful with all children. Indeed, most feel that they are working as hard as they can and are being blamed for problems that are beyond their control, and most parents would like to be supportive of schools. What, then, is the problem? What is needed to address it?

Our work and that of others suggests that by promoting student development in school, academic learning and student behavior can be significantly improved; relationship and behavior problems can be greatly reduced. These outcomes can be brought about by helping practitioners understand the role of development and how to create school environments that enable them to promote it. When we can overcome the ill effects of inadequate staff knowledge about student development, theory and research of all kinds can be used more often and more effectively in practice (Comer, Joyner, & Ben-Avie, 2004; Darling-Hammond, 1997).

This is not an easy task. Human resistance to change is well known. Change that calls for promoting student development is even more difficult because it goes against the cultural grain. In our mainstream American culture, individuality and/or individual capacities are so highly valued that we often deny the benefits of our own personal developmental experiences to uphold the "intelligence and will" myth. We are taught to believe that we achieve and succeed on the basis of our individual ability and effort. Our readiness for learning and success through development is almost totally downplayed.

The individual educator's belief about his or her own academic ability, professional development, and rewards for practice that put little emphasis on development all reinforce the notion that success is due to one's ability and will. The cultural belief of innate ability, reinforced by experience and internalized, stand as formidable barriers to the notion that the full expression of one's intelligence and even motivation or will are in large part a product of one's developmental experience. All children are limited by educators' failure to recognize the importance of support for development in learning and behavior and our failure to promote it in school. Children of the poor and children of color are hurt most by this wrong notion because they more often experience preschool conditions that limit development.

Moving against traditional beliefs and conformity in an organization—even when there is some understanding of how doing so can improve conditions—requires taking social and psychological risks and even employment and income risks. Schools are usually asked to improve without a change mechanism or framework, consultation, practice, or the kind of support that will reduce threat and anxiety. Most cannot reorganize the forces that created dysfunction in the first place without such help.

In this chapter, we describe a school improvement approach, the Yale Child Study Center School Development Program (SDP), that is based on child and adolescent development and behavior theories that are widely accepted in the social and behavioral sciences but that met with much resistance when we attempted to put them into practice: first in inner-city schools and later in schools across the socioeconomic spectrum. We describe how we designed a conceptual and operational framework that promoted the six developmental pathways, which overcame school-based contextual challenges, and eventually addressed challenges outside the pilot setting and in other parts of the education enterprise. It should be noted that the framework evolved as we encountered new obstacles over time.

PILOT PHASE

The SDP is an action research model that requires a moderate-to-high level of involvement by stakeholders at every step of the change process. It is informed by knowledge bases from public health, child and adolescent development, organizational behavior, pedagogy, and the management sciences. It recognizes behavior—child and adolescent and adult—as an interactive process and an outcome of individual and contextual factors; as much, sometimes more, than it is an outcome of individual capacities, feelings, thinking, and action. Because interactive forces in complex systems can be asynchronous to the point of dysfunction, the model works toward synchrony and synergy.

A five-, sometimes six-member Yale Child Study Center mental health team—psychiatrist, social worker(s), special education teacher, and psychologist—began work in two inner-city elementary schools in New Haven,

Connecticut in 1968. It was a joint project with the New Haven Public School System. The children served were almost all African American and almost all poor. Based on a 1969 measure, they had the lowest achievement and attendance and the highest behavior problem records in the city.

The underlying problem was that many of the students were underdeveloped or not prepared for school. School people did not have the preparation needed to understand and respond to student performance in a helpful way. As a result, staff, students, and parents were acting out in ways that made matters worse. The schools were a "beehive" of harmful activity. Everybody was busy putting out fires that should not have existed in the first place. Nonetheless, the resistance to change was palpable.

Our Child Study Center SDP team lived in the schools as the mental health providers and directly experienced the harmful interactions between staff, students, and parents as well as their source and cause. Without a child development perspective, the school staff viewed the students as good or bad or smart or slow rather than underdeveloped. The schools were largely punitive, and the majority of the students were consistently held to low expectations. Parents sensed the low regard that the teachers had for their children and attributed it to race or class discrimination. There was no leadership structure or mechanism in the schools that could empower staff and parents to understand these behaviors differently and gain the skills and dispositions needed to respond appropriately. Effective teaching and learning could not take place in such an environment.

Our SDP team had no official authority other than an invitation to participate. Thus, we could not lay out a plan and force compliance, nor did we want to do so. Such a program would not endure. We attempted to provide a rational/empirical approach based on what we knew about child development in the hope that the staff would act in ways that would support development and learning: in their own self-interest and in that of the students. However, many who agreed with the principles could not apply them in real-world practice.

Before we could change the group's norms or culture or use the reeducative approach, most people would have to buy into the idea and feel safe in thinking and working differently. An appeal to the heart helped to interest many in change—"for the good of the children." However, significant movement toward change could not take place until the educators could observe some benefits of working differently and recognize that the change process was not too complicated or painful. They needed to feel that they owned the change and would be responsible for generating and sustaining it.

We gradually overcame the initial resistance by using our clinical skills in team meetings and one-on-one sessions to help teachers and administrators become more effective with some of the most challenging students. We were able to help staff and parents learn how to balance tasks and relationships, provide descriptive rather than judgmental feedback, and apply user-friendly data collection and evaluation techniques to improve school outcomes. This raised the value of our group and in time won the trust of most staff. This enabled us to help the participants put in place a problem-solving organization and management framework based on child and adolescent development knowledge and an understanding of organizational behavior.

The framework is both conceptual and operational because it is difficult to understand unless you are using it. As you use it, you gain ownership and understanding. As a result, change is eventually brought about through intrinsic rather than extrinsic efforts. The use of collaborative planning, no-fault problem solving, and consensus decision making throughout the system creates a culture that supports change at all levels of the system.

Unlike other reform models, SDP's intervention, in keeping with its public health and interactive or ecological perspective, targets the entire building staff and related stakeholder groups as the system. The framework is designed to create synchronous operations in the organization and management of schools, which in turn promote gratifying personal and interpersonal experiences and development and learning among all involved. The nine elements or components of the model grew out of an effort to address the three conditions most responsible for troublesome schools—again, ineffective organization and management, limited capacity to promote student development, and inadequate teaching and learning strategies.

The model components are as follows: three teams or mechanisms, three operations, and three guiding principles.

The Three Teams

1. The School Planning and Management Team (SPMT) serves as the major decision-making body allowing representatives from the various constituent groups (school staff, parents, and sometimes students) of the school to have input in decisions and comprehensive planning. It oversees the change process and provides all school participants with a sense of influence and ownership. Schools have typically identified 12 as the maximum number of members on the team because a larger group has proven to be unwieldy. Broader participation is secured through participation on subcommittees.

2. The Student and Staff Support Services Team brings child development and behavior knowledge to bear in all aspects of the school program. It addresses the psychosocial and health needs of individual or groups of students and helps the school to develop a preventive focus by identifying and correcting inappropriate institutional practices. This team also works with family-service providers within the broader community, often inviting

them to meetings to develop strategies and creating a seamless network of child and adolescent support services for students. It provides clinical feedback to staff that may be struggling to work effectively with students experiencing difficulties. The number of members on this team corresponds to the social services staff in the school.

3. The Parent Team (PT) connects the home and the school in support of child development. It involves parents at all levels of school life, especially parents who have typically not been involved in their children's education due to feeling uncomfortable in the school. Level 1 involves general support activities including attendance at the Parent Teacher Association (PTA), Parent Teacher Organization (PTO), or Parent Teacher Student Association (PTSA) meetings, social events, and other school activities. At the second level, some parents serve in school buildings as volunteers or paid assistants in the library, cafeteria, or classrooms. At the third level, parents are selected by their fellow parents to represent them on the SPMT. As members of the SPMT, parents transmit the views and opinions of the general parent body on issues related to academic, social, and staff development needs of the school.

The PT bridges the gap between home and school. It reduces the dissonance that disadvantaged students experience as they attempt to adjust from one environment to the other. By empowering parents, schools provide consistency and continuity in children's lives. Empowerment can also serve to strengthen families and help them become resilient supporters of their children's development. Empowerment stems directly from parents working with school staff to create a plan to insure that their children receive the level of intellectual and personal development that is critical for success in and beyond school. This level of active participation energizes parents by giving them a voice and choice in school matters that do not require the level of professional training received by teachers, social service staff, and administrators.

The SDP views parental involvement as the cornerstone for success in developing a school environment that stimulates the total development of its students. Parents are expected to

1. Select their representatives to serve on the SPMT.
2. Review the school plan developed by the SPMT.
3. Work with staff in developing and carrying out activities of the parent–teacher general membership group (PTA, PTO, PTSA) in line with the overall school plan.
4. Support the efforts of the school to assist students in their overall development.
5. Encourage new parents to become involved in school activities.

The Three Operations

The SPMT is responsible for managing three operations. We note that this team does not supersede the legal-jurisdictional authority of the principal but works with school leadership to develop proactive school improvement strategies. Its major responsibility is to develop a 1- to 2-year Comprehensive School Plan that has both an academic and social focus. The Plan identifies instructional priorities and develops programmatic responses to students' developmental and academic needs. The Plan creates a sense of direction, and it is the standard the participants use to hold themselves accountable.

The final Plan should reflect the collective wisdom of staff and parents and should include a calendar of important events associated with the Plan's life cycle. Collective wisdom is assured by using the SPMT as the structure and process that both staff and parents use to examine critical information that provides a window onto the current reality of the school on measures of student success. The data is used to identify areas in need of improvement, and these priorities are translated into strategies that are likely to generate improvement. The final Plan is submitted to the larger school community for further review and final approval.

The Plan should contain measurable goals and objectives. As its second operation, it is the SPMT's responsibility to monitor and assess the achievement of these goals. Action research is the preferred method to use in schools attempting to solve their own problems. It allows its users to

1. Gather data in the diagnostic and planning process involved in identifying areas in need of improvement within the school.
2. Develop working theories of what is needed to generate better results.
3. Develop specific plans that are measurable.
4. Implement the plans.
5. Measure the impact using formative and summative evaluation of the resultant data and make the needed adjustments.

The stipulation that goals be measurable is the first step in the action research process. The baseline of where the school is on a specific outcome (such as the reading achievement of students) can be examined monthly to assess progress or regression. Schools are asked to do a midyear evaluation to look at changes in the data and make adjustments. The summative assessment at the end of the year helps to provide a baseline for the next year's Plan.

The staff uses data to ask three essential questions regarding expected outcomes: What went well? What did not go as well as expected? What corrective adjustments must we make to achieve desired results?

Staff development is the third operation administered by the SPMT. In a school district, there should be three levels of staff development. District-level staff development should address needs common to all district staff. School-based staff development should arise out of the unique needs of the individual school. Clusters of schools—for instance, those in a common feeder pattern facing common needs—should consolidate their resources to develop cost-effective staff development strategies for the needs of the cluster.

The Three Guiding Principles

Collaborative diagnosis and planning, "no-fault" problem solving, and consensus decision making are the guiding principles of the SDP. The three guidelines, when all parts of the framework are functioning adequately, make it possible for all the adults and students to interact with each other in a reasonably desirable way.

Collaboration requires that representative stakeholders work together across various roles to make key decisions related to school improvement. This strategy allows participants to develop a comprehensive agenda for change with widespread input from constituents. No-fault problem solving allows team members to focus on solving problems instead of looking for someone or something to blame. This approach channels energy toward solutions instead of toward useless, divisive finger pointing. The drive toward consensus encourages teams to reach a decision that can be supported by the whole organizations. Decisions reached by a simple majority do not necessarily reflect broad input and consequently do not receive broad support. Working an issue through to consensus gives participants the opportunity for deeper and broader exploration of problems and their causes. It is important for decision-making bodies to accept that any decision is subject to modification when new information reveals a more suitable alternative.

This nine-element or component framework is the core of our SDP. The structures or mechanisms create the processes that bring about good relationships and a school context that enables adults and peers to support the development of students and enables the staff to carry out an academic program that promotes learning. The framework manages the interactions that often lead to dysfunction in a way that produces synchrony and synergy.

The framework, based on theory and research and applied to practice, brought about a context of good relationships that then made further use of theory and research possible in the schools (Comer, Haynes, & Hamilton-Lee, 1987). This led to thinking about how children grow and behave as they attempt to cope with various situations and challenges. It shifted staff thinking to helping students grow and cope rather than thinking about containment and control. These considerations led to our interest in developmental pathways.

DEVELOPMENTAL PATHWAYS

The absence of a significant knowledge base about child development and behavior made it difficult to discuss teacher–child–parent interactions. This was the major reason that lecturing to the staff about child development or the rational/empirical approach to promoting change was not effective. The knowledge base and perception problem was made crystal clear after a discussion about an eight-year-old transfer student who panicked, kicked his teacher, and ran out of the room.

The initial impression of the teacher and her colleagues was that he was a bad boy. However, he had lost a warm, supportive support network in a far away state. After they thought about the fear and anxiety he had experienced and the limited behavior responses available to a child of his age, they began to understand how the situation, developmental level, and management capabilities come together to affect behavior. With this understanding, they created a more child-friendly and helpful classroom, school-transfer policies and practices, and displayed more empathy than anger and negative expectations.

Here is proof of the problem. When I (J. P. Comer) commented at the end of the discussion that this was a case of fight and flight as opposed to fight or flight, the faces of the staff were blank, reflecting puzzlement. The most junior mental health person would have understood. However, teachers on the front line of the child-rearing opportunity, if not battle, did not know this concept and could not apply it to understand and address the student's challenge.

We encountered this problem often. This led to our use of the concept of the developmental pathways in helping educators, other staff, and parents to think about how children develop, behave, and learn. Obviously, we did not invent the concept. Erickson (1985), Freud (1965), Vygotsky (1978), and Piaget (1930) were the first in modern times to use the idea of developmental lines or pathways to denote progression over or through increasingly complex tasks and capacities to maturity in particular domains. We brought this approach from our discipline and used it in a way that was not being used in schools or anywhere within the education enterprise.

Discussions about the developmental pathways helped the staff and parents to begin to regularly think about development and the way it is related to learning and behavior and the need and possibility of promoting it in school. Gradually, they began to ask the question of what was going on with a child who was having a learning or behavior problem rather than to immediately assume that the child was "dumb" or bad. This was particularly helpful in our setting where unconscious race and class stereotypes could suggest that the problem was the latter.

The pathways are as follows: physical including brain functioning, social-interactive, psycho emotional, ethical, linguistic, and intellectual cognitive. Children grow along these pathways as they imitate, identify with,

and internalize the attitudes, values, and ways of the adults they are interacting with. Almost all of the interactions that children have with adults and
peers—before and in school—influence their growth and development.

The interactions with meaningful others, or people from their social networks of friend and kin, are particularly influential. Thus, children who are
interacting with meaningful people who are engaged in activities that are
the precursor to learning along all the developmental pathways are usually
better prepared for school. However, we have found that by creating a good
school culture, school people can become meaningful in a way needed to
provide the children who have not had good preparatory experiences with
many of these relationships and experiences in school.

SOCIAL SKILLS CURRICULUM

Such thinking led us to design an activity that enabled the school to focus on
providing the children with experiences that supported their growth along
all the developmental pathways. The activity was called "A Social Skills Curriculum for Inner-City Children" and was initiated in 1977. After discussion
with parents about what they wanted for their children and reflection on the
kinds of experiences they would need to be able to achieve these goals, a project that integrated the teaching of basic academic skills, social skills, and appreciation of the arts was initiated. In what would have been free or leisure
time, units designed in this way were carried out in the four areas identified as
those in which the students would need skills—politics and government,
business and economics, health and nutrition, and spiritual and leisure time.

This approach was extraordinarily successful. It further energized an already much improved school climate in the project schools. These activities
improved the interactions between the staff, students, and parents. They
improved the perception of the staff about the skills of and possibilities for
the students. After the 1st year at Martin Luther King Jr. School in New Haven, there was a 7-month jump in academic achievement over the previous
year. This continued at a 2 month per year improved rate until they were
above grade level (Comer, 1993).

This approach requires a well-functioning school or learning community. Thus, when we began field testing our model, the Social Skills Curriculum could not be carried out in full, and during the dissemination phase, it
was carried out only in the best functioning schools. Our intent, however, is
to be able to do so in all schools.

THE FIELD-TESTING PHASE

Between 1968 and 1988 (pilot and field-testing stages of the program), direct service was used to inform, train, and support districts and schools that

were part of the SDP's relatively small network. We and two or three staff members were involved in service delivery. We used the nine-element theoretical and empirical framework that emerged out of our pilot project. Our major goal was to determine whether this framework could be used to change other schools.

The districts selected were Benton Harbor, Michigan and Norfolk, Virginia along with expansion efforts in New Haven. By 1986, outcome data from controlled studies in these three districts showed significant gains in achievement, attendance, and behavior for students in SDP schools when compared to students in matched control schools (Haynes, Emmons, Gebreyesus, & Ben-Avie, 1996). Analyses of data in Prince George's County, Maryland also showed impressive gains for students in schools implementing the SDP.

DISSEMINATION AND CONSULTATION

By 1987, the Rockefeller Foundation recognized that a gap existed in the school reform movement, and it was attracted to the conceptual views and demonstrated effectiveness of the SDP. In a joint effort with the Melville Corporation, the Foundation decided to support an expanded training program through what was called the Comer Project for Change in Education. The strategy was to introduce our SDP child development centered program through Yale-based training and initial follow-up coaching and consultation in the field. The schools were expected to be able to sustain the change with gradually decreasing outside support.

This required a turnkey trainer of trainer model. Successful school improvement approaches cannot be brought to scale without an intrinsic capacity for continued adjustment to people and policy challenges at every level.

Training Program

Our staff, led by E. Joyner, established a training and consultation program. It was designed to transfer knowledge and skills to a participating school district through a "Comer Facilitator." The facilitator would teach and coach others in using the model back in their local schools and be supported with coaching and consultation from our SDP staff. Some facilitators that demonstrated outstanding change agent skills in their own districts, when available, were asked to serve on our national faculty of trainers.

The training began and continues at Yale but has evolved and is now also carried out at regional sites. Knowledge and skills are transferred through several academies. The initial academy, Leadership 101, is carried out at Yale and in regional sites. Its goal is to assure that participants

- Can organize and deliver orientation sessions on the Comer Process (Comer, Joyner, & Ben-Avie, 2004).
- Have a working knowledge of the nine components of the Comer Process.
- Understand the six developmental pathways.
- Are prepared to apply change strategies.
- Develop specific strategies for implementing the Comer Process in their own schools or districts.
- Know how the Comer Process fits in with other local initiatives.

Districts are expected to send a team representative of all the stakeholders—parents, teachers, central office administrators, board members, and principals or a combination of these. These participants are expected to return to their school districts with enough information to enable them to explain the program to other school and parent groups and to begin the SDP in new schools.

Leadership Training 102 is at Yale. It is especially important for those who are going to be district facilitators, either at the central office or at the school level. It builds on the skills and information gained in Leadership 101. It is designed to strengthen facilitators' skills at developing effective school teams. The week of training also provides opportunities for our Yale staff to give constructive feedback to individuals and teams and to process the communications among members. The content of this week includes curriculum and instruction, child development, and action research. This training also focuses on the Comer child-centered planning process. Participants in this academy

- Work in a collaborative fashion.
- Serve as facilitative leaders and resource developers.
- Support the school teams.
- Maintain the focus of the school on child development, relationships, and curriculum.
- Monitor the implementation of the curriculum.
- Interact with staff, students, and parents in ways that promote shared decision making.
- Acquire in-depth understanding of how the child-centered planning process integrates child development theory, assessment and modification, comprehensive school planning, staff development, and change theory.

There is also a 5-day Academy for Developmentally Centered Education at Yale. In SDP schools, the principles of child and adolescent development serve as the knowledge base from which the adult stakeholders make decisions and set priorities to address the learning and teaching needs of the students. Training during this week helps members of the School Planning and Management Team, the Student and Staff Support Team, and the Parent Team acquire the understanding of developmental principles they need to function effectively under the Comer Process operating system. Most important, they learn how to apply these principles in a way that establishes good relationships and a school climate that can support child and adolescent development and improved student achievement.

To help administrators work differently, we developed a Principals' Academy. Principals of schools implementing the Comer Process attend this Academy after at least one complete year of implementing the process. This Academy is designed to enable participants to

- Work in a collaborative fashion.
- Serve as facilitative leaders and resource developers.
- Support the school teams.
- Maintain the focus of the school on child development, relationships, and curriculum and instruction.
- Monitor the implementation of the curriculum.
- Interact with staff, students, and parents in ways that promote shared decision making.
- Acquire in-depth understanding of how the child-centered planning process integrates child development theory, assessment and modification, comprehensive school planning, staff development, and change theory.

Many of our colleagues doubted that the trainer of trainers' approach could work because transmitting the spirit of the work (that academic improvement is possible among poor children) is more difficult than transmitting the content. Providing consultative support from a distance is difficult, and local resistance to change could be as strong, if not stronger, at distant sites than it was in our pilot project in New Haven. We learned how to provide training that engendered the spirit, understanding, content, and skills during our field-test phase and through continuous feedback from all our training.

One of the things we have observed directly and have often received comments about is the enthusiasm generated among the trainees, during the training and back at home. Many were sent to the training as skeptical representatives of their schools. One facilitator of a district that has had dramatic improvement over the last 3 years told us that she came first as a teacher representative determined to learn about the approach to argue against using it in their school. By the third day of training, she was a convert and eventually a very effective facilitator for the district.

Many practitioners have a sense that they are not adequately prepared to meet the challenges in their schools. In their preparation, they received bits and pieces of the "pedagogical whole." Our training integrates child and adolescent development theory, pedagogy, and practice in a way that the application to practice, and how to do it, becomes more apparent. In the case of this good veteran teacher, she recognized that the framework pulled things together in a way that would work for her and her school.

We initially undertook a school-by-school approach. The thought was that we would try to create a large nucleus of successful schools that others would want to emulate. However, as we worked, we began to realize that many factors beyond the building have a powerful impact on what goes on in a school and on whether change can take place and be sustained. Some schools that improved over 3 to 5 years would decline quickly when a new principal or superintendent was appointed that did not support our SDP approach. Even bringing in several new teachers without training led to decline. These and other experiences pointed to the need for district or system-level support as well as a need to work with schools of education that could provide local support as they changed their own methods.

The Rockefeller Foundation supported an initiative that enabled us to create school district–university partnerships. The strategy was to share our SDP's perspectives, principles, and practice with university staff who would in turn work with and strengthen schools in a local school district and to work with their own university staff to reform teacher education programs. To help further disseminate the process, a 13-part "how to" video series titled "For Children's Sake" was developed.

Charleston Southern University, Eastern Michigan University, Drury University, Hampton University, Long Island University, San Francisco State, Southern University at New Orleans, Southern Connecticut State University, University of North Carolina at Charlotte, and Washburn University are institutions that we have worked with to improve schools and influence the content that is used to prepare professionals for the field.

In 1992, the SDP embarked on two additional major initiatives: systemic or district-wide implementation and the development of Regional Professional Development Centers. By then, we had long realized that many problems in school were created or complicated by policies and practices in education enterprise organizations beyond the school, and we were already working with schools of education, a part of the education enterprise that has an important impact on what goes on in classrooms, buildings, and districts. However, having watched successful schools lose ground because of the lack of district-level support, we felt that district-wide or system use of a child development oriented framework would be helpful.

Changes in policies and practices at the board and central-office levels could support the implementation of the SDP in buildings. Three districts were selected to begin the systemic drive: New Haven, Connecticut; Washington, DC; and Community School District 13 in Brooklyn, New York. The Guilford County School District in North Carolina decided to use the SDP as the organizing governance and management infrastructure for school change across the district without support from Rockefeller Foundation.

The systemic initiative presses for changes in the way policy is developed as well as for changes in central office and school building relationships. The school is embedded in the district and in a broader community that can either support or oppose its efforts to improve. Consequently, we recognized the need for the district to adopt a systemic view regarding school improvement and to recognize that school reform is a perpetual series of activities that must engage all critical stakeholders. Our dissemination strategy had always involved requesting general and fiscal support from the school board and superintendent before we enter a district. This new approach was designed to involve the many elements of a district in collaborative activity guided by a common focus of the development of children.

To facilitate a changed view and way of working, a district steering committee was created that makes it possible for educators at this level not only to understand the principles of the model but to better support their schools. We now routinely begin work in new districts by setting up a steering committee. Their first task is to assist in making the final decision about the feasibility of adopting the program.

The District Steering Committee provides oversight of the change process. The superintendent and representative leaders from relevant stakeholder groups within the system (which may vary from community to community) make up the membership. They meet quarterly, or as often as needed, to monitor progress and to address major implementation problems. This team, as with all teams, commits to using the three SDP guiding principles: collaboration, no fault, and consensus.

REGIONAL TRAINING CENTERS

Along with the effort to work district wide or systemically, we developed regional centers. The Regional Training Centers (RTCs) were designed to facilitate regional training activities. The selected RTC sites were Prince George's County, Maryland; Eastern Michigan University; and Chicago, Illinois. These Centers offer orientation programs to schools considering using the SDP, Leadership 101 training for some school staffs, and consultation to districts in their region.

The Centers are sponsored and staffed by people and programs who have been successfully implementing our SDP model. Some of the same staff also help with the training during our academies at the Yale Child Study Center.

They have also served another important function. From the beginning of our work, due to changing policies and emphases in education, we encountered major problems that made good school functioning and student growth difficult. We worked out pilot projects that addressed these often critical issues within the context of SDP schools. The systemic and regional activities made it possible to field test these projects within reasonably well-functioning but distant school sites. We discuss three pilot projects here:

- Essentials of Literacy.
- Teachers Helping Teachers.
- Balanced Curriculum process.

In the Essentials of Literacy project, students who have beyond the usual reading problems are given a rich, highly stimulating, developmentally appropriate instruction at six different workstations that represent essential aspects of literacy. They are helped to achieve mastery at each station with the support of trained teachers, parents, student volunteers, and other caring adults.

Our Teachers Helping Teachers project is designed to enable trained teachers to help their colleagues use best teaching practices to meet the learning needs of students. It allows them to take time together to reflect in-depth on their teaching and how children develop and learn.

Through the Balanced Curriculum project, teachers learn how to work together to develop priorities for curriculum, instruction, and assessment by aligning and balancing students' developmental needs and abilities; standards and test requirements of the state, local, and national levels; textbooks and other resources; teacher assessment of student work; and teacher's own expectations, knowledge, skills, and beliefs. It allows the schools or districts to examine the continuity of instructional practice and curriculum between and within grades and courses.

We have recently added

- The Comer Kids' Leadership Academy to the training.
- The Policy Institute, designed to inform policymakers about the role of development in schools and how they can support it.

The Comer Kids' Leadership Academy is a 2-day summer event in which the students learn to function in accordance with the guiding principles of the Comer Process. The Academy also teaches students to use the developmental pathways and guiding principles as tools for identifying and solving problems and for taking responsibility for their own learning. They are expected to provide leadership back in their own schools. This Academy takes place during the period of the Principals' Academy, so they are accompanied by participating administrators, teachers, and parents.

We developed a summer Policy Institute in 1999. These 2½-day sessions brought together practitioners from schools and districts using the model as well as university and school of education people working with them. Policymakers from state boards of education, school boards, school union heads, national organizations such as the PTA, community organizations, city councils, state legislators, and the United States Congress have participated.

An important module of each institute has been student presentations of their perspectives on their education experience. The adults consider, from their varied positions, how they can better shape their work to facilitate the developmental needs of students. Our SDP team has an interest in learning how all the education enterprise players can work together to bring coherence to education policy and practice.

Alliances

Also, our dissemination efforts led to alliances with colleagues and groups that shared our philosophy and could add value to our work. These alliances have included the Comer–Zigler Initiative; Authentic Teaching, Learning, and Assessment for All Students; SDP–Developmental Studies Center; and SDP–National Urban Alliance.

EVALUATION AND RESEARCH

Research and documentation has played a vital role in the work of the SDP. We have combined context and needs assessments, process documentation, and quality of implementation studies with quantitative, including quasi-experimental, methodologies that focus on outcomes. Our SDP research unit evaluates the SDP's training and consultation services to determine if the content, skills, and support offered by the organization meet the needs of our clients, and it has conducted research studies. We have had about a dozen major external evaluations over the past decade.

Results

Numerous studies by our evaluation unit have shown significantly improved test scores, improved school climate, and reduced behavior problems in some of the most difficult communities in our country (Haynes, Emmons, & Woodruff, 1998; Noblit, Malloy, & Malloy, 2001). A quasi-experimental research study (Cook & Murphy, 2001) in a large urban district in Illinois carried out by highly regarded researchers showed that SDP schools had greater gains than the district as a whole and that the students have sustained the lead over 5 years. The schools also showed improved climate and reduced behavior problems.

Our two lowest wealth pilot elementary schools in New Haven went from 32nd and 33rd of 33 schools in 1970 and to 3rd and 4th highest levels of achievement by 1984. A low-wealth kindergarten through eighth grade school in New Jersey went from 34th to 1st in its district; and it equaled high-wealth suburban schools in mathematics for 3 years until it experienced major staff turnover problems. It is gradually recovering. The lowest wealth school in a large urban district in Michigan had the highest fourth-grade test scores on the state mastery exams in 2000.

We have also shown that schools that implement the SDP process well do significantly better than poor implementers in the same district. These findings, and about a dozen external evaluations, attest to the effectiveness and promise of this work. Finally, with regard to test scores, a recent meta-analysis (Borman, Hewes, Overman, & Brown, 2002) conducted by a respected research group funded by the U.S. Department of Education found that only 3 of the 29 school reform groups raised test scores, one being our SDP.

Although SDP was not designed to raise test scores, the finding is not unexpected. It supports our belief that when students are developing well, they will learn and score at improved levels. Our contribution was the provision of a framework that enabled school people and others to change and to support student development in school.

Also, the work has shown promise in helping schools of education to better prepare staff to work in challenging communities, and it appears to reduce staff turnover problems. The positive outcomes and anecdotal comments from staff, students, parents, and others are too numerous to discuss here (Comer, 2004; Williams, 2003).

SUMMARY AND CONCLUSIONS

Our SDP transferred theory and research from the behavioral and social sciences, public health, and organization and management to education, initially through work in two elementary schools. We created a change process that allows school practitioners to gain knowledge and skills that enable them to promote the development and learning of students in school and to become continuous consumers of theory and research knowledge in the service of improving their practice. This makes continuous intrinsic learning—or learning communities—and change possible.

We field tested the process, made adjustments, and began direct service dissemination. We developed a trainer of trainer model of transfer that permitted local facilitators to receive training at Yale, with representative and supportive home teams, and then implement the SDP process back in their home districts and schools. We began working with facilitators from universities and schools of education in a way that enabled them to support local school districts to use the SDP process with continued but decreasing support from our staff while simultaneously helping their university colleagues address child development issues.

We have had effective district-wide implementation of the model in about a dozen places. We have worked with community organizations, business, government, and other policymakers to share development knowledge and skills and to understand their challenges and limitations. We have involved students themselves in thinking about and in helping to promote their own development and in the creation of school contexts that can be helpful.

In short, the synchrony that the SDP process brings to the asynchronous conditions of many schools makes the impermeable membrane more permeable and the transfer of theory and research into education practice more possible, and the process, with all its related theory and research, is transferable through training trainers.

REFERENCES

Borman, G. D., Hewes, G. M., Overman, L. T., & Brown, S. (2002, November). Comprehensive school reform and student achievement: A meta-analysis. *Center for Research on the Education of Students Placed at Risk (CRESPAR), 59,* 1–45.

Bransford, J. D., Brown, A. L., & Cockings, R. R. (Eds.). (2002). *How people learn: Brain, mind, experience, and school.* Washington, DC: National Academy Press.

Comer, J. P. (1993). Update. In *School power: Implications of an intervention project* (pp. 189–210). New York: Free Press.

Comer, J. P. (2004). Voices from the schoolhouse. In *Leave no child behind: Preparing today's youth for tomorrow's world* (pp. 24–49). New Haven, CT: Yale University Press.

Comer, J. P., Haynes, N. M., & Hamilton-Lee, M. (1987). School power: A model for improving black student achievement. *The Urban League Review, 111,* 187–200.

Comer, J. P., Joyner, E. T., & Ben-Avie, M. (Eds.). (2004). *The field guide to Comer Schools in action: When children develop well, they learn well.* Thousand Oaks, CA: Corwin Press.

Cook, T. D., & Murphy, R. F. (2000). Comer's School Development Program in Chicago: A theory-based evaluation. *American Educational Research Journal, 37,* 535–597.

Darling-Hammond, L. (1997). *The right to learn: A blueprint for creating schools that work.* San Francisco: Jossey-Bass.

Darling-Hammond, L. (2004, June). Standards, accountability, and school reform. *Teachers College Record, 106, 6,* 1047–1085.

Epstein, J. L., & Salinas, K. C. (2004). Partnering with families and communities. *Educational Leadership, 61*(8), 12–18.

Erickson, E. (1985). *Childhood and society.* New York: Norton.

Freud, A. (1965). *Normality and pathology in childhood: Assessments of development.* New York: International Universities Press.

Hardiman, M. M. (2003). *Connecting brain research with effective teaching: The brain-targeted teaching model.* Lanham, MD: Scarecrow Press.

Haynes, N. M., Ben-Avie, M., & Ensign, J. (Eds.). (2003). *How social and emotional development add up: Getting results in math and science education.* New York: Teachers College Press.

Haynes, N. M., Emmons, C. L., Gebreyesus, S., & Ben-Avie, M. (1996). The School Development Program evaluation process. In J. P. Comer, N. M. Haynes, E. T. Joyner, & M. Ben-Avie (Eds.), *Rallying the whole village* (pp. 123–146). New York: Teachers College Press.

Haynes, N. M, Emmons, C. L., & Woodruff, D. W. (1998). School Development Program effects: Linking implementation to outcomes. *Journal of Education for Students Placed at Risk, 3,* 71–85.

Healy, J. M. (2004). *Your child's growing mind: Brain development and learning from birth to adolescence.* New York: Broadway Books.

Henderson, A. T., & Mapp, K. L. (Eds.). (2002). *A new wave of evidence: The impact of family, school, and community connections on student achievement.* Austin, TX: Southwest Educational Development Laboratory.

Noblit, G. W., Malloy, W. W., & Malloy, C. E. (2001). *The kids got smarter: Case studies of successful Comer Schools.* Cresskill, NJ: Hampton.

Piaget, J. (1930). *The child's conception of the world.* New York: Harcourt, Brace, and World.

Shonkoff, J. P., & Phillips, D. (Eds.). (2002). *Neurons to neighborhoods: The science of early childhood development.* Washington, DC: National Academy Press.

Vygotsky, L. (1978). *Mind in society: The development of higher psychological processes.* Cambridge, MA: Harvard University Press.

Williams, J. A. (2003, November/December). Fundamental success. *The Crisis, 110*(6), 30–33.

8

The School of the 21st Century

Edward Zigler and Matia Finn-Stevenson
Yale University

We discuss in this chapter the School of the 21st Century (21C), a school based child care and family support program we developed in 1988. 21C is based on child development research and has been implemented in over 1,300 schools around the country. These schools provide services beginning at the birth of the child through age 12 in an effort to ensure the optimal development of children and their success in school. As you will see in the course of this chapter, 21C brings about many changes in the way the schools operate. However, it is unique among school reform efforts because it does not focus on specific academic issues and pedagogy but rather on the provision of nonacademic support services.

Numerous school reform programs have been developed during the past two decades. Indeed, the years since the publication in 1983 of *A Nation At Risk: The Imperative for National Reform* (National Commission on Excellence in Education, 1983) have been a period of sustained attention to educational improvements. Nevertheless, significant numbers of children continue to fail in school. In an effort to address the problem, some education reform programs are being refined, and new ones are being developed. There are also legislative reforms, most notably the No Child Left Behind (NCLB) Act of 2001. The purpose of NCLB is to ensure that all children have a fair, equal, and significant opportunity to obtain a high-quality education. Various provisions are included in NCLB as the means by which to accomplish this purpose; among these are increased student assessments, changes in academic standards and accountability, and the promotion of school-wide reforms that

173

focus on academic content and reading. Appropriations for two grant programs—Reading First, for students in kindergarten to third grade and Early Reading First, for preschool age children—are included among other provisions such as funding for school libraries.

NCLB and other program and legislative reforms may have merit, but in and of themselves, they are insufficient. The focus on the school is important given the critical role of the school environment and its impact on children's development (Rutter, 1983). However, these efforts fail to address the broader context within which children are growing up—the family and the neighborhood, for example—and the circumstances that affect their development and ability to profit from instruction. It is our contention, which we elaborate in this chapter and have reflected in the 21C program, that for us to ensure that all children have an opportunity to succeed academically, educators must not only make fundamental changes in teaching and the school environment; but must also provide various child and family support services, some of these beginning at the birth of the child, so as to optimize the growth and development of children.

Calls for the provision of support services are not new, although they have traditionally been made on behalf of children of poverty (see, e.g., Lee & Burkam, 2002). We believe that not only poor children but all children and families should have access to support services. The attention to all children through universally accessible programs is noted given current considerations of the concepts of "disadvantage" and "deprivation" as extending beyond income. There are also studies showing that although poverty is a serious risk for children (Brooks-Gunn & Duncan, 1997), there are other risk factors as well. Barnett and Hustedt (2003) note that although poverty as a risk for educational failure affects many children, as many as 50% of children have some other risk factor such as disability, maternal depression, parents with less than high school education, parents who do not speak English, and parents who are recent immigrants.

21C

The provision of universal programs—evident in several European countries where all children have access to basic services such as child care and early education, and poor children receive additional help—is getting increased attention in the United States with regards to preschool education. The 21C program is a universal program accessible to all children regardless of their families' income. As indicated earlier, 21C has been implemented in over 1,300 schools across the country, and in many of these schools, it has been in operation for over a decade. Several factors account for 21C's widespread implementation and continuation over time. Before discussing these, we describe the program and the rationale underlying its conceptualization.

What is the 21C?

The 21C is often referred to as "a" program, but it is actually made up of several programs and services that are provided in the school from birth to age 12. At the core of 21C are child-care programs. First, all day, year round child care for children ages 3 and 4 prior to their entry to kindergarten is a key part of 21C. We refer here to developmentally appropriate care that ensures that children have opportunities for play and social interactions as well as preschool education activities, thus enabling children to acquire skills that are important for later learning. A second important component of 21C is the provision of before and after school and vacation care for children from kindergarten to age 12. Whereas the focus of many such school-age, child-care programs is on providing enrichment activities that are academic in focus, in 21C, the emphasis is on providing children with the opportunity to choose among various types of activities including, but not limited to, academic enrichment and homework. The rationale here is that for optimal development, children need time off from academic tasks. Some school-age programs focus entirely on the provision of instruction on reading and math rather than on—or in addition to—opportunities for the children to engage in nonacademic recreational activities.

Also included in 21C are several outreach services. One is a home visitation program to families with newborns and young children, from birth to age 3, patterned after the Parents As Teachers (PAT) program. This enables parent educators to visit the home and provide information to parents about their children's development and screen the children for any potential developmental and learning problems. This provides opportunities for referral to early intervention services before the problem becomes exacerbated. The 21C also includes outreach to family child care and other child-care providers in the community; information and referral for various services families may need; health, mental health, and nutrition education and services; and other services that may be needed in different communities. These services are all part of the 21C "umbrella" and are coordinated as a whole.

Need for and Rationale for the Program

IMPACT OF SOCIETAL CHANGES ON CHILDREN'S
DEVELOPMENT

The need for child and family support services in general and 21C in particular is noted in several developments, many of these related to societal changes that have occurred over the past several decades: changes in the family structure, including divorce and increases in the number of children living in single-parent families; high mobility, especially in families with young children; and what some have come to term as lack of social capital and "social poverty," referring to the dearth of adults in the lives of children and weak ties between families and their neighbors and kin (Putnam, 1995). The result has been increased isolation and alienation, which leave parents to raise children without any help and support.

These societal changes, as well as the fact that many children live in poverty, create stressful conditions under which children are growing up. They are often associated with child maltreatment and dysfunction in family life that can have profound developmental and educational consequences, evident not only in low academic achievement but also in juvenile delinquency and other social problems (Brooks-Gunn & Duncan, 1997; Shonkoff & Phillips, 2000; Vinson, Baldry, & Hargreaves, 1996). The stress in children's lives often stems from several sources rather than a single source. For example, children whose parents divorce may live in a single family as well as experience periods of poverty. The more stress factors children encounter, the greater the likelihood that they will suffer developmental consequences (Rutter, 1980), although children who have access to some form of support show resilience in the face of adversity (Garmezy, 1985; Rutter, 1979).

The Early Years and School Readiness

The children likely to be affected by difficult life conditions are very young. The early years, from the prenatal stage and the birth of the child to about age 5, represent an important developmental period during which children are vulnerable to risks but also receptive to interventions. These points are underscored in a recent review of the research by Shonkoff and Phillips (2002) who note that a number of core concepts have come to frame our understanding of the nature of human development including among these that

1. *Human development is shaped by the ongoing interplay among sources of vulnerability and sources of resilience.*
2. *The timing of early experiences can matter, but, more often than not, the developing child remains vulnerable to risks and open to protective influences throughout the early years of life and into adulthood.*
3. *The course of development can be altered in early childhood by effective interventions that change the balance between risk and protection, thereby changing the odds in favor of more adaptive outcomes* (p. 3).

Social science research of the past several decades has contributed to our knowledge base regarding the early years and the importance of interventions. This knowledge was reflected in policies during the 1960s and 1970s that led to the development of such programs as Head Start (Zigler & Val-

entine, 1979), which provide various educational, nutrition, and health services for low-income preschool children. More recently, there has been
renewed interest in the early years and policy emphasis on school readiness.
The concept of school readiness recognizes that children's experiences before they even start kindergarten have profound implications for development and later schooling and can determine whether children will succeed
or fail in school. Interest in school readiness is noted in the 1990 National
Education Goals, Goal 1 of which states that "all children in America will
start school ready to learn" (National Education Goals Panel, 1991).
Included in Goal 1 are several objectives:

> That all disadvantaged children will have access to high quality and develop-
> mentally appropriate preschool programs to help them prepare for school;
> that every parent in America will be the child's first teacher and will devote
> time each day to helping his or her preschool child learn, and that parents
> will have access to training and support they need to accomplish this; that
> children will receive nutrition and health care needed to arrive at school with
> healthy minds and bodies, and that the number of low birth weight babies
> will be significantly reduced through enhanced prenatal health systems (Na-
> tional Education Goals Panel, 1991, p. 61).

Policy interest in the early years was noted not only at the federal level but
at the state level as well. Forty-two states have preschool programs for at-risk
children, although only 10 of these states have a sizable program (Children's
Defense Fund, 2002). This interest in the early years has been strengthened
in part by recent studies on the brain that support much of what is known
from the social sciences regarding early experiences (Zigler, Finn-Stevenson,
& Hall, 2002). The current federal policy focus, however, has some limitations, one of which is the emphasis on literacy and cognition in early childhood. This emphasis, which includes a focus on academics, effectively
ignores the concept of the whole child and the fact that several developmental pathways besides cognition are critical for overall development and children's ability to succeed academically. Also ignored in the current policy
approach is the notion that learning, especially in young children, occurs in
numerous ways—including play and social interactions—and in a variety of
contexts.

Besides the narrow view of development and learning, current policy attention to early education and school readiness is not backed by any substantial financial assistance (Gilliam & Zigler, 2001). Subsequently, policymakers
target low-income children, and even under the best circumstances, only a
portion of eligible low-income children can be served as is the case with Head
Start. The same is true at the state level. Although, the states have made much
progress in supporting early childhood programs, these serve only 12% of
the eligible low-income children (American Federation of Teachers, 2003;
Barnett, Finn-Stevenson, & Henrich, in press).

The Need for Child Care

Perhaps the most difficult and universal of the conditions under which young families today live is the inability to find good quality, affordable child care. The lack of good quality, affordable child care has reached crisis proportions with detrimental consequences for children, many of whom are in poor-quality programs. The need for child care is evident in the statistics: 65% of mothers with children under age 6 and 78% of mothers with children ages 6 to 13 are in the labor force, and among mothers with infants under age 1, 59% are in the labor force or actively looking for work (U.S. Department of Labor, 2000). With their parents working, 13 million infants and preschool children—or 3 out of every 5 children—are in child care. Among school-age children, the situation is even worse, with an estimated 7 million children left home alone while their parents are working. The child-care arrangements for the children vary, but increasingly, parents are using child-care centers, and smaller numbers of parents utilize family child care (where a woman takes care of several children in her own home), in-home caregivers, or care provided by a relative.

There are numerous issues related to child care besides the lack of availability and access to good quality, affordable programs. Examples include lack of care for children whose parents work in nontraditional fields and different shifts (U.S. Bureau of the Census, 1997), lack of child care in poor neighborhoods (Queralt & Witte, 1998), and the fact that not much is known about issues related to child care for children with disabilities (Shonkoff & Phillips, 2000). We cannot explore these and other issues within the scope of this chapter, but they are detailed in other publications (Finn-Stevenson & Zigler, 1999; Zigler et al., 2002; Zigler & Lang, 1991).

Also, although we focus here on child care for very young children, the need for good quality, affordable, and accessible care extends to school-age children as well. Because school schedules and vacations do not coincide with work schedules, school-age children need to be in child care, but when it is unavailable or too expensive, they are left home alone. Studies have found that children who are left home alone or with their peers when school is out are at risk for a host of problems including crime, substance abuse, and behavioral problems (Fight Crime/Invest in Kids, 1997; Vandell & Shumow, 1999). Two other points are of relevance: One, the consequences for children of being left unsupervised when school is out include low academic achievement, and two, children's academic performance may be enhanced by attending school-age child care; children attending good, quality, school-age care programs have been found to have better academic work habits and fewer behavioral problems than children who are home alone when school is out (Miller, O'Connor, Stringnano, & Joshi, 1996).

21C: A Response to the Child-Care Crisis

The issues we raise, albeit briefly, point to the fact that there is no system of child care in the United States. Rather, we have a collection of child-care services that differ in quality and make up a patchwork nonsystem. It is not merely additional services and more money that are needed to address the problem but rather the establishment of a system because the current nonsystem we have is difficult to tap into and improve. The 21C program seeks to establish a much-needed child-care system not by creating entirely new structures but by joining with and making use of the already existing educational system.

Guiding Principles

The 21C program was conceptualized on the basis of six guiding principles.

First, to address the needs of all children and ensure their optimal development, a child-care system must become a national priority and part of the very structure of our society as is the case with education. Stable, reliable, good quality care—vital to children's development and well-being as well as their education—must be a central element of such a national system. In using the words *good quality care,* we refer to care that is developmentally appropriate, as opposed to basic supervision or mere babysitting, and that provides children with the opportunity for play, learning, and social interactions with peers and adults.

Second, good quality care should be accessible to every child regardless of ethnic or socioeconomic group to avoid a two-tier system wherein some children receive good quality care and others do not. Like education, child care can only be universally available if it is primarily a state-based system. The federal government's role is both to subsidize the care of the most needy, as it currently does, as well as support research, evaluation, and other efforts to enhance the system and ensure the provision of good quality care.

Third, the child-care system in this country must be based on the optimal development of children and should emphasize a whole-child approach that places equal weight on all developmental pathways: social, emotional, physical, and cognitive. For purposes of research, social scientists often regard each developmental domain separately and have in the past given more weight to cognitive development. However, it has become widely recognized that in reality, all aspects of growth and development are interdependent and occur simultaneously and should thus be given equal attention. This third principle not only acknowledges the child as a whole; it also reflects the fact that although child care may be regarded as a service for parents, it is first and foremost an environment where children spend a significant amount of time. As such, its quality affects their growth and development.

Fourth, parents and those who care for and educate children must work together; hence, the importance of parent involvement, which has been shown to be essential for optimal development of children. The importance of parent involvement is noted not only for programs for preschool and younger children but also when children are in school.

The fifth principle calls for recognition, support, and decent pay for child-care providers because they play a crucial role in the quality of care children receive. This principle also encompasses the need for ongoing provider training as well as appropriate pay upgrades.

Sixth, a national child-care system must be flexible and adaptable. Because every family has particular child-care needs, a universal system must be able to provide a range of choices for child care. Inherent in this principle is the recognition that there are differences not only among families but also among communities.

If such a child-care system is to be readily accessible in terms of cost as well as location to all families, the most efficient way to implement it would be to tap into the already existing educational system. Our country has a trillion-dollar investment in public school buildings, which are supported by tax dollars and only used for part of the day, 9 months a year. By capitalizing on this investment and incorporating a child-care system into the already existing public school system, as a nation, we would be able to increase the supply of child care as well as ensure equitable and affordable, good quality care to all children.

Two issues must be emphasized with regard to the concept of universally accessible child care. One, *universal* is a term that qualifies access to good quality, affordable care. As such, it does not mean that child care should be compulsory. Rather, it means that it should be accessible to those who need and want such care. Two, given limited public funds, one cannot expect support for child care for all children. Hence, in 21C, the provision of child care is based on parental fee for service. However, a sliding scale fee system calibrated to family income is included, and subsidies are used to support low-income families.

FROM CONCEPT TO REALITY

The guiding principles outlined previously represent 21C's theoretical framework and spell out the steps to be undertaken to ensure the optimal development of children and their ability to succeed in school. The principles also provide an initial direction for the implementation of the program moving it from concept to reality.

Implementation of 21C in Schools

Recall from the previous pages that 21C includes several different programs and services: all day, year round child care for preschoolers; child care for school-age children during times when school is out; and several other outreach and support services, all of these provided in the school. The use of the school is one of the unique aspects of 21C. However, 21C calls for more than simply utilizing space in the school building. Rather, the program is actually administered by and becomes part of the very fabric of the school.

Schools that implement 21C are changed substantially, opening their doors to young children and beginning to work with parents soon after the birth of the child. The academic calendar is changed as well, with schools operating programs the entire day—from 6:00 a.m. in the morning to 6:00 p.m. in the evening—year round. One such school in Bridgeport, Connecticut is simply known as "Six to Six." It is not only the provision of services that accounts for the change but more important, the transformations that occur when educators take responsibility for addressing the various nonacademic needs children and families may have.

Anticipating Change

When schools adopt any reform initiative, they do so because they want to bring about change, focusing on ultimately enabling students to do better academically. However, other changes occur as well in the way the school operates and in the relationship between parents and educators and among educators in the school building. This is true in any reform program and can be a source of problems that impede implementation unless anticipated and addressed at the outset (Desimone, 2000; Fullan, 2001).

In 21C, some of the changes are logistical and are important to understand; the changes not only affect the way the school operates, they can be a source of confusion, disruption, and negativity. Revisions in the school calendar, for example, necessitate maintenance and transportation changes as well as additional staff and costs. There are numerous other such changes. However, none of these can be more disruptive than the changes brought about due to the use of space. Lack of dedicated space for 21C services often means sharing classrooms, which can be a point of contention or an opportunity for collaboration, depending on how it is addressed.

Those who oppose the provision of support services in the school often point to the lack of space as a reason against the program. However, space availability is cyclical in nature and comes up whether or not support services are included. That is, enrollments rise and fall depending on changes in birth rates and other factors (e.g., economic changes in the community), either making whole school buildings superfluous or necessitating the building of new structures. The existence of so many 21C schools is indicative of the fact that the space issue, although difficult, can be addressed by the use of a modular building as one example. Dryfoos (1994) points out that how the space issue is addressed is often a reflection of the school's, district's, and community's commitment to the program. This has been our experience, reflected in three (of many) examples: fifth-grade teachers in one school deciding to move to a modular unit so the early childhood classrooms can be made to feel welcomed and part of the school, several districts' allocation of funds for the purchase of modular units, and one community's support of a bond issue for new early childhood buildings to be built on the grounds of each of the elementary schools. We note a broader response to the issue in Ontario, Canada where through legislation, all new school buildings are required to include classrooms to be used for such support services as before and after school child care.

Another change that should be anticipated is related to staff relations. When schools are providing school-based services such as child care, there is need to hire additional staff. Besides policy decisions regarding staff qualifications, schools have to make an effort to treat the entire staff as a whole rather than treat the child-care staff as separate from the academic faculty. Such separation, which means in effect that the various child and family support services are being considered merely as an add-on, can stand in the way of the programs becoming part of the very core of the school's operation (Jehl & Kirst, 1992). The support services can indeed function autonomously within the buildings by simply using the physical space made available in the school with no attempt being made to conceptualize the programs as part of the school. However, the services are more likely to realize their potential and have positive outcomes if they are an integral aspect of the school's operations and culture.

Conceptualizing the provision of early care and family support as an integral facet of the school would lead to such activities as having representation of the entire staff early in the planning process and making provisions for regular whole-staff meetings. This facilitates interactions among the staff as well as instilling the notion that the academic as well as the nonacademic support services are important functions of the school as a whole.

Staffing issues are usually considered at the school level. However, changes associated with the implementation of nonacademic programs also involve educational administrators in the central district office as well as the custodians and others who work at the school building whose support of the effort may be crucial. In some 21Cs, for example, the principal or program coordinator has responsibility for opening and closing the schools early in the morning and late in the evening. However, in some of the schools, this is the responsibility of the custodial staff. To ensure the support of as many of its academic and nonacademic staff as possible in the implementation of 21C, one school district established a policy of enabling the children of anyone on its staff, even if they lived out of the district, to participate in the program at a reduced fee, and this proved to be an important benefit to many of the faculty and other staff members.

It is also important to ensure that all players understand the rationale behind the provision of services and support the initiative. For example, teachers who have not participated in such orientation prior to the implementation of 21C might regard early education or after school child care as extraneous efforts that drain educational resources and as such, stand in the way of their ability to teach academic subjects. In such cases, not only resentments but also continued infighting over space and materials can result. However, if the teachers are made aware, for example, that children who are left home alone after school present behavior and academic problems and that the provision of good quality early care would ensure that children come to school ready to learn, they would understand the relevance of the programs and their potential to facilitate rather than inhibit their ability to teach.

We have learned in the course of studying the implementation of 21C that even though the teachers, as part of the school's academic program, do not provide the direct support services associated with 21C, their role is critical to the success of the initiative:

> Teachers have a critical role in any school change initiative. By understanding the philosophy behind the School of the 21st Century, and working with full knowledge of the scope of its programs and services, teachers can help each student and each family to make the most out of the available services and programs. Teachers provide the machinery to make school reform a reality. No meaningful efforts to make schools better can succeed when imposed from the outside. It is only with the enthusiasm and involvement of teachers in each classroom that schools can be ... made better. (The Bush Center in Child Development and Social Policy, 1995, p. 11)

Fullan (1992, 2001) underscores the importance of orientation and staff development workshops, noting that these should be aspects of any school reform program. Fullan (1992, 2001) emphasizes, however, that even when enabling all players to participate early on in the process of change, not all of them would necessarily understand the significance of the effort nor be entirely supportive of it immediately. Fullan (2001) recommends that provisions for continued staff development be made. Huberman (1992) makes a similar point when describing several educational reform programs. Huberman (1992) notes that initially, staff commitment to the programs was fragile, in part because not every one understood the significance of the efforts and their relevance: *"It was only when teachers had undergone a few cycles of experimentation ... that they got on top of the [programs] in conceptual terms. This, in turn, strengthened their technical mastery and heightened their commitment"* (p. 10).

Factors Facilitating Implementation

The 21C program presents unique challenges to schools because establishing a system for child care and working with young children are outside the traditional mission of the school. Nevertheless, our experiences with its implementation have been similar to those of designers of school reform programs that have a traditional focus on teaching and learning. It appears that no matter what the actual reform is, there are common factors that facilitate effective implementation. This point is made by Rand researchers (Kirby, Berends, & Naftel, 2001) in a study of schools in the New American School initiative. Kirby et al. found that several factors influenced implementation, among them the principal's leadership, the school's prior experience with program implementation, teachers' perception of the need for the effort, and the support of the district. In studies on the implementation of 21C, similar findings are noted, indicating several prerequisites to successful implementation.

Commitment.   One such prerequisite is commitment to change. Change is a characteristic of and indeed the goal of any school reform effort. In the 21C and other programs (see, e.g., Elmore, 2000), change is unlikely to occur unless there is commitment to the effort at all levels. One level of commitment is at the district level even in cases in which the reform implicates only one school rather than all schools in the district (Fullan, 2001; Slavin, 2003). The implementation of 21C occurs on a school-by-school basis. However, because we seek to provide services to all children, the expectation is that all schools in the district will eventually implement the program; therefore, school districts interested in implementation have to make a commitment to phasing in implementation so that eventually, the program is available in all of the district's schools. The school district, headed by the school board and superintendent, is the primary organizational structure of the public school system, providing the schools with the external supports and infrastructure they need. As such, the district's support is essential if programs are to be implemented effectively, withstand leadership changes—which is bound to happen over time—as well as grow and develop (Ucelli, 2001). In 21C, commitment on the part of the school board and superintendent is essential to success not only for these reasons but for several other reasons as well, one of the most important of these being the financial support needed for the effort. The resources needed to implement 21C are substantial (Zigler & Finn-Stevenson, 1996), especially during the first year of operation (after that start-up period, parental fees support the program in part). Because there are no funds dedicated in school budgets for the type of services included in 21C, the superintendent and board members have to raise money and/or facilitate the allocation of staff development and other funds for purposes of the program.

Equally important is commitment to the program at the building level, especially on the part of the principal. This means that principals have to provide not only leadership and support for the program; they also have to be actively involved in the implementation process. Studies on the implementation of 21C and other programs have shown that schools where principals report spending 10% to 20% of their time during the 1st year on the program are more successful in implementation and sustainability than schools where principals report spending 5% or less of their time (Finn-Stevenson, 1992). There needs to be a point person to assume daily coordination of 21C, but it is the principal who sets the tone for the reform, encourages change, and initiates and maintains enthusiasm and high levels of effort.

In addition to the commitment and involvement of the principal, there has to be an understanding of the need for the effort and support on the part of the teachers, a point that becomes clear later in the chapter. Strategies to secure and maintain commitment to the program at all levels include continued training, the dissemination of information about the program and its impact, and the establishment of activities (e.g., conferences and newsletters) to enable educators from across the country to share their experiences with 21C implementation.

Locally Driven Approach to Implementation. Although, as we discuss later, there are external factors that can facilitate implementation, change cannot be imposed on a school but should be initiated from within. A locally driven approach to implementation is embedded in the design of 21C. It means the program is the responsibility of educators in the school and is adapted to needs of the school and community. The 21C program does not mandate the provision of all service components that make up the program, nor a uniform method for its implementation. Rather, it provides a blueprint for action and requires schools to develop and implement services on the basis of the needs of the community. The result is variations among 21C schools around the country. However, all 21C schools share a common goal—the optimal development of children through the provision of child care and support services—and they adhere to the guiding principles we described earlier. Although variations in scope of effort is noted, the majority of the schools grow to provide all of the core services of the program as well as additional services implemented in response to need and requests by parents.

Phase-in Approach. Implementation is phased in over a 3- to 5-year period as opposed to implementing all services at one time. This is essential in 21C, given the numerous services that make up the initiative, but it is also important for other reform efforts, as it provides a strong foundation on which growth is made possible (Fullan, 2001). In 21C, the decision about which services to begin with and whether or not to add additional services is made on the basis of a plan of action. The plan of action is part of the initial planning process, but it remains important in later years as well and evolves and changes over time. It is made on the basis of (a) an assessment of the needs of families and an inventory of services in the community and (b) an organizational audit, the purpose of which is to determine what strengths exist and what financial and other resources and capabilities the school district and individual schools have and what else is needed to facilitate implementation.

External Factors.   So far in our discussion, we have focused our attention on the local context. However, external factors are critical as well and can hinder or facilitate implementation because schools are part of and operate within the larger social context. External factors have influenced the development of 21C in several ways. On the negative side, opposition to schools' role in the provision of child care has been voiced by some in the child-care community. For the most part, schools are able to reach out to and work with community based child-care providers, but in the spirit of collaboration, some of the schools have been unable to lower the cost of care or upgrade staff salaries above a level consistent with what other child-care facilities are paying. On the positive side, federal and state policies, cited by Fullan (2001) as outside factors that influence implementation, have facilitated the implementation of 21C. Policy changes in the use of Title I funds, for example, have enabled the implementation of the program in low-income, urban communities by allowing schools to use these funds to support the salaries of early childhood educators. Changes in the use of Head Start funds are facilitating the integration of 21C, and Head Start in many schools, and the 21st Century Community Learning Center grant program is enabling many schools to begin 21C by implementing school-age child care. At the state level, appropriations for Family Resource Centers (the name for 21C as used in some places) created opportunities for implementing the program in some states such as Kentucky where the implementation of the program has been extensive because provisions for funding the programs were established by court order (an equity case) and were included in the 1990 Kentucky Educational Reform Act (Goetz & Debertin, 1991). In Kentucky, the importance of external factors is noted not only in funds appropriated to all schools in low-income communities but also in the provision of state-supported training to staff implementing the program.

Widespread Implementation and Sustainability.   The ultimate goal in school reform is, of course, to move beyond the implementation of the program in a few schools and scale up the effort beyond the individual school and even the individual district. Although programs are often successful in moving from the concept stage to implementation in one or several schools, the development of programs with widespread implementation has been difficult to achieve. This point is made by Schorr and Schorr (1998; Schorr, 1997) and Elias (1997) who contend that although effective programs and services exist, they often represent isolated instances of excellence and are not widely implemented. This problem is not new. The issues are not only difficulties in scale up of program implementation but also in some cases lack of consistency and failures in implementation when programs are replicated (Elias, Gager, & Leon, 1998; Fullan, 2001). There is also the problem of poor quality implementation or, over time or in different places, implementing the program in such a way as to dilute the intervention. All reform programs face this latter problem, but early care and family support services such as 21C are especially vulnerable; financial constraints can lead to program changes or to cutting corners that not only dilute the effort but may result in the provision of poor quality programs that can impede rather than enhance children's development.

The failure to implement programs to scale or having widespread implementation at a cost—namely, poor quality implementation—are common. In part, difficulties in scaling up are attributed to the way programs are developed, with far more attention paid to the idea and initial design of a program rather than to its implementation beyond the model demonstration or pilot site. That is, program developers tend to put all their energies and resources in one school to demonstrate the effectiveness and feasibility of the initiative, evaluating the effort and claiming success only to find out later that such success is limited to the demonstration site; many of the conditions that factored into the success of the program—foremost among these being the constant attention of program developers and the coaching, nurturing, as well as the resources they provide to educators during the implementation process—cannot be replicated. The results are efforts that do not resemble the original program and fail to produce positive outcomes (Elmore, 2000). Because making available good quality child care is the reason for our starting 21C, we help schools develop and maintain good quality programs. Studies on 21C indicate that the schools are succeeding in that regard, with the majority scoring high marks on the widely used quality measure known as the Early Childhood Environmental Rating Scale (Henrich, in press; Finn-Stevenson, Ginicola, & Yekelchik, 2005).

In conceptualizing 21C, our intent at the outset was to ensure widespread implementation because our goal was to ensure the optimal development and education of all children by providing good quality and affordable child care. Rather than limit our work to one or several pilot sites, we took a service-oriented approach to developing 21C that entailed building our staff capacity to enable us to work with multiple schools interested in implementation. The need to provide schools with assistance in the implementation of reform programs is emphasized by Ucelli (2001) who notes that schools have few places, if any, to turn to for support in implementing reforms. Berends et al. (2000) also found that implementation is effective only in instances in which schools have access to continued assistance from program designers.

Technical Assistance and Training

Our approach to providing schools with support in implementation is two-fold: the provision of technical assistance and the establishment of a national network. To facilitate our support of schools, we developed a training protocol and provide on-site and off-site technical assistance and training on the implementation of the program. The technical assistance staff, referred to as Implementation Associates, are based at Yale and have a designated number of schools in their region, working with each of the schools by providing on-site technical assistance several times a year for 2 years. As the schools become more proficient and implementation is underway, the Associates assume an advisory role and provide only occasional consultation by phone.

Peer Training.   The implementation staff is assisted by superintendents, principals, program coordinators, and others who have successfully implemented 21C. We have selected from among them several peer trainers and have found that pairing them with their counterparts in schools beginning the implementation is an effective and efficient training approach. It not only enables educators to learn from one another but also provides an informal support system that can be an invaluable source of strength during the initial phases of implementation. This peer approach to training is especially effective when we pair educators from similar districts or those likely to experience similar problems.

Training Events.   Peer training opportunities also exist at the 21C National Academy, which is an annual orientation and training conference, as well as at smaller training events held in several regional areas. Such regional training events focus on the specific needs of 21C schools in that area and provide, in addition to training, opportunities for 21C educators to coalesce, network, and share lessons learned.

National Network

The second aspect of our effort to facilitate widespread implementation is the establishment of a 21C National Network. 21C schools have already established informal relations and helped each other in implementation. However, as the program continues to grow nationally, it has become imperative to ensure that services at the local level maintain a high level of quality and that we are able to address the training needs of educators at established sites: hence, the creation of the National Network. The National Network entails the development of standardized professional materials on various aspects of implementation (e.g., how to create a plan of action or how to conduct a needs assessment) and the codification of procedures for working with schools with varying levels of training needs and/or experiencing changes (e.g., an increase in the number of immigrant children). Also included is a tiered, fee-based, Network membership structure. The latter provides opportunities for schools to continue to be formally affiliated with the program by becoming members, even when they have successfully completed implementation (meaning they have fully implemented all aspects of 21C and have operated these for at least 3 years). It also provides a quality ladder so schools can continually refine their efforts, eventually attaining status as 21C Schools of Excellence. A quality ladder includes several steps to achieving quality. For example, schools have to become 21C Demonstration Sites before they can become 21C Schools of Excellence. Besides being meaningful to schools, the quality ladder is important from our perspective, enabling us to maintain contact with and continue to influence the schools.

These approaches to widespread implementation have enabled us to respond to the interest schools have in implementing the program as well to maintain enthusiasm for the effort once the program has been implemented. This national perspective is an essential ingredient of scale-up efforts that have been adopted by other initiatives such as Success for All (Slavin, Dolan, & Madden, 1994). However, in and of itself, it is not sufficient. Also important is an understanding of the local level we described earlier and the practical information—what difficulties to expect, how to overcome these, and what specific steps to take—about program implementation (Fullan, 1992). Such information can only be obtained when program developers work with several schools, when they immerse themselves into the local settings and contexts ... and extend their ranks through participation in implementation (Elias, 1997, p. 285).

Challenges to Widespread Implementation

Our success to date is noted at three levels: One, over 1,300 schools have implemented the program and in many cases have operated the program for over a decade; two, Connecticut and Kentucky appropriate funds for state-wide implementation of the program; and three, an emerging state-wide effort in Arkansas is funded by the Winthrop Rockefeller Foundation, paving the way for philanthropic support of the program in other states. Although implementation of 21C has been extensive, from a national perspective, we are meeting only a fraction of the need. Some external factors, such as federal and state legislation, may be needed if we are to become truly national. Because ours is only one of many other reform efforts and school-based initiatives, continued success in scaling up may depend on whether we can indicate positive effects associated with the program.

Evaluations leading to documentation of program effects are essential aspects of any school reform program, especially at the scale-up phase. Funding for the program as well as legislation supporting the effort can only be obtained if positive outcomes are documented. Program evaluations entail not only outcome studies but also process studies to determine what has been implemented and how. Several process studies have been conducted in 21C schools, the findings of which—many of them we reported previously—have informed our efforts and facilitated the growth of the program. Outcome studies have been more difficult to conduct, although there have been some outcome studies (e.g., Finn-Stevenson, Desimone, & Chung, 1998; Finn-Stevenson, Ginicola, & Yekelchik, 2005), and currently, a longitudinal evaluation of the impact of 21C is ongoing, with five school districts participating in the study.

This study has already yielded important findings indicating, as we noted earlier, that overall, the schools are providing high-quality programs. Although we expect other findings once the data are analyzed, there are limitations to the study such as the inability to utilize a rigorous experimental design and random assignment. This limitation is not unique to the evaluation of 21C, nor are other evaluation difficulties. Even in programs in which the focus is on one outcome, such as on increased reading scores, difficulties in evaluation are noted. In 21C and other comprehensive reform initiatives, there are multiple services and goals, the achievement of which depends on interactions throughout the system. Such programs are not implemented all at once but rather over time, and even when stable, they are characterized by a constant process of adaptation and change. The complex, flexible, and evolving nature of the programs render evaluations difficult, and the difficulties are exacerbated given the breadth of the range of outcomes that comprehensive programs pursue (Kubisch, Weiss, Schorr, & Connell, 1995). In 21C, there are several intermediate and long-term outcomes; reduction in parental stress, greater parent involvement, enhanced school readiness and school achievement among participating children, fewer retentions in grade, and fewer behavior problems among participating children are some possible outcomes.

To address some of the difficulties with evaluation, researchers have employed as we did what Weiss (1995) calls "theories of change"—how and why an initiative works—as the basis for evaluation. This necessitates defining the underlying assumptions behind the cause and effect relations that programs wish to achieve and developing data collection and analysis to track the unfolding of the assumptions. Researchers are cautioned, however, that it is usually not effective to investigate a wide range of variables (Miller, 1988), so in our evaluation, we have had to be specific and focus only on some of the expected outcomes.

There are other difficulties such as the need to conduct evaluations over a long period of time to document positive outcomes. Zigler (1980), who has long held the view that there is no quick fix, and Brooks-Gunn (2000) note that if we expect positive outcomes after a year or two of program participation, we may be engaging in "magical thinking." Among other difficulties, schools providing 21C may also provide other reforms, such as literacy programs, sometimes putting these in place after the evaluation began. This presents obvious problems regarding attribution of effects and necessitated one, careful selection of districts to participate in the study and two, the need to include in the evaluation not only the documentation of outcomes but also taking into account the context, which we are doing in each one of the five districts participating in the evaluation.

Funding.   At the local level, obstacles to program growth stem from funding issues. The 21C program is designed to operate on a fee-for-service basis, but schools still need funds for start-up expenses, for the financial support of those services for which fees cannot be assessed, as well as for child-care subsidies for families who are not able to pay. The challenge is not only to find funds but also, if successful in this regard, to coordinate the various different funding sources.

There are two issues regarding funds for nonacademic services in the school. First, public funds are limited, so private sources of funding must be looked into as well. Second, even if we just consider the public sector, there are many disparate sources of potential funds. Schorr (1997) writes in reference to numerous early childhood programs, many of which are based in the school, noting that these programs "exist in the midst of fragmented and contradictory policies and hopelessly inadequate funding" (p. 241). Schorr (1997) claims that public funds are not only insufficient, but federal subsidies for early childhood alone come from 90 different programs located in 11 federal agencies and 20 offices (p. 241). It is not only difficult to know about the numerous public funds, but once a school is successful in getting grants, there are innumerable details that have to be attended to to meet the various different guidelines and reporting procedures (Iscoe, 1995). Larger school districts may have personnel who can devote the time needed to make sense out of the funding opportunities that exist, but smaller districts have to rely on the entrepreneurial and creative skills of the superintendent, principal or program coordinator.

It is important to emphasize, however, that although the funding issue places a burden on educators implementing reform initiatives, the availability of money in and of itself will not always ensure success. The

Annenberg Challenge initiative (Olson, 1997), for example, funded several schools with over $500 million over a 5-year period. The central assumption was that giving money to educators at the local building level would result in needed change. Within the first 3 years, however, it became apparent that although money is necessary, it is not sufficient to bring about effective implementation (Olson, 1997).

CONCLUSION

Our understanding about these and other points regarding program implementation has grown in the process of our work with 21C schools, underscoring the fact that there is reciprocity in the link between knowledge and practice; knowledge and theory are important aspects of school reform and other programs, and in the same way, what we learn from the process of program implementation enriches the theory and adds to our knowledge base. This has been our experience with our work on other social issues as well. Zigler (1980), Zigler and Finn-Stevenson (1987, 1993), and Zigler and Hall (2000) have championed a new subdiscipline in developmental psychology known as child development and social policy bringing to the policy arena our knowledge of children's development. The 21C program is a prime example of work in this regard. The need for child-care policy has played a critical role in the conceptualization of 21C, and what we have learned over the years in the context of research and outcome and process evaluation studies of early interventions provided the basis for the guiding principles of the program. To illustrate the link between research and policy, it is important to underscore that any effort to improve the education of children and their ability to succeed in school should include not only changes in pedagogy but also attention to children's and families' need for support programs. One such support is child care. Child care should not be thought of as a service for working parents and their employers, as it is first and foremost an environment that influences children's development and learning. The impact of child care on children's development is noted in several national studies we cited in this chapter that have indicated that poor quality child care is taking its toll; children in poor quality child care have been found to be delayed in language and reading skills and to display behavior problems, whereas children in high-quality care have greater mathematical and other academic abilities and fewer behavioral problems than children in poor quality care. These findings clearly point to the need to upgrade the quality of care children receive and to include good quality, affordable and accessible child care as part of school reform efforts. Yet, current policies (e.g., the NCLB Act of 2001) favor instead an emphasis on student assessments, cognitive development, and literacy programs. This approach represents a narrow view of development because all developmental pathways—social, emotional, physical, and cognitive—occur together and hence the importance of a whole-child approach. Also, children learn in different contexts that include, but are not limited to, schools and in a variety of ways. Young children in particular learn through play and social interactions. Any effort to ensure that children have an opportunity to succeed academically should be based on this understanding drawn from child-development research.

REFERENCES

American Federation of Teachers. (2003). *At the starting line: Early childhood education programs in the fifty states*. Washington, DC: Author.

Barnett, W. S., Brown, K., Finn-Stevenson, M., & Henrich, C. (in press). From visions to systems in universal preschool. In L. Aber, D. Phillips, & K. T. McLearn (Eds.), *Child development and social policy: Knowledge to action*. Washington, DC: American Psychological Association.

Barnett, W. S., & Hustedt, J. (2003). Preschool—The most important grade. *Educational Leadership, 60, 71*, 54–57.

Berends, M., Kirby, S., Naftel, S., & McKelvey, C. (2000). *Implementation and Performance in New American Schools: Three years into scale up*. Santa Monica, CA: Rand.

Brooks-Gunn, J. (2000). Do you believe in magic? What we can expect from early childhood intervention programs. *Social Policy Report, Society for Research in Child Development, 17*, 1–14.

Brooks-Gunn, J., & Duncan, C. (1997). The effects of poverty on children. *The Future of Children, 7, 2*, 51–71.

Children's Defense Fund. (2002). *Child care basics*. Washington, DC: Author.

Desimone, L. (2000). *Making comprehensive school reform work*. New York: Clearinghouse on Urban Education, Teachers College.

Dryfoos, J. (1994). *Full service schools: A revolution in health and social services for children, youth, and families*. San Francisco: Jossey-Bass.

Elias, M. (1997). Reinterpreting dissemination of prevention programs a widespread implementation with effectiveness and fidelity. In R. Weissberg, T. Gullotta, R. Hampton, B. Ryan, & G. Adams (Eds.), *Establishing preventive services* (pp. 283–289). Thousand Oaks, CA: Sage.

Elias, M., Gager, P., & Leon, S. (1998). Spreading a warm blanket of prevention over all children: Guidelines for selecting substance abuse and related prevention curriculum for use in the school. *Journal of Primary Prevention, 19*, 239–260.

Elmore, R. (2000). *Building new structures for school leadership*. Washington, DC: The Albert Shanker Institute.

Fight Crime/Invest in Kids. (1997). *After school crime or after school programs. Report to the U.S. Attorney General*. Washington, DC: Author.

Finn-Stevenson, M. (1992). *Iowa's innovative program for at-risk elementary school students: First phase evaluation*. Des Moines, IA: Iowa Department of Education.

Finn-Stevenson, M., Desimone, L., & Chung, A. (1998). Linking child care and support services with the school: Pilot evaluation of the School of the 21st Century. *Children and Youth Services Review, 20*, 177–205.

Finn-Stevenson, M., Ginicola, M., & Yekelchik, A. (2005). *Annual evaluation of the School of the 21st Century in Arkansas*. New Haven, CT: Zigler Center, Yale University.

Finn-Stevenson, M., & Zigler, E. F. (1999). *Schools of the 21st century: Linking child care and education*. Boulder, CO: Westview Press,

Fullan, M. G. (1992). *Successful school improvement: The implementation perspective and beyond.* Philadelphia: Open University Press.

Fullan, M. (2001). *The new meaning of educational change.* New York: Teachers College Press.

Garmezy, M. (1985). Stress resistant children: The search for protective factors. In J. E. Stevenson (Ed.), *Recent research in developmental psychopathology.* Oxford, England: Pergamon.

Gilliam, W., & Zigler, E. (2001). A critical meta-analysis of all evaluations of state funded preschool from 1977 to 1998: Implications for policy, service delivery and program evaluation. *Early Childhood Research Quarterly, 15,* 441–473.

Goetz, S. J., & Debertin, D. L. (1991). *Rural education and 1990 Kentucky Educational Reform Act: Funding, implementation, and research issues.* Retrieved from University of Kentucky College of Agriculture www.uky.edu

Henrich, C. (in press). *Quality outcomes in the School of the 21st Century Program.*

Huberman, M. (1992). Critical introduction. In M. Fullan (Ed.), *Successful school improvement* (pp. 1–20). Philadelphia: Open University Press.

Iscoe, L. (1995). *The project coordinators: A key to the school of the future.* Austin, TX: Hogg Foundation.

Jehl, J., & Kirst, M. (1992). Getting ready to provide school-liked services: What schools must do. *The Future of Children, 2*(1), 95–106.

Kirby, S., Berends, M. & Naftel, S. (2001). *Implementation in a longitudinal sample of new American schools.* Santa Monica, CA: Rand.

Kubisch, A., Weiss, C. H., Schorr, L. B., & Connell, J. P. (1995). New approaches to evaluating community initiatives: Concepts, methods, and contexts. In J. Connell et al. (Eds.), *Evaluating comprehensive community initiatives* (pp. 1–18). Washington, DC: Aspen Institute.

Lee, V., & Burkam, D. (2002). *Inequality at the starting gate: Social background differences in achievement as children begin school.* Washington, DC: Economic Policy Institute.

Miller, S. H. (1988). The Child Welfare League of America's Adolescent Parents Project. In H. B. Weiss & F. H. Jacobs (Eds.), *Evaluating family programs* (pp. 371–388). New York: Aldine de Gruyter.

Miller, B., O'Connor, S., Stringnano, S., & Joshi, P. (1996). *Out of school time in three low income communities.* Wellesley, MA: Center for Research on Women.

National Commission on Excellence in Education. (1983). *A nation at risk: The imperative for national reform.* Washington, DC: U.S. Department of Education.

National Education Goals Panel. (1991). *The National Education Goals Report.* Washington, DC: Author.

No Child Left Behind Act of 2001, Pub. L. No. 117-10, 115 Stat. 1425 (2002).

Olson, L. (1997, July 25). Annenberg challenge proves to be just that. *Education Week, 1,* 30–32.

Putnam, R. (1995). Bowling alone: America's declining social capital. *Journal of Democracy, 6,* 65–78.

Queralt, M., & Witte, A. (1998). Influences on neighborhood supply of child care. *Social Service Review, 72,* 17–47.

Rutter, M. (1979). Protective factors in children's responses to stress and disadvantages. In M. E. Kent & J. E. Rolf (Eds.), *Primary prevention of psychopathology: Vol. I. Promoting social competence and coping in children* (pp. 130–139). Hanover, NH: University Press of New England.

Rutter, M. (1980). *Changing youth in a changing society.* New York: Cambridge University Press.

Rutter, M. (1983). School effects on pupil progress: Research findings and policy implications. *Child Development, 54,* 1–29.

Schorr, L. (1997). *Common purpose: Strengthening families and neighborhoods to rebuild America.* New York: Anchor Books.

Schorr, L., & Schorr, D. (1988). *Within our reach: Breaking the cycle of disadvantage.* New York: Doubleday.

Shonkoff, J., & Phillips, D. (2000). *From neurons to neighborhoods.* Washington, DC: National Academy Press.

Slavin, R. (2003, March 5). Converging reforms. Changing schools? Changing districts? How the two approaches can work together. *Education Week,* p. 64.

Slavin, R., Dolan, L., & Madden, N. (1994). *Scaling-up: Lessons learned in the dissemination of Success for All.* Baltimore: Johns Hopkins University, Center for Research on the Education of Students Placed at Risk.

The Bush Center in Child Development and Social Policy. (1995). *The role of the teacher in the School of the 21st Century.* New Haven, CT: Author.

Ucelli, M. (2001). *From school improvement to systems reforms.* New York: Rockefeller Foundation.

U.S. Bureau of the Census. (1997). *Who is minding preschoolers?* Washington, DC: U.S. Department of Commerce.

U.S. Department of Labor. (2000). *1999 national occupational employment estimates.* Washington, DC: U.S. Government Printing Office.

Vandell, D., & Shumow, L. (1999). After school child care. *The Future of Children, When School is Out, 9*(2) 64–80.

Vinson, T., Baldry, E., & Hargreaves, J. (1996). Neighborhoods, networks and child abuse. *British Journal of Social Work, 26,* 523–543.

Weiss, C. H. (1995). Nothing as practical as good theory: Exploring theory-based evaluation for comprehensive community initiatives for children and families. In J. P. Connell, A. C. Kubisch, L. B. Schorr, & C. H. Weiss (Eds.), *New approaches to evaluating community initiatives: Concepts, methods, and contexts* (pp. 33–50). Washington, DC: Aspen Institute.

Zigler, E. (1980). Welcoming a new journal. *Journal of Applied Developmental Psychology, 1,* 1–6.

Zigler, E. F., & Finn-Stevenson, M. (1987). *Children, development and social issues.* Lexington, MA: D. C. Heath.

Zigler, E., & Finn-Stevenson, M. (1996). Funding child care and public education. *The Future of Children, 6*(2), 104–121.

Zigler, E. F., & Finn-Stevenson, M. (1993). *Children in a changing world: Development and social issues.* Pacific Grove, CA: Brooks/Cole.

Zigler, E. F., Finn-Stevenson, M., & Hall, N. (2002). *The first three years and beyond: Brain development and social policy.* New Haven, CT: Yale University Press.

Zigler, E. F., & Hall, N. (2000). *Child development and social policy: Theory and applications.* Boston: McGraw-Hill.

Zigler, E., & Lang, M. (1991). *Child Care Choices.* New York: Free Press.

Zigler, E., & Valentine, J. (1979). *Head Start: The legacy of the war on poverty.* New York: Free Press.

III

TRANSLATION OF THEORY AND RESEARCH INTO EDUCATIONAL PRACTICE TO BUILD INTELLECTUAL CAPACITY

Commentary

Mark A. Constas and Robert J. Sternberg

Attempts to translate theory and research into practice in education are most frequently focused on building content area mastery (e.g., mathematics, science) or on establishing a fundamental skill base (e.g., reading). Authors in the third part of *Translating Educational Research and Theory into Practice* are concerned with a set of abilities that cut across content areas and across skill domains. The author in this set of chapters describe some of the challenges encountered in the general domain of intelligence and creative ability. Although the authors in each chapter provide well-detailed descriptions of the difficulties of translating theory and research into practice, each does so from a different perspective and with a different set of outcomes. Sternberg et al. (chap. 9, this volume) provide a conceptual analysis of practical problems that suggests a theory of context on which translation-focused research may be based. As a highly detailed narration of over 25 years of work on giftedness and creativity, Renzulli (chap. 10, this volume) provides a set of instructive insights about the professional challenges and political nuances of work that seeks to build more productive connections between theory and practice. In the analysis provided by Kornhaber and Gardner (chap. 11, this volume), the authors describe the challenges of what could be referred to as a case of unintended translation or naturalized implementation. Viewed collectively, the authors of the three chapters in this part of the book show how new views of abilities can inform educational research.

TOWARD A THEORY OF CONTEXT AND THE CHALLENGES OF IMPLEMENTATION VARIATION

What happens when the scale of intervention moves from a small number of schools to a larger number of more varied schools? What are the main sources of implementation variation that should be studied as one tries to understand why some efforts to translate research and theory into practice are more effective than others? One of the most important features of the chapter by Sternberg et al. (chap. 9, this volume) is that it brings into focus the importance of contextual variation as a way to answer questions such as these. Elements of an inchoate theory of contextual variation Sternberg et al. propose is comprised of structural features (e.g., policies, mandates, student abilities), training issues (e.g., logistics, training consistency within groups, and distinctiveness between groups), intervention concerns (e.g., experimental controls, implementation fidelity), and analytic issues (e.g., equating of achievement scores, sampling bias). These concepts and their empirical referents suggest an array of variables that could be useful in the formulation of models of context. Such models could guide efforts to translate research and theory into practice. Context is frequently cited as source of variation in research studies of practical settings. Context, however, is not usually proposed or developed as a formal construct. By suggesting a set of concepts and a set of empirical indicators to study context, Sternberg et al. move the academic discourse on context to a higher level.

The focus on "upscaling" is another feature of the chapter by Sternberg et al. (chap. 9, this volume) that distinguishes it from most analyses of the problems of translating theory and research into practice. As a generic concern, the question of how to translate research into theory does not address the question of the scope of translation. As Sternberg et al. point out, a distinct set of challenges emerges when one attempts to implement interventions at different scales (e.g., across classrooms, schools, school districts). In response to these challenges, Sternberg et al. recommend that the problem of "scaling up" be approached theoretically by applying Brunswik's notion of "representation." What is perhaps most interesting about this suggestion is that it offers a different way of exploring, through empirical means, the notion of generalization.

NATURALIZED IMPLEMENTATION AND THE INVERSION OF TRANSLATION PRACTICES

Distance between the planned structure of an intervention and its actual implementation is a problem commonly experienced by those who attempt to translate research and theory into practice. The fact that multiple intelligences (MI) has been adopted by many educators is surprising not just because there has not been a widespread deliberate effort to support adoption but because the theory itself dedicated so little attention to educational practice. As Korhnaber and Gardner (chap. 11, this volume) note, the original work did not attempt to establish connections, abstract or practical, between MI and "curriculum, instruction, pedagogy, teachers, or testing" (p. 00). No support staff were provided, and no guidelines were published. Without deliberate efforts from researchers and without a system of supports, the theory of MI was readily adopted and used by educators around the world. This appears to have happened quite naturally without the force of policy mandates and without the participation incentives (e.g., pay compensation, course credit, training offers) that are often provided by sponsoring researchers.

As a response to the phenomenon of naturalized implementation, Kornhaber and Gardner (chap. 11, this volume) pose two fundamental questions: (a) What is it about MI that has led to its widespread adoptions?, and (b) What can be done to address quality-control problems that arise from variations in implementation? As an answer to the first question, Kornhaber and Gardner summarize reports from teachers that describe why the theory of MI was adopted. Focusing on reports from teachers, Kornhaber and Gardner argue that MI validated existing practice and helped teachers think about ways to organize and extend their practice. Focusing on organizational issues, Kornhaber and Gardner argue that school culture, readiness (to change), school leadership, and collaboration are integral components of education.

Kornhaber and Gardner (chap. 11, this volume) link their observations of teachers' natural receptiveness to and adoption of MI to the notion of the "zone of proximal development" (Vygotsky, 1978). This is a novel and generative extension of a well-known cognitive theory to the problem of how to think about the relative success of efforts to translate theory into practice. On a different level, the arguments offered by Kornhaber and Gardner might also be viewed as activating latent tendencies related to self-efficacy (Bandura, 1986) and establishing generative possibilities for the codification of professional knowledge. It appears that the inadvertent, completely unplanned capacity of MI to both satisfy a psychological need (i.e., self-efficacy) and to extend and organize educational practice is what accounts for the success of MI.

Some may view the positive effects reported by Korhnaber and Gardner (chap. 11, this volume) as an artifact of self-selection. After all, the empirical reports of MI's implementation have come from the populations of teachers who both viewed the theory as having value for their educational practice and had positive outcomes with MI. We know little about those who did not value MI, either through an unsuccessful attempted use or through outright rejection without attempted application. None of this, however, vitiates the value of the insights provided by Kornhaber and Gardner. Those interested in efforts to purposefully translate educational theory into practice may want to consider closely the observations related to the validation of practice, congruence of practice, organization of practice, and extension of practice reported by Kornhaber and Gardner. These are features that could be incorporated into future work that seeks to effectively translate research and theory into practice.

CHALLENGES AND REWARDS OF BEING A PROFESSIONAL HYBRID

The conventional researcher occupies a professional space that is safely removed from the everyday complexities of the communities to which research findings might be applied. Renzulli (chap. 10, this volume) offers a richly detailed account of his experiences as a researcher who has consistently sought to bridge the divide between theory and practice. Renzulli's identity as researcher and theoretician has always been influenced by a deep interest in the problems of practice. Although many view theory and practice as points in a natural chronology, Renzulli argues for the integration of theory development and practice. Renzulli's work provides an instructive example of what Stokes, in his description of Louis Pasteur's research, referred to as "use-inspired research" (1997, p. 74). In such research, the temporal, empirical, and analytic separation between the laboratory and the field is eliminated and is replaced by efforts to identify positive tensions between research and practice.

Responsibility is one of the main themes of Renzulli's chapter (chap. 10, this volume). Researchers frequently cite the complexities of the setting or the inadequacies of practicing professionals as explanations for an intervention's failure. Renzulli argues that failures in the translation of theory into practice should cause researchers to raise questions about the validity and completeness of the theoretical frameworks on which practices are based. Locating his work in what he considers the fertile middle ground between theory and practice, Renzulli encourages other researchers to consider both the theoretical aspects and practical implications of their own work. Nested within the discussion of learning models that forms the substantive core of his work, Renzulli's emphasis on inductive modes of learning offers insights about how researchers might better understand the setting and populations to which their work might be applied and translated into practice. As a practical tool to support his work, Renzulli refers to a "research-into-action strategy" that seeks to establish a series of collaborative relationships between researchers and stakeholders. On a sociological level, Renzulli also describes what happens when one advocates a position that challenges normative views about "best practice." According to Renzulli (chap. 10, this volume), investigators need to think carefully about how to "sell" their research to varied audiences (e.g., teachers, administrators, parents) that make up the educational community. As a way to formulate a more effective response to this need, Renzulli argues that the problem of how to translate educational theory and research can be related to issues of persuasion, communication, and relevancy. Renzulli's accomplishments illustrate the effectiveness of substantive and professional hybrids that offer a fecund blend of theoretical formulations, social insights, and political sensibilities.

REFERENCES

Bandura, A. (1986). *Social foundations of thought and action: A social cognitive theory.* Englewood Cliffs, NJ: Prentice Hall.

Brunswik, K. E. (1956). *Perception and representative design of psychological experiments.* Berkeley, CA: University of California Press.

Stokes, D. (1997). *Pasteur's quadrant: Basic science and technological innovation.* Washington, DC: Brookings Institute.

Vygotsky, L. S. (1978). *Mind in society: The development of higher psychological processes.* Cambridge, MA: Harvard University Press.

9

From Molehill to Mountain: The Process of Scaling Up Educational Interventions (Firsthand Experience Upscaling the Theory of Successful Intelligence)

Robert J. Sternberg
Tufts University

Damian Birney
University of Sydney, Australia

Alex Kirlik
University of Illinois at Urbana–Champaign

Steven Stemler
Wesleyan University

Linda Jarvin and Elena L. Grigorenko
Yale University

Embedded into the question of how to translate research into practice are a number of issues, one of which is scale. Once the effectiveness of an intervention has been established at a limited scale in a fairly controlled environment (e.g., a classroom or school), what steps need to be taken to ensure that efforts to translate research into practice at larger scales (e.g., school district, multiple school districts, state, regions), where a high level of control of implementation is not feasible, will be successful? Over the past few years, increasing numbers of researchers have begun to consider how interventions may "scale up."

Some educational interventions successfully scale up; others do not. Little—arguably, almost nothing—is known about the factors that lead to successful upscaling. Our goal in this chapter is to identify a number of these factors through a disciplined and methodologically rigorous approach. In addition, we discuss some lessons learned through our own efforts to upscale an educational intervention based on the theory of successful intelligence (Sternberg 1997, 1999).

This chapter is based on the idea that Brunswik's (1956) theory of probabilistic functionalism, and more specifically, his notion of representativeness, provides a theoretical framework suited to meeting the goals of upscaling and to addressing the problem of identifying the conditions under which educational interventions to improve pre-kindergarten to Grade 12 learning will succeed when applied on a broad scale. To understand scalability, it is necessary to conduct careful investigations guided by the prescriptions of representativeness. These investigations should focus on both the characteristics of educational programs and the descriptions of environmental conditions toward which educational interventions should be targeted.

WHY IS UPSCALING HARD TO DO?

The problem of moving an educational intervention from one location to many locations is beginning to receive considerable attention in the research literature (e.g., Berends, Kirby, Naftel, & McKelvey, 2001; Elmore, 1996; Fullan, 2000; Ramey & Ramey, 1998; Slavin & Madden, 1996). In principle, it might seem that scaling up would be a simple, even trivial, task: One simply takes an intervention that has been used on a small scale and applies it on a large scale. In practice, however, there are many difficulties associated with scaling up. These difficulties might be broadly summarized as falling into two classes: (a) difficulties associated with interventions (i.e., is a particular program suitable for upscaling?) and (b) difficulties associated with the social and human contexts in which interventions are implemented (i.e., what contexts are suitable for upscaling?).

With regard to the first class of difficulties, the first characteristic is obvious—the intervention itself should be of high quality. Elmore (1996) highlights a number of other key features of programs suitable for successful upscaling. For example, the program must create realistic expectations about the amount of time required for teachers and principals to master and deliver the program. Programs often work on a small scale because they are adopted by highly motivated individuals. Yet, these same programs fail to successfully upscale because the initial sample of the program's deliverers was not representative of the larger population. Moreover, the program must provide sufficient scaffolding for teachers navigating and delivering the program for the first time. The program must also be one that teachers can cope with, given their competencies and skills, and that they can implement with a reasonable amount of in-service instruction given the other demands on their time.

With regard to the second class of difficulties, there are also several groups of problematic issues. The first has to do with getting people to adopt the program (i.e., the diffusion of the innovation). The second problem relates to the degree to which the program is successfully implemented. The issue of adoption is relevant to the problem of upscaling because no intervention ever can be upscaled if educators do not buy it. Of relevance here are Rogers's (1995) Diffusion of Innovations and Ely's (1976) Conditions of Change models of educational change. The Diffusion of Innovations framework emphasizes the impact of characteristics of the innovation on the rate of adoption, whereas the Conditions of Change model calls attention to circumstances that predispose an environment toward change.

However, even reasonably good educational interventions might fail the upscaling test if educators do not commit themselves to implementing them (Elmore, 1996). For example, there is some research suggesting that even during peak reform periods, only about 25% of teachers are interested in experimenting with reform efforts (Cuban, 1990; Elmore, 1996). Thus, even a good program might fail to upscale successfully as a result of the resistance of those who are expected to carry out the upscaling.

It is often assumed that a good program or a great idea will sell itself. Perhaps one of the major breakdowns in upscaling happens because good programs have failed to address the critical need to disseminate their findings in a way that communicates effectively with educators. In other words, innovators need to know what educators, who make the critical decisions with regard to bringing innovations to school, consider while these decisions are made. These aspects of the "consumer mentality" of educators in adopting specific interventions have not been well studied. The second issue, implementation, is also relevant to the problem of upscaling. Even when a decision to adopt successful interventions is made, adopting institutions have to consider all kinds of factors (e.g., institutional and individual competence of the program implementers and social and structural conditions of implementations) that influence upscaling (Fullan, 1982; Fullan & Miles, 1992).

In addition, there are a number of themes that have been developed in the organizational psychology literature that link adoption and implementation (Armenakis & Bedeian, 1999; Brink et al., 1995; Goodman & Steckler, 1989; Goodman, Steckler, Hoover, & Schwartz, 1993). These four research themes are (a) content, which pertains to the substance of the

change; (b) context, which involves existing forces or conditions in an organization's external and internal environments; (c) process, which addresses
actions undertaken during the enactment of intended change; and (d) criterion, which deals with outcomes or markers for tracking the likelihood
that necessary behaviors are enacted to achieve the desired changes. A
number of ideas from the organizational-change literature have been successfully used in studies of upscaling in schools (e.g., Blumenfeld et al.,
2000). Yet, none of these approaches or theories has been adopted in the
field of education. Correspondingly, there is a need both to explore
developed theories and to propose new approaches.

THEORETICAL FRAMEWORK FOR UPSCALING

One angle from which the scalability issue can be approached is that of scientific generalization (Brunswik, 1956). Reformulated in the context of educational interventions, the issue of scientific generalization can be stated
as follows: What characteristics of a given educational program have the potential to transcend the context of discovery (i.e., the immediate context in
which the program was developed) and to be validly implemented in contexts unlike the context of discovery? The hypothesis of the existence of
such characteristics originates from practices of natural sciences for which
there are universal laws applicable to all (or almost all) contexts. However, a
growing apprehension exists in the field of educational sciences that many
cognitive and social phenomena may never adequately yield to a description or explanation in terms of "universal" characteristics or laws. For example, as a result of extensive research indicating the importance of
phonological skills in mastery of reading, many reading-intervention programs based on teaching phonemic skills have been developed. However,
not all children respond equally well to the direct teaching, phonics-based
approach—some other interventions are needed to address the needs of a
diverse group of children with reading difficulties. (For discussion of this issue, see Blachman, 1997.)

Because universal laws in education are lacking, the task of assessing or
attempting to ensure the generalizability of educational research products
will have to be based instead on the logic of representativeness. An example
of such a task would be determining whether a newly proposed educational
intervention emerging from a psychological laboratory or a specific limited
educational setting will scale up to the realities of the modern educational
environment. The term *representativeness* was introduced into discussions of
psychological methodology by Brunswik (1956) to indicate the level of similarity between the context in which a scientific investigation is performed
and the target class of contexts toward which research products are intended to generalize. As such, the concept of representativeness embraces

the notion that outcomes of any learning process are highly dependent on the context in which this learning unfolds (e.g., Sternberg & Wagner, 1994). At the same time, however, the concept of representativeness provides a logical basis for assessing and assuring generalizability, and thus, it plays an important role both in the authors' general theoretical approach and in our specific research plan for contributing knowledge to better enable the upscaling of educational interventions.

Thus, a functionalist program focuses on principles of adaptation to particular environments rather than on context-free mechanisms. Consequently, the corresponding methodology needs to include characteristics of educational interventions, students to whom these interventions are administered, and the environmental conditions under which these programs are run (Hammond & Stewart, 2001). Because the environments in which schooling and learning take place vary and because schooling is "applied" to all kinds of children at different levels of abilities and of different backgrounds, the generalizations should be based on statistical sampling of the environments as well as on statistical sampling of participants in the process of schooling. The latter is common today: Educational studies routinely employ large numbers of participants to ensure reliable generalization of results beyond the particular participants studied to the wider population to which the investigator intends to generalize his or her results. What is still rather rare is statistical sampling of the environmental conditions toward which generalization is intended. Just as in participant sampling, a crucial factor determining the success of a representative design is accurately specifying and describing the properties of the environmental (in the context of this chapter, educational) settings toward which the research results are intended to apply (or again, to scale up). As with participant sampling, the specification of the target environments toward which generalization is desired should be performed prior to the performing a study.

In our own work, we have used many of the principles described previously, starting with small-scale studies and then upscaling them in what we believe are appropriate ways.

LESSONS FROM A SCALE-UP OF THE THEORY OF SUCCESSFUL INTELLIGENCE: WHAT IS SUCCESSFUL INTELLIGENCE?

The Definition of Successful Intelligence

Intelligence Is Defined in Terms of the Ability to Achieve Success in Life in Terms of One's Personal Standards, Within One's Sociocultural Context. The field of intelligence has at times tended to put the cart before the horse, defining the construct conceptually on the basis of how it is operationalized rather than vice versa. This practice has resulted in tests that stress the academic aspect of intelligence, as one might expect given the origins of modern intelligence testing in the work of Binet and Simon (1905/1916) in designing an instrument that would distinguish children who would succeed from those who would fail in school. However, the construct of intelligence needs to serve a broader purpose, accounting for the bases of success in all areas of one's life.

The use of societal criteria of success (e.g., school grades, personal income) can obscure the fact that these operationalizations often do not capture people's personal notions of success. Some people choose to concentrate on extracurricular activities such as athletics or music and pay less attention to grades in school; others may choose occupations that are meaningful to them but that never will yield the income they could gain doing work that is less personally meaningful. Although scientific analysis of some kinds requires nomothetic operationalizations, the definition of success for an individual is idiographic. In the theory of successful intelligence, however, the conceptualization of intelligence is always within a sociocultural context. Although the processes of intelligence may be common across such contexts, what constitutes success is not. Being a successful member of the clergy of a particular religion may be highly rewarded in one society and viewed as a worthless pursuit in another culture.

One's Ability to Achieve Success Depends on One's Ability to Capitalize on One's Strengths and Correct or Compensate for One's Weaknesses. Theories of intelligence typically specify some relatively fixed set of abilities, whether one general factor and a number of specific factors (Spearman, 1904), seven multiple factors (Thurstone, 1938), eight multiple intelligences (Gardner, 1983, 1999), or 150 separate intellectual abilities (Guilford, 1982). Such a nomothetic specification is useful in establishing a common set of skills to be tested. However, people achieve success, even within a given occupation, in many different ways. For example, successful teachers and researchers achieve success through many different combinations of skills rather than through any single formula that works for all of them.

A Balance of Abilities Is Achieved to Adapt to, Shape, and Select Environments. Definitions of intelligence have traditionally emphasized the role of adaptation to the environment ("Intelligence and Its Measurement," 1921; Sternberg & Detterman, 1986). However, intelligence involves not only modifying oneself to suit the environment (adaptation) but also modifying the environment to suit oneself (shaping) and sometimes finding a new environment that is a better match to one's skills, values, or desires (selection).

Not all people have equal opportunities to adapt to, shape, and select environments. In general, people of higher socioeconomic standing tend to have more opportunities than do people of lower socioeconomic standing.

The economy or political situation of the society also can be factors. Other variables that may affect such opportunities are education and especially literacy, political party, race, religion, and so forth. For example, someone with a college education typically has many more possible career options than does someone who has dropped out of high school to support a family. Thus, how and how well an individual adapts to, shapes, and selects environments must always be viewed in terms of the opportunities the individual has.

Success Is Attained Through a Balance of Analytical, Creative, and Practical Abilities. Analytical abilities are the abilities primarily measured by traditional ability tests. However, success in life requires one not only to analyze one's own ideas and the ideas of others but also to generate ideas and to persuade other people of their value. This necessity occurs in the work world as when subordinates try to convince superiors of the value of their plan, in the world of personal relationships as when children attempt to convince their parents to do what the children want or when spouses try to convince their partners to do things their preferred way, and in the world of school as when students write an essay arguing for a particular point of view.

According to the proposed theory of human intelligence and its development (Sternberg, 1980, 1984, 1985, 1990, 1997, 1999), a common set of processes underlies all aspects of intelligence. These processes are hypothesized to be universal. For example, although the solutions to problems that are considered intelligent in one culture may be different from the solutions considered to be intelligent in another culture, the need to define problems and translate strategies to solve these problems exists in any culture.

Metacomponents, or executive processes, plan what to do, monitor things as they are being done, and evaluate things after they are done. Examples of metacomponents are recognizing the existence of a problem, defining the nature of the problem, deciding on a strategy for solving the problem, monitoring the solution of the problem, and evaluating the solution after the problem is solved.

Performance components execute the instructions of the metacomponents. For example, inference is used to decide how two stimuli are related, and application is used to apply what one has inferred (Sternberg, 1977). Other examples of performance components are comparison of stimuli, justification of a given response as adequate although not ideal, and actually making the response.

Knowledge-acquisition components are used to learn how to solve problems or simply to acquire declarative knowledge in the first place (Sternberg, 1985). Selective encoding is used to decide what information is relevant in the context of one's learning. Selective comparison is used to bring old information to bear on new problems, and selective combination is used to put together the selectively encoded and compared information into a single and sometimes insightful solution to a problem.

Although the same processes are used for all three aspects of intelligence universally, these processes are applied to different kinds of tasks and situations depending on whether a given problem requires analytical, creative, or practical thinking or a combination of these kinds of thinking. In particular, analytical thinking is invoked when components are applied to fairly familiar kinds of problems abstracted from everyday life. Creative thinking is applied when the components are applied to relatively novel kinds of tasks or situations. Practical thinking is used when the components are applied to experience to adapt to, shape, and select environments.

More about the theory can be found in Sternberg (1985, 1997). Because the theory of successful intelligence comprises three subtheories—a componential subtheory dealing with the components of intelligence; an experiential subtheory dealing with the importance of coping with relative novelty and of automatization of information processing; and a contextual subtheory dealing with processes of adaptation, shaping, and selection—the theory has sometimes been referred to as triarchic.

EDUCATIONAL INTERVENTIONS BASED ON SUCCESSFUL INTELLIGENCE

In early studies (Sternberg & Clinkenbeard, 1995; Sternberg, Ferrari, Clinkenbeard, & Grigorenko, 1996; Sternberg, Grigorenko, Ferrari, & Clinkenbeard, 1999), the question of whether conventional education in school systematically discriminates against children with creative and practical strengths has been explored. Motivating this work was the belief that the systems in most schools strongly tend to favor children with strengths in memory and analytical abilities. However, schools can be unbalanced in other directions as well. One school R. Sternberg and E. L. Grigorenko visited in Russia in 2000 placed a heavy emphasis on the development of creative abilities—much more so than on the development of analytical and practical abilities. While on this trip, they were told of yet another school—catering to the children of Russian businessman—that strongly emphasized practical abilities and where children who were not practically oriented were told that eventually, they would be working for their classmates who were so oriented.

We used the Sternberg (1993) Triarchic Abilities Test, which measures analytical, creative, and practical abilities, in some of our instructional work. The test was administered to 326 children around the United States and in some other countries who were identified by their schools as gifted by any standard whatsoever. Children were selected for a summer program in (college-level) psychology if they fell into one of five ability groupings: high analytical, high creative, high practical, high balanced (high in all three abilities), or low balanced (low in all three abilities). Students who came to Yale were then divided into four instructional groups. Students in all four groups used the same introductory-psychology textbook (a preliminary version of Sternberg, 1995) and listened to the same psychology lectures. What differed among them was the type of afternoon discussion section to which they were assigned. They were assigned to an instructional condition that emphasized either memory, analytical, creative, or practical instruction. For example, in the memory condition, they might be asked to describe the main tenets of a major theory of depression. In the analytical condition, they might be asked to compare and contrast two theories of depression. In the creative condition, they might be asked to formulate their own theory of depression. In the practical condition, they might be asked how they could use what they had learned about depression to help a friend who was depressed.

Students in all four instructional conditions (Sternberg et al., 1999) were evaluated on their performance on homework, a midterm exam, a final exam, and an independent project. Each type of work was evaluated for memory, analytical, creative, and practical quality. Thus, all students were evaluated in exactly the same way. The results suggested the utility of the theory of successful intelligence. This utility showed itself in several ways.

First, students in the high-creative and high-practical groups were much more diverse in terms of racial, ethnic, socioeconomic, and educational backgrounds than were students in the high-analytical group, suggesting that correlations of measured intelligence with status variables such as these may be reduced by using a broader conception of intelligence. Thus, the kinds of students identified as strong differed in terms of populations from which they were drawn in comparison with students identified as strong solely by analytical measures. More important, just by expanding the range of abilities measured, Sternberg et al. (1999) discovered intellectual strengths that might not have been apparent through a conventional test.

Second, Sternberg et al. (1999) found that all three ability tests—analytical, creative, and practical—significantly predicted course performance. When multiple-regression analysis was used, at least two of these ability measures contributed significantly to the prediction of each of the measures of achievement. Perhaps as a reflection of the difficulty of deemphasizing the analytical way of teaching, one of the significant predictors was always the analytical score. (However, in a replication of Sternberg et al.'s [1999] study with low-income African American students from New York, Coates [personal communication, 1997] of the City University of New York found a different pattern of results. Coates's data indicated that the practical tests were better predictors of course performance than were the analytical measures, suggesting that what ability test predicts what criterion depends on population as well as mode of teaching.)

Third and most important, there was an aptitude–treatment interaction whereby students who were placed in instructional conditions that better matched their pattern of abilities outperformed students who were mismatched. In other words, when students are taught in a way that fits how they think, they do better in school. Children with creative and practical abilities, who are almost never taught or assessed in a way that matches their pattern of abilities, may be at a disadvantage in course after course, year after year.

Follow-up studies (Sternberg, Torff, & Grigorenko, 1998a, 1998b) have examined learning of social studies and science by third graders and eighth graders. The 225 third graders were students in a very low-income neighborhood in Raleigh, North Carolina. The 142 eighth graders were largely middle- to upper middle-class students in Baltimore, Maryland, and Fresno, California. Students were assigned to one of three instructional conditions. In the first condition, they were taught the course they would have learned had there been no intervention. The emphasis in the course was on memory. In a second condition, students were taught in a way that emphasized critical (analytical) thinking. In the third condition, they were taught in a way that emphasized analytical, creative, and practical thinking. All students' performance was assessed for memory learning (through multiple-choice assessments) as well as for analytical, creative, and practical learning (through performance assessments).

As expected, students in the successful-intelligence (analytical, creative, practical) condition outperformed the other students in terms of the performance assessments. One could argue that this result merely reflected the way they were taught. Nevertheless, the result suggested that teaching for these kinds of thinking succeeded. More important, however, was the result that children in the successful intelligence condition outperformed the other children even on the multiple-choice memory tests. In other words, to the extent that one's goal is just to maximize children's memory for information, teaching for successful intelligence is still superior. It enables children to capitalize on their strengths and to correct or compensate for their weaknesses, and it allows children to encode material in a variety of interesting ways (Sternberg, Torff, & Grigorenko, 1998a, 1998b).

Thus, the results of three sets of studies suggest that the theory of successful intelligence is valid as a whole. Moreover, the results suggest that the theory can make a difference not only in laboratory tests but in school classrooms and even the everyday life of adults as well.

More recently, Grigorenko, Jarvin, and Sternberg (2002) reported on three studies that extended the work on applying the theory of successful intelligence in the classroom with the goal of improving reading performance. As in the earlier studies, Grigorenko et al. attempted to help teachers do better what they were already doing (e.g., teaching reading) rather than giving them a new curriculum that they most likely would reject for lack of time. Hence, in these studies, the goal was to supplement standard reading instruction—which included both phonic and whole-language elements—with a specifically creative, analytical, practical (CAP) intervention.

In brief, Grigorenko et al. (2002) worked with the reading curricula at the middle and high school levels. In this study of 871 middle school students and 432 high school students, Grigorenko et al. taught reading either triarchically or through the regular curriculum. At the middle school level, reading was taught explicitly. At the high school level, reading was infused into instruction in mathematics, physical sciences, social sciences, English, history, foreign languages, and the arts. Teachers in the control condition were shown how to apply mnemonic strategies.

To illustrate, in one of the studies Grigorenko et al. (2002) conducted with fifth graders, vocabulary and comprehension were assessed on multiple occasions throughout the academic year. Students in the successful intelligence condition improved over time in memory–analytical, practical, and creative tasks. Students in the control condition displayed a very different performance profile over time: They did not show improvement on memory–analytical tasks, improved on practical tasks, and declined on creative tasks. Hence, students taught using triarchic (successful intelligence) methods profited more over time from instruction than students not taught this way. Grigorenko et al.'s Studies 2 and 3 explored the impact of triarchic teaching on reading in broader academic contexts with upper middle school and high school students. Once again, a distinct triarchic advantage was demonstrated in these samples. In all settings, students who were taught triarchically substantially outperformed students who were taught in standard ways (Grigorenko et al., 2002).

In our Interagency Education Research Initiative-funded project, which was aimed at upscaling the earlier work, we created Grade 4 curriculum materials in three subject areas—language arts (5 units), mathematics (5 units), and science (4 units). The materials were designed for presentation in one of three instructional modes: triarchic (CAP), critical thinking (CT), and memory (M). Across the 14 curricular units, multiple assessments from 7,702 students were collected in the first 2 years of the program. Here, we present the preliminary findings based on a subset of the data. Again, the triarchic advantage is evident. For example, in the "Wonders of Nature" language arts unit, analyses of data showed that significantly greater gains over time were achieved by CAP students compared with both CT and M students. Similar results were found in an analysis of the available data in the "Equivalent Fractions" math unit: CAP students had significantly higher levels of gain than did students in the CT condition and tended to outperform the M students, although the effect vis-à-vis memory has not reached $p < .05$ significance for the subset of data analyzed.

Taken as a whole, the data collected at the elementary, middle, and high school levels are supportive of the utility of the triarchic model of instruction and justify further explorations into the scalability of the triarchic pedagogical approach.

FACTORS ASSOCIATED WITH SUCCESSFUL UPSCALING: LESSONS FROM THE FIELD

In our own research, we have identified some of the empirical factors that can make successful upscaling a challenge. Here we list some of them briefly:

1. Heterogeneity of content and skills standards across states, districts, and schools.
2. Heterogeneity of students' ability levels across and within schools.
3. Heterogeneity of districts: (a) political environment, (b) commitment, and (c) teachers/administrators' levels of experience.
4. Large-scale training of teachers, especially with regard to (a) scheduling, (b) availability, and (c) comparability of training within the groups of trained teachers with regard to (a) distances, (b) budget, (c) quality control, and (d) confidentiality.
5. Lack of control of intervention: (a) experimental (randomization), (b) administrative, (c) accountability, (d) implementation, (e) delivery of materials, and (f) communication with teachers.
6. Variability in technological resources across schools.
7. Equating achievement indicators across schools.
8. Quantification of the outcomes of the programs.
9. Developing assessments of program outcomes and understanding variables that influence assessment task difficulty: (a) ability to generate new tasks and (b) ability to generate alternate forms of the same tasks.
10. Complexity of data analysis: (a) comparability of information and data available for comparable analyses and (b) sources of variability that are controlled and uncontrolled across samples.

Although these factors have been elicited empirically from our own experience in the field, there is a body of general literature on innovation supporting their importance (e.g., Rogers, 1995). Specifically, Veir (1990) used stepwise regression analysis to identify the key context variables for implementing staff-development programs in rural schools. Eight predictor variables were found to be important in explaining whether the program would be successfully implemented in schools. The variables were training time, socioeconomic profile of the student body, administrative participation, proximity to an institution of higher education, provision of incentives, number of high school level teachers, number of administrators in the district, and the presence of a trainer from a higher educational institution.

As we indicated at the onset of the chapter, we find the concept of representativeness especially valuable because it embraces all the empirical observations we made while trying to upscale the successful intelligence intervention. The absolute and relative contributions of all the factors just listed have yet to be quantified, but when considered simultaneously, they provide enough dimensions to compare contexts in which innovative interventions are to be applied on a large scale so that the success of the application can be predicted.

CONCLUSION

Earlier, we noted that educational contexts are characterized by high levels of heterogeneity along many dimensions, creating a challenge to successful upscaling. This, coupled with a theory of successful intelligence acknowledging that learning outcomes are highly context dependent, leads us directly to the view that there is there is simply no magic bullet for the upscaling problem other than to sample and represent this heterogeneity in empirical research. We hope that the diversity and progression of the studies described in this chapter amply illustrate this point.

As evidenced by our framing of upscaling in terms of the more general issue of statistical generalization, it should not come as a surprise that we are not the first to note the need to sample diverse contexts in educational science. More than 60 years ago, in his text on statistical methods for educational research, Lindquist (1940) suggested that interventions be evaluated using a random selection of schools. Nor is the upscaling problem specific to education: Educational scientists must draw on lessons learned by those performing practically relevant research in neighboring psychological disciplines. Successful upscaling is a challenge any time theoretically motivated interventions are applied in specific contexts that were not the primary empirical foundation for theory. Consider, for example, what the human factors pioneer Chapanis (1988) had to say on this point:

> There are two ways one can go about doing studies that will extrapolate to a wide variety of situations. The first is by deliberately building heterogeneity into studies, a tactic recommended by Brunswik (1956) over 30 years ago; the second is by replication. (pp. 253–267).

As scientists striving for robustness and generality in our educational research, we are clearly not alone in embracing Brunswik's (1956) method of representative design as a basis for the design of effective psychological interventions. We believe achieving the goal of generality or robustness is best achieved by iteratively creating, testing, modifying, and retesting theory in heterogeneous contexts.

Representative design solves the problem of generalization by requiring that the integrity and heterogeneity of contextual variables in the target educational environment be preserved in one's fundamental research. To the extent that our discussion and examples have persuaded others to join us in this venture, we note that representative design places one additional requirement on research design and communication. This requirement concerns the need to treat the educational ecology as an object of scientific study on a par with internal psychological activities or processes.

Embracing this aspect of representative design requires an appreciation of Brunswik's (1956) deep understanding of the inherently social nature of scientific conduct and progress. Brunswik noted that truly cumulative knowledge about the contextual influences on cognition and behavior will be achievable only if those conducting and reporting research provide descriptions or theories of their research contexts as precise and detailed as the descriptions or theories psychologists have provided for phenomena such as learning, intelligence, and the like. By requiring this type of "equal treatment" for theories of internal and contextual aspects of cognition and behavior, empirical findings can bear not only on the truth or utility of related phenomena such as learning and intelligence but also on the truth or utility of theory related to the contextual influences on these activities.

By making contextual descriptions and theories explicit in this way, the educational science community as a whole can participate in what Brunswik (1956) called the large, concerted group project that is necessary to realize the promised fruit of representative design. For educational science, this fruit would be a detailed understanding of what contextual factors matter in upscaling and applying interventions, what factors tend not to matter, and what factors matter in what ways. Naturally, these factors may be intervention specific, with the result that what is learned through research is which types of interventions work in which contexts.

When the contextual theories and descriptions underlying educational research are explicitly stated and communicated and findings shared, questions about the robustness and generality of those findings become empirically decidable and thereby scientific. One researcher, for example, may not find a particular effect in an educational environment in which a theory's contextual components suggest she or he should find one. This evidence can then be used to revise the contextual theory, growing one's collective understanding of the contextual variables that matter. We encourage others to join us in this effort, as we believe it to be the most promising path toward improving the scalability of educational interventions as we work to translate research and theory into practice across a diverse range of settings, and upscale and disseminate the most successful and effective research and theory.

ACKNOWLEDGMENTS

Preparation of this article was supported by Grant REC–9979843 from the National Science Foundation. Grantees undertaking such projects are encouraged to express freely their professional judgment. This article, therefore, does not necessarily represent the positions or the policies of the U.S. government, and no official endorsement should be inferred. We thank Cynthia Matthew for review of the relevant organizational psychology literature.

REFERENCES

Armenakis, A. A., & Bedeian, A. G. (1999). Organizational change: A review of the theory and research in the 1990's. *Journal of Management, 25,* 293–315.

Berends, M., Kirby, S., Naftel, S., & McKelvey, C. (2001). *Implementation and performance in New American Schools: Three years into scale-up.* Santa Monica, CA: Rand Education.

Binet, A., & Simon, T. (1916). *The development of intelligence in children.* Baltimore: Williams & Wilkins. (Original work published 1905)

Blachman, B. (Ed.). (1997). *Foundations of reading acquisition.* Mahwah, NJ: Lawrence Erlbaum Associates.

Blumenfeld, P., Fishman, B. J., Krajcik, J., Marx, R. W., & Soloway, E. (2000). Creating usable innovations in systemic reform: Scaling up technology-embedded project-based science in urban schools. *Educational Psychologist, 35*(3), 149–164.

Brink, S. G., Basen-Engquist, K. M., O'Hara-Tompkins, N. M., Paviel, G. S., Gottlieb, N. H., & Koyato, C. Y. (1995). Diffusion of an effective tobacco prevention program. Part I: Evaluation of the dissemination phase. *Health Education Research, 10,* 283–295.

Brunswik, E. (1956). *Perception and the representative design of psychological experiments* (2nd ed.). Berkeley: University of California Press.

Chapanis, A. (1988). Some generalizations about generalization. *Human Factors, 30,* 253–267.

Cuban, L. (1990). Reforming again, again, and again. *Educational Researcher, 19*(1), 3–13.

Elmore, D. R. (1996). Getting to scale with good educational practices. *Harvard Educational Review, 66,* 1–26.

Ely, D. P. (1976). Creating the conditions for change. In S. Fabisoff & G. Bonn (Eds.), *Changing times, changing libraries* (pp. 150–162). Champaign: University of Illinois Graduate School Library.

Fullan, M. (1982). *The meaning of educational change.* New York: Teachers College Press.

Fullan, M. (2000). The return of large-scale reform. *Journal of Educational Change, 1,* 1–23.

Fullan, M. G., & Miles, M. B. (1992). Getting reform right: What works and what doesn't. *Phi Delta Kappan, 73,* 744–752.

Gardner, H. (1983). *Frames of mind: The theory of multiple intelligences.* New York: Basic Books.

Gardner, H. (1999). Are there additional intelligences? The case for naturalist, spiritual, and existential intelligences. In J. Kane (Ed.), *Education, information, and transformation* (pp. 111–131). Upper Saddle River, NJ: Prentice Hall.

Goodman, R. M., & Steckler, A. (1989). A model for the institutionalization of health promotion programs. *Family and Community Health, 11,* 63–78.

Goodman, R. M., Steckler, A., Hoover, S., & Schwartz, R. (1993). A critique of contemporary community health promotion approaches: Based on a qualitative review of six programs in Maine. *American Journal of Health Promotion, 7,* 208–220.

Grigorenko, E. L., Jarvin, L., & Sternberg, R. J. (2002). School-based tests of the triarchic theory of intelligence: Three settings, three samples, three syllabi. *Contemporary Educational Psychology, 27,* 167–208.

Guilford, J. P. (1982). Cognitive psychology's ambiguities: Some suggested remedies. *Psychological Review, 89,* 48–59.

Hammond, K. R., & Stewart, T. R. (Eds.). (2001). *The essential Brunswik: Beginnings, explications, applications.* Oxford, England: Oxford University Press.

Intelligence and Its Measurement: A symposium. (1921). *Journal of Educational Psychology, 12,* 123–147, 195–216, 271–275.

Lindquist, E. F. (1940). *Statistical analysis in educational research.* Boston: Houghton Mifflin.

Ramey, C., & Ramey, S. (1998). Early intervention and early experience. *American Psychologist, 53,* 109–120.

Rogers, E. (1995). *Diffusion of innovations* (4th ed.). New York: Free Press.

Slavin, R. E., & Madden, N. A. (1996, November). *Scaling up: Lessons learned in the dissemination of Success For All.* Retrieved April 13, 2002, from http://www.csos.jhu.edu/crespar/Reports/report06entire.html

Spearman, C. (1904). "General intelligence," objectively determined and measured. *American Journal of Psychology, 15,* 201–293.

Sternberg, R. J. (1977). Component processes in analogical reasoning. *Psychological Review, 84,* 353–378.

Sternberg, R. J. (1980). Sketch of a componential subtheory of human intelligence. *Behavioral and Brain Sciences, 3,* 573–584.

Sternberg, R. J. (1984). Toward a triarchic theory of human intelligence. *Behavioral and Brain Sciences, 7,* 269–287.

Sternberg, R. J. (1985). *Beyond IQ: A triarchic theory of human intelligence.* New York: Cambridge University Press.

Sternberg, R. J. (1990). *Metaphors of mind: Conceptions of the nature of intelligence.* New York: Cambridge University Press.

Sternberg, R. J. (1993). Sternberg Triarchic Abilities Test. Unpublished manuscript.

Sternberg, R. J. (1995). *In search of the human mind.* Orlando, FL: Harcourt Brace College Publishers.

Sternberg, R. J. (1997). *Successful intelligence.* New York: Plume.

Sternberg, R. J. (1999). The theory of successful intelligence. *Review of General Psychology, 3,* 292–316.

Sternberg, R. J., & Clinkenbeard, P. R. (1995). The triarchic model applied to identifying, teaching, and assessing gifted children. *Roeper Review, 17,* 255–260.

Sternberg, R. J., & Detterman, D. K. (1986). *What is intelligence?* Norwood, NJ: Ablex.

Sternberg, R. J., Ferrari, M., Clinkenbeard, P. R., & Grigorenko, E. L. (1996). Identification, instruction, and assessment of gifted children: A construct validation of a triarchic model. *Gifted Child Quarterly, 40*(3), 129–137.

Sternberg, R. J., Grigorenko, E. L., Ferrari, M., & Clinkenbeard, P. (1999). A triarchic analysis of an aptitude–treatment interaction. *European Journal of Psychological Assessment, 15,* 1–11.

Sternberg, R. J., Torff, B., & Grigorenko, E. L. (1998a). Teaching for successful intelligence raises school achievement. *Phi Delta Kappan, 79,* 667–669.

Sternberg, R. J., Torff, B., & Grigorenko, E. L. (1998b). Teaching triarchically improves school achievement. *Journal of Educational Psychology, 90,* 374–384.
Sternberg, R. J., & Wagner, R. K. (Eds.). (1994). *Mind in context.* New York: Cambridge University Press.
Thurstone, L. L. (1938). *Primary mental abilities.* Chicago: University of Chicago Press.
Veir, C. (1990). *Context variables for successful staff development in rural schools.* (ERIC Document Reproduction Service No. ED331184)

10

Swimming Upstream In a Small River: Changing Conceptions and Practices About the Development of Giftedness

Joseph S. Renzulli
University of Connecticut

> Conflicts between incompatible, staunchly held, sincere beliefs make up what we may call the little wars of science, little wars which, except for size and consequences differ in pattern no whit from the big wars between nations or, for that matter, the persecution of a religious minority by a majority.

> —Edwin G. Boring (1963, p. 246)

Translating theory into practice is all about the process of change—policy change, organizational change, and perhaps most important, change in the attitudes and behaviors of practitioners directly responsible for implementing a theory-driven method that differs from current practice. If policy adoption, organizational sponsorship, and practitioner support are all present, change is likely to take place more smoothly than if one element is missing. In popular parlance, both "top-down" and "bottom-up" approaches are most effective in bringing about any kind of social, political, or educational change. Purely top-down change, whether or not it is theory driven or research supported, will not achieve prolonged implementation if the power elite dictating particular changes do not win the "minds and hearts" of practitioners.

The main strategy for winning the minds and hearts of leaders and practitioners and for bringing about the sustained implementation of new ideas
is persuasion. Persuasion is dependent on effective communication, which
in turn is a function of the exchange of relevant information for particular
constituencies. Organizations such as school districts and state departments of education are concerned with issues such as research support, tangible benefits at low costs, minimal disruption of existing routines, how the
change fits in with already adopted initiatives, and political considerations
related to equity, public relations, and popular support. Practitioners (e.g.,
teachers, principals, school psychologists) are more concerned with how
the proposed change will affect their day-to-day work and how much time
and new knowledge will be required to implement a new initiative. However, practitioners also have informal theories and beliefs about the best
ways to provide educational services, and in this regard, they may be a more
sophisticated and demanding audience than policymakers or organization
managers. Practitioners always care about whether a proposed change
makes sense in terms of what they believe are the best ways to accomplish a
particular objective.

These differences in the targets for persuasive activity mean that strategies for change, and especially the genre of communication, must be carefully crafted to meet the needs of various audiences. An article or workshop
for teachers, for example, should include some "practical theory" that answers questions about why they should consider a proposed change, and
some information about research results based on data from schools that resemble the workplace of teachers (rather than laboratory experiments with
college sophomores) is also useful in helping them to reach conclusions
about adopting a particular strategy. However, the essence of persuasive
communication for teachers should mainly address concerns about what is
expected from them in bringing about a proposed change, how these expectations relate to their own beliefs and daily activities, and what practical
materials and strategies can be provided that will make their implementation easier.

Although my work has dealt with theory development, I have given equal
attention to how practical materials and strategies figure into the communication and change process. In this chapter, I discuss the two main theories
that have been the basis for my work over the past 25 years and the strategies I have used to persuade policymakers, organizations, and educational
practitioners to implement practical applications of these theories. This
work has focused on (a) a human potential theory dealing with the conceptualization of giftedness and talent potential in young people and (b) a pedagogical theory that is intended to produce a particular "brand" of learning
that promotes what I refer to as gifted behaviors. These theories have been
described in great detail elsewhere (Renzulli, 1977a, 1978, 1986) and

therefore, I only summarize them briefly in this chapter. My focus in the chapter is on the strategies that have resulted in "selling" these ideas to the gifted-education establishment and to the general education community. Because these two theories parallel one another and are complimentary in purpose and implementation, I discuss the strategies for gaining acceptance as a single set of entities.

All theorists are promoters, but most theorists leave practical applications to others. This orientation is especially prevalent among psychologists, even if they believe that their work has applications in practical education settings. "Here is my brilliant idea—I leave its implementation to you educators" (condescension sometimes implied). Because education is my major affiliation for both theoretical and applied work and having an impact in schools a major professional goal, one of the characteristics of my work is that it has proceeded simultaneously along both theoretical and practical lines. For better or worse, I have never been content with developing theoretical concepts without devoting equal or even greater attention to creating instruments, procedures, staff development strategies, or instructional materials for implementing the various concepts. This approach has both advantages and disadvantages! An eye toward implementation enables theory testing in practical settings—the kinds of places for which the work was intended and where the uncertainty of personalities, politics, and variations among schools and populations allow examination of impact in the so-called real world. The disadvantage is, of course, less than rigorous experimental control and thus the susceptibility to design-related criticisms.

A second advantage of pursuing practical as well as theoretical contributions is it has enabled me to stay in touch with the sights, sounds, and smells of real schools and classrooms and the practical and political challenges of people working in them. Theory in an applied field does not have much value if it is not compatible with real-world conditions such as how schools work, teachers' ways of knowing, the politics of innovation, and the practices that can reasonably be expected to endure beyond the support usually accorded to pilot or experimental studies or the guiding influence of a patron saint who originated or shepherded the program in its initial implementation. The opportunity to generate research data can lend credence to the theory and point out directions where additional work needs to be done in both theory development and, perhaps even more important, in fitting theory-guided practices into the complexity of diverse school settings. In fact, the evolution of my work over the years is a direct result of these realities, for it is from direct experience that my ideas have taken new directions.

A third advantage of a theory-into-practice approach is it has afforded me the opportunity to collaborate with exceptionally talented practitioners, many of whom have expanded both the theoretical and practical dimensions of the ideas and suggested further research needs to enhance understanding, application, and credibility. One of the main lessons learned from my combined theory and practice approach is that the best ways to bridge the theory-into-practice gap is for the "ivory tower" people and the people "in the trenches" to listen to one another.

The negative side of a combined theoretical/practical approach is the vulnerability of partially or poorly implemented practices. In most cases, it is the implementation rather than the theory that is the object of scrutiny. When I visit classrooms, for example, where every student has produced cookie cutter copies of the same project while simultaneously claiming that these projects are examples of what I have defined as Type III enrichment (i.e., individual and small-group investigations of real problems), it reminds me of the quote about the shadow that falls between the idea and the reality. Nevertheless, even negative experiences have value. Mainly, they point out that the originator of the theory has not engineered the proper conditions for implementation, communicated effectively with practitioners, provided the appropriate training and resources, overestimated what works in the real world, or all of the above! Many innovative programs work well at the experimental level because supplementary funds and highly committed research teams and patron saints support these factors. The bench chemist might be able to make a new drug work in an experimental setting, but producing millions of gallons for wholesale use is the job of chemical engineers. I view theory development that is paralleled by practical procedures for implementation as the best combination of ideas and engineering.

In the sections that follow, I summarize the two major theories underlying my work: the three-ring conception of giftedness and the enrichment triad model. Also interrelated with this phase is a subtheory that defines a procedure for regular curriculum modification called curriculum compacting.

THE THEORIES BRIEFLY DESCRIBED

The Three-Ring Conception of Giftedness

The three-ring conception of giftedness is a theory that attempts to portray the main dimensions of human potential for creative productivity. The name derives from the conceptual framework of the theory—namely, three interacting clusters of traits (above-average ability, task commitment, and creativity) and their relationship with general and specific areas of human performance (see Fig. 10.1). The theory distinguished between what I have called schoolhouse or lesson-learning giftedness on one hand and creative/productive giftedness on the other (I discuss this following). Perhaps the most salient aspect of this theory is that it is the interaction between and

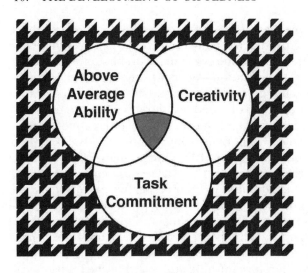

FIG.10.1. The three-ring conception of giftedness.

among these clusters of traits brought to bear on a particular problem situation that creates the conditions for the creative productive process to commence. A second aspect of the theory is that whereas abilities (especially general intelligence and aptitudes) tend to remain constant over time, creativity and task commitment are contextual, situational, and temporal. They emerge in certain people, at certain times, and under certain circumstances. The enrichment triad, which I briefly describe following, is a compatible learning theory that attempts to prescribe learning environments that create the conditions for stimulating interaction among the three rings.

Above-average ability encompasses both general abilities (e.g., verbal and numerical reasoning, spatial relations, memory) and specific abilities (e.g., chemistry, ballet, musical composition, experimental design), and ability-dependent performance is the most constant of the rings. That is, any student's performance within the parameters of this ring is minimally variable at any given point in time, capable of being developed over time, and can be measured with higher degrees of reliability than the other two clusters of traits. The reason that this ring makes reference to above-average ability (as opposed to, e.g., "the top 5%" or "exceptional ability") derives from research that highlights minimal criterion validity between academic aptitude and high levels of creatively productive accomplishment. In other words, research suggests that beyond a certain level of general ability, real-world achievement is less dependent on ever increasing cognitive ability than on other personal and dispositional factors (e.g., task commitment and creativity; Albert, 1975; Bloom, 1964; Holland & Astin, 1962; Simonton, 1994; Wallach & Wing, 1969). This realization highlights the limitations of intelligence tests and the innumerable aptitude and achievement tests that are used for identifying candidates for "gifted programs."

Task commitment represents a nonintellective cluster of traits found consistently in creative/productive individuals (e.g., perseverance, determination, willpower, positive energy). It may best be summarized as a focused or refined form of motivation—energy brought to bear on a particular problem or specific performance area. The significance of this cluster of traits in any definition of giftedness derives from numerous research studies as well as autobiographical sketches of creative-productive individuals (Albert, 1975; Barron, 1969; Bloom & Sosniak, 1981; McCurdy, 1960; Nicholls, 1972; Roe, 1952; Zuckerman, 1979). Simply stated, one of the primary ingredients for success among persons who have made important contributions to their respective performance areas is their ability to immerse themselves fully in a problem or area of intense interest for an extended period of time and to persevere even in the face of obstacles that may inhibit others. The role of interests in generating task commitment is crucial in the development of creative/productive giftedness and therefore must be addressed in the pedagogical theory.

Creativity is that cluster of traits that encompasses curiosity, originality, ingenuity, and a willingness to challenge convention and tradition. In this regard, I view creativity as both cognitive and nonintellective traits that are interactive. For example, there have been many gifted scientists throughout history, but the scientists whose work we revere, whose names have remained recognizable among both the scientific community and the general public, are those scientists who have used their creativity to envision possibilities, to find and focus previously unidentified realms of inquiry, and ultimately to help resolve scientific questions in new and original ways. Einstein is a perfect case in point. Clearly, he had above-average ability and task commitment, but it was his creative approach to looking at the world (in conjunction with the former two trait clusters) that led him to what were truly brilliant theories about how the natural world functions. Einstein is a household name because of his creativity; certainly there are countless other scientists whose intellect and commitment were commensurate with Einstein's, but they were unable to visualize problems in as creative a way as did Einstein.

By way of summary, the most salient point to make in discussing the three-ring conception of giftedness is that it is the overlap and the interaction among the three clusters of traits that create the conditions for making giftedness. There are many personal and environmental conditions (represented in the houndstooth background of Fig. 10.1) that give rise to the clusters of traits; and it is sometimes a team effort that brings the traits together for particular problem-solving endeavors. Before moving on to the pedagogical theory underlying my work, it is useful to review the continuum of learning theories presented by other scholars.

THE CONTINUUM OF LEARNING THEORIES

All learning exists on a continuum ranging from deductive or didactic approaches at one end to inductive or constructive approaches at the other. This continuum exists for learners of all ages—from toddlers to doctoral students—and it exists in all areas of curricular activity. The continuum also exists for learning that takes place in the nonschool world, the kinds of activities that young people and adults pursue as they go about acquiring new skills for their jobs or working in the kitchen, the garden, or the workshop in the basement. (There are, of course, occasions when a particular approach falls between the two ends of the continuum. However, for purposes of clarifying the main features of deductive and inductive learning, I treat the two models as polar opposites.) Both models of learning and teaching are valuable in the overall process of schooling, and a well-balanced school program must make use of basic and high-end approaches as well as the combined approaches between the two ends of the continuum.

The Deductive Model of Learning

Although many names have been used to describe the theories that define the ends of the continuum, I simply refer to them as the deductive model and the inductive model. The deductive model is familiar to most educators and guides the majority of activity that takes place in classrooms and other places where formal learning is pursued. The inductive model, on the other hand, represents the kind of learning that typically takes place outside formal school situations. A good way to understand the difference between these two types of learning is to compare how learning takes place in a typical classroom with how someone learns new material or skills in real-world situations. Classrooms are characterized by relatively fixed time schedules; segmented subjects or topics; predetermined sets of information and activities, tests and grades to determine progress, and a pattern of organization that is largely driven by the need to acquire and assimilate information and skills that are deemed important by curriculum developers, textbook publishers, and committees who prepare lists of standards. The deductive model assumes that current learning will have transfer value for some future problem, course, occupational pursuit, or life activity.

Deductive learning is based mainly on the factory model or human engineering conception of schooling. The underlying psychological theory is behaviorism, and the theorists most frequently associated with this model are Pavlov, Thorndike, and Skinner. At the center of this ideology is the ability to produce desirable responses by presenting selected stimuli. In an educational setting, these theories translate into a form of structured training for purposes of knowledge and skill acquisition. A curriculum based on the deductive model must be examined in terms of both what and how something is taught. The issue of what is (or should be) taught has always been the subject of controversy ranging from a conservative position that emphasizes a classical or basic education curriculum to a more liberal perspective that includes contemporary knowledge and life adjustment experiences (e.g., driver's education, sex education, computer literacy). Overall, American schools have been very effective in adapting what is taught to changes taking place in society. Recent concerns about the kinds of skills that a rapidly changing job market will require have accelerated curricular changes that prepare students for careers in technological fields and a postindustrial society. Nowhere is this change more evident than in the emphasis currently placed on thinking skills, interdisciplinary approaches to curriculum, and the use of technology in the learning process. These changes are favorable developments, but the deductive model still limits learning because it restricts both what is taught and how the material is taught.

Although most schools have introduced teaching techniques that go beyond traditional drill and practice, the predominant instructional model continues to be a prescribed and presented approach to learning. The textbook, curriculum guide, or lists of standards prescribe what is to be taught; and the material is presented to students in a predetermined, linear, and sequential manner. Educators have become more clever and imaginative in escaping the restrictiveness of highly structured deductive models, and it is not uncommon to see teachers using approaches such as discovery learning, simulations, cooperative learning, inquiry training, problem-based learning, and concept learning. More recent approaches include simulated problem solving through interactive computer technology. Some of these approaches certainly make learning more active and enjoyable than traditional, content-based deductive learning, but the bottom line is that there are certain predetermined bodies of information and thinking processes that students are expected to acquire. The instructional effects of the deductive model are those directly achieved by leading the learner in prescribed directions. As I indicated previously, there is nothing inherently "wrong" with the deductive model; however, it is based on a limited conception of the role of the learner. It fails to consider variations in interests and learning styles, and it always places students in the roles of lesson learners and exercise doers rather than authentic, first-hand inquirers.

The Inductive Model of Learning

The inductive model, on the other hand, represents the kinds of learning that ordinarily occurs outside formal classrooms in places such as research laboratories; artists' studios and theaters; film and video production sets;

business offices; service agencies; and almost any extracurricular activity in which products, performances, or services are pursued. The names most closely associated with inductive learning are Dewey (1956), Montessori (1964, 1967), and Bruner (1966, 1990). The type of learning advocated by these theorists can be summarized as knowledge and skill acquisition gained from investigative and creative activities that are characterized by three requirements. First, there is a personalization of the topic or problem—the students are doing the work because they want to. Second, students are using methods of investigation or creative production that approximate the modus operandi of the practicing professional, even if the methodology is at a more junior level than that used by adult researchers, filmmakers, or business entrepreneurs. Third, the work is always geared toward the production of a product or service that is intended to have an impact on a particular audience. The information (content) and the skills (process) that are the substance of inductive learning situations are based on need-to-know and need-to-do requirements.

For example, if a group of students is interested in examining differences in attitudes toward dress codes or teenage dating between and within various groups (e.g., gender, grade, students vs. adults), they need certain background information. What have other studies on these topics revealed? Are there any national trends? Have other countries examined dress code or teenage dating issues? Where can these studies be found? Students will need to learn how to design authentic questionnaires, rating scales, and interview schedules and how to record, analyze, and report their findings in the most appropriate format (e.g., written, statistical, graphic, oral, dramatized). Finally, they will need to know how to identify potentially interested audiences, the most appropriate presentation formats (based on a particular audience's level of comprehension), and how to open doors for publication and presentation opportunities. This example demonstrates how knowledge and skills that might otherwise be considered trivial or unimportant become instantaneously relevant because they are necessary to prepare a high-quality product. All resources, information, schedules, and sequences of events are directed toward this goal; and evaluation (rather than grading) is a function of the quality of the product or service as viewed through the eyes of a client, consumer, or other type of audience member. Everything that results in learning in a research laboratory, for example, is for present use. Therefore, looking up new information, conducting an experiment, analyzing results, or preparing a report is focused primarily on the present rather than the future. Even the amount of time devoted to a particular project cannot be determined in advance because the nature of the problem and the unknown obstacles that might be encountered prevent rigid, predetermined schedules.

To sum up, the deductive model has dominated the ways in which most formal education is pursued, and the track record of the model has been less than impressive. One need only reflect for a moment on his or her own school experience to realize that with the exception of basic language and arithmetic, much of the compartmentalized material learned for some remote and ambiguous future situation is seldom used in the conduct of daily activities. The names of famous generals, geometric formulas, the periodic table, and parts of a plant learned outside an applicable, real-world situation are usually quickly forgotten. This is not to say that previously learned information is unimportant, but its relevancy, meaningfulness, and endurance for future use is minimized when it is almost always learned apart from situations that have personalized meaning for the learner.

Inductive learning, on the other hand, focuses on the present use of content and processes as a way of integrating material and thinking skills into the more enduring structure of the learner's repertoire. It is these more enduring structures that have the greatest amount of transfer value for future use. When content and processes are learned in authentic, contextual situations, they result in more meaningful uses of information and problem-solving strategies than the learning that takes place in artificial, preparation-for-the-test situations. If individuals involved in inductive learning experiences receive some choice in the domains and activities in which they are engaged and if the experiences are directed toward realistic and personalized goals, this type of learning creates its own relevancy and meaningfulness.

If people do, in fact, learn important content and skills outside of formal classroom situations, then it is important to examine the dimensions of this type of learning and the ways in which real-world learning can be brought into the school. However, bringing anything new into the school can be tricky business. The track record in this regard has been one of overstructuring and institutionalizing even the most innovative approaches to learning. Many educators can remember how the much heralded concept of Discovery Learning (Bruner, 1967; Snelbecker, 1974) ended up being what one teacher called "sneaky telling" and how a focus on thinking skills and creative thinking fell prey to the same types of formulas and prescribed activities that characterized the content-based curriculum that has been criticized so strongly by thinking-skills advocates. Even the present fascination with computers and online learning is in some cases turning out to be little more than tutoring with electronic worksheets. However, if we, as educators, can learn to view the Internet and other media as a vast treasure chest of categorical and searchable information that can be sought out on a need-to-know basis, then we will begin to tap the true value of this resource for inductive learning experiences.

Human beings are inherently curious, problem-solving creatures who take action and endeavor to evoke positive change when their interests are sincere and personal. Therefore, the environment in which humans take action with commitment and enthusiasm must be natural (as opposed to contrived or forced), and resources (e.g., expert opinion, valid information and knowledge, appropriate equipment and materials, and authentic strategies) must be accessible within that environment to facilitate taking action.

The Enrichment Triad Model

The enrichment triad model (Renzulli, 1977a) is pedagogical theory based on inductive approaches to learning and the ways in which people learn in an authentic (natural) environment. Enrichment conceptually represents opportunities for students to capitalize on external stimulation, internal curiosity, necessity, or combinations of these three sources of action for the purpose of effecting positive change or creating meaningful products in real-world, problem-solving ways that often transcend the traditional learning mode and thus the traditional, "artificial" classroom setting. This model is an organizational pattern for systematically applying enrichment teaching and learning into a variety of learning environments.

The three types of enrichment I describe following are designed to work in harmony with one another, and it is the interaction among the types of enrichment that produce the dynamic properties represented by the arrows in Fig. 10.2 that are as important as the cells in achieving the goals of this inductive approach to learning. Type I enrichment includes general, exploratory activities that expose students to problems, issues, ideas, areas of study, theories, skills—in sum, possibilities that may lead to various follow-up opportunities. Often, this type of enrichment serves as a catalyst for curiosity and internal motivation—it helps to create interests that may lead

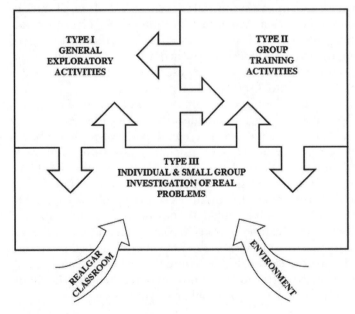

FIG.10.2. The enrichment triad model.

to task commitment. Type I enrichment is one method for externally stimulating students toward internal commitment and purpose. These activities should be made available to all students—a highlight of the model that underscores the philosophy behind the three-ring conception of giftedness in that task commitment and creativity are crucial to the development of potentially gifted students who may "rise to the challenge" in unexpected ways or at unexpected times given the proper environment.

Type II Enrichment involves group training activities in a variety of cognitive, metacognitive, methodological, and affective skills. This type of enrichment prepares the students to produce tangible products and/or generate resolutions to real-world problems through its emphasis on research skill development, information gathering, and the development of professional quality communication skills. It is not enough to be curious and moved toward action; one must also be equipped to tap and utilize resources to take action. Type I activities endeavor to capture students' interests—to inspire—whereas Type II activities endeavor to teach students how to move from inspiration to action. Type II activities are contingent on the students' developmental levels and as such should vary in complexity and sophistication with personal and academic maturity. Generally, there are five categories of Type II activities, all of which may be considered "process skills": (a) cognitive training; (b) affective training; (c) learning-how-to-learn training; (d) research and reference procedures; and (e) written, oral, and visual communication procedures. Type II enrichment can be used as a follow-up to Type I experiences, or it can be independent activities that have general value in skill development. Type II enrichment oftentimes generates as much or more interest as Type I experiences, and when young people learn a research skill and the excitement of creative or investigative opportunities, the acquisition of the skill, in and of itself, often causes students to generate research problems that can also serve as points of entry into Type III involvement.

Although Types I and II enrichment are recommended for all students or for targeted populations (e.g., all students with a strong interest in poetry or technology), Type III activities are investigations of real-world problems that have been selected by individuals or small groups with common or complimentary interests. Thus, Types I and II enrichment should be viewed as identification situations—not identifying who is or is not gifted but rather who and under what circumstances young people might want to go on to higher levels of involvement. The "height" of the follow-up is, of course, a function of (a) the level of traits in each of the three rings in the conception theory that an individual learner or small group brings to a potential Type III situation, (b) the degree of interaction between and among the rings, and (c) the expertise and commitment of teachers or other adult facilitators of this type of real-world problem solving.

Real-world problems are defined in this theory as those problems with a personal frame of reference for students, those with no existing or unique resolution, and those that are designed to have an impact on one or more targeted audience. As with Type II activities, the sophistication and depth of Type III activities is contingent on students' developmental levels. Regardless of students' age or level of performance, all such activities encompass five main objectives:

1. To experience enjoyment in and a commitment to the process of authentic inquiry and creative productivity; to guide future education, career, and non-school/work decision making; and to explore one's efficacy and sense of power to change things.
2. To acquire advanced-level understanding of the knowledge and methodology used within particular disciplines, artistic areas of expression, and interdisciplinary studies.
3. To develop authentic products or services that are primarily directed toward bringing about a desired impact on one or more specified audiences.
4. To develop self-directed learning skills in the areas of planning, problem finding, and focusing, management, cooperativeness, decision making, and self-evaluation.
5. To develop task commitment, self-confidence, feelings of creative accomplishment, and the ability to interact effectively with other students and adults who share common goals and interests.

Type III experiences are the culmination of natural learning, representing a synthesis and an application of content, process, and personal involvement through self-motivated work. These activities serve as the vehicles within the total school experience through which everything from basic skills to advanced content and processes "come together" in the form of student-developed products and services. In this regard, I sometimes refer to them as "the assembly plant of mind." Clearly, the student's role is transformed from one of lesson learner to firsthand investigator or creator; and the teacher's role must shift from that of instructor or disseminator of knowledge to some combination of coach, promoter, manager, mentor, agent, guide, and sometimes even colleague.

THE ROCKY ROAD OF EDUCATIONAL CHANGE CIRCA THE LATE 1960S AND EARLY 1970S

Obstacles related to bringing about educational change can occur on multiple levels. In the late 1960s, when I first began work on the three-ring conception of giftedness and the enrichment triad model, I never dreamed (a) that my work would become popular enough to form the basis for a new look at what makes giftedness and the means for serving high-potential students and (b) that it would become the basis for a good deal of controversy in the field. This work was greeted by a less than enthusiastic reception from the gifted establishment of the time, including rejections of my writing by all the main journals in the field of gifted education, admonitions about my work by state directors of gifted programs to school districts seeking consultation, and rejections of papers from state and national conference organizers. My convictions about a broadened view of human potential caused me to seek an audience outside the gifted community, and in 1978, the *Phi Delta Kappan,* a general education journal, published my article entitled "What Makes Giftedness: Reexamining a Definition" (Renzulli, 1978). In the ensuing years scholars, practitioners, and policymakers began to encounter my work, and this awareness led to an appreciation of more flexible attitudes toward the meaning of this complex phenomenon called giftedness. The 1978 *Phi Delta Kappan* article (Renzulli, 1978) is now the most widely cited publication in the field. I mention this fortunate turn of events mainly to call attention to the always expectant hope that people can change their minds about a long-cherished belief and to acknowledge the courage of Cole, the then *Phi Delta Kappan* editor, who was willing to take a chance on what was at the time a decidedly unpopular point of view (as pointed out to him by field reviewers). Similarly, after agreeing to publish the triad model as a three-part series, a gifted education journal editor inexplicably decided not to publish the second or third installments. Once again, I sought audiences outside the gifted education establishment by submitting work to nongifted education publications and by offering independent workshops around the country. If there is a strategic lesson to be learned from this scenario, it is simply that an end-run strategy is sometimes effective to go around organizational power brokers (i.e., "The Establishment") to bring your message directly to the consumer. A basic principle of economics is that supply creates its own demand. When practitioners began to see value in the approaches I advocated, this bottom-up strategy resulted in gaining the sometimes-reluctant attention of the persons who select articles for publication, invite speakers to conferences, and recommend practices to schools.

A bottom-up strategy is not without its roadblocks and pitfalls. In the years since I originally published the enrichment triad model (Renzulli, 1977a), and the three-ring conception of giftedness (Renzulli, 1978), a wide variety of reactions have appeared in the literature and on the professional conference circuit. These reactions have ranged from a highly positive article entitled "Renzulli Is Right" (Busse & Mansfield, 1980) to a scathing criticism that branded my work as "a national disease in gifted education" (Jellen, 1983). Also, this work seems to have generated enough controversy to cause some authors and speakers, regardless of the topic they are addressing, to weave into their work what Treffinger (1987) referred to as "cheap shots" about the ideas I have set forth.

To be certain, I was fully aware that the triad model and the three-ring conception of giftedness challenged the traditional orthodoxy that dominated the field at that time, but I never thought that state directors of gifted programs would prohibit me from speaking or consulting with school districts in their states or that the editors of professional journals in the field would reject my articles because, as one person put it, "I disagree philosophically with your ideas." To understand the discrepancy regarding the popularity of these theories in more recent years versus the early resistance to it, it is necessary to turn back the calendar and revisit the climate in the gifted education field in the late 1960s and early 1970s. This was a time period prior to the landmark theories of Sternberg (1984, 1985, 1999) and Gardner (1983) and before the publication of influential research on talent development by Bloom (1985), Csikszentmihalyi (1991), Albert (1975), Simonton (1978, 1994), and others. Although some people were beginning to question the predominance of the single criterion, IQ score cutoff approach to the identification of students for special programs, state guidelines and regulations that were in existence or being enacted at that time still harkened back to the work of Terman (1916) and the belief that a certain level of traditionally measured intelligence was synonymous with giftedness. The only controversy within this very conservative conception of giftedness was how high to set the cutoff scores on IQ tests! Some people argued that it should be the top 1%, which was Terman's definition (1916, pp. 6,12), and others argued for a 3% or 5% percent criterion. Regardless of the cutoff level, however, there was no mistaking the absolutist belief that a person was either gifted or not gifted; and chances were that they would retain their respective designations despite evidence to the contrary, especially if that evidence was based on information other than test scores.

It is easy to understand the wide acceptance of the cutoff score approach if one also examines historically (a) the ways in which designated students were commonly served in the early days of the movement and (b) the emergence of state guidelines and especially state funding formulas. Most programs separated identified students into full-time special classes or part-time resource room arrangements for preselected students. Typical school-based programs consisted mainly of accelerated content or conglomerations of disconnected enrichment activities frequently based on individual teachers' favored topics and units of study, the most recent make-it-and-take-it workshops attended, or trendy thinking skill activities that claimed to be based on Bloom's (1985) Taxonomy of Educational Objectives. The advent of state funding, almost always based on a "body count" approach to reimbursement (x number of dollars per identified gifted student), placed additional pressure on schools to come up with tidy lists of exactly who qualified according to state-imposed guidelines. In an effort to address this very entrenched tradition, it was necessary to raise questions about the rationale for having special programs in the first place and to be prepared to examine the criticisms that are the inevitable weapons of the little wars mentioned in my opening quote by Boring (1963).

THE PURPOSE OF IDENTIFICATION AND SPECIAL PROGRAMS FOR THE GIFTED

The Why Question.   When I came on the scene in the late 1960s and early 1970s, a number of observations helped shape what eventually became the three-ring conception of giftedness and the enrichment triad model. The first observation had to do with the purpose of special programs. Implicit in any effort to define and identify a targeted group is the assumption that one will make special services available that capitalize on the characteristics that brought certain young people to one's attention in the first place. In other words, the why question supersedes the who and the how questions. Little attention had been given to the why question in gifted education literature, although many people had strongly held beliefs about why special programs and services are necessary supplements to general education. The discussion that follows about two types of giftedness and status versus action information was an early attempt on my part to bring the why question into the dialogue on gifted education. When attempting to sell a theory or new idea, it is sometimes necessary to deal with these larger (some would say, philosophical) issues to lay the groundwork for a proposed change in orientation. Getting someone into the "right" frame of mind can make a theory more palatable, especially if persons have not previously thought about the larger issues.

The literature on the gifted and talented has indicated that there are two generally accepted purposes for providing special education for high-potential youth. The first purpose is to provide young people with opportunities for maximum cognitive growth and self-fulfillment through the development and expression of one or a combination of performance areas in which superior potential may be present. The second purpose is to increase society's reservoir of persons who will help to solve the problems of contemporary civilization by becoming producers of knowledge and art rather than mere consumers of existing information. This second purpose, sometimes referred to as the "cure-for-cancer argument," was especially useful in gaining legislative and financial support. Most people would agree that the two goals are mutually supportive of one another. In other words, the productive and creative work of scientists, authors, artists, and leaders in all walks of life provide benefits to society and also result in feelings of accomplishment, self-fulfillment, and a positive attitude about one's self; and these characteristics are, in turn, important contributors to self-efficacy (Bandura, 1977), the belief that one is capable of subsequent and usually more advanced expressions of creative productivity.

Two Types of Giftedness. General consensus about these two purposes of special education for the gifted served as a rationale for both the conception of giftedness and the programming theories. Keeping the interaction of the two purposes of gifted education in mind, it is safe to conclude that special services and supplementary expenditures of public funds should be geared primarily toward increasing society's supply of potentially creative and productive adults. This conclusion has important implications for both the who and how questions, but most important, it led me to propose the difference between two types of giftedness—lesson-learning or "schoolhouse" giftedness on one hand and creative productive giftedness on the other.

Schoolhouse giftedness is the kind most easily measured by standardized ability tests, and therefore the type most conveniently used for selecting students for special programs. The competencies young people display on cognitive ability tests are exactly the kinds of abilities most valued in traditional school learning situations, especially those situations that focus on analytic skills rather than creative or practical skills. Research has shown a high correlation between schoolhouse giftedness and the likelihood of getting high grades in school and that superior lesson learning and test taking remain stable over time. Schoolhouse giftedness exists in varying degrees, can easily be identified through standardized and informal assessment techniques, and we should therefore do everything in our power to make appropriate modifications for students who have the ability to cover regular curricular material at advanced rates and levels of understanding than their age peers. These conclusions led me to develop one aspect of our programming model known as curriculum compacting (Renzulli, Smith, & Reis, 1982). Research on curriculum compacting (Reis et al., 1992) has shown that with as little as 3 hours of systematic training, teachers can eliminate up to 50% of regular curricular material for high-achieving students without causing any declines in standardized achievement test scores.

Although schoolhouse giftedness is valued and accommodated in our work, mainly through curriculum modification and replacement techniques, a major focus of the work has been on the second type of giftedness, which I have termed *creative productive giftedness*. Creative productive giftedness describes those aspects of human activity and involvement in which a premium is placed on the development of original ideas, products, artistic expressions, and areas of knowledge that are purposefully designed to have an impact on one or more target audiences. Learning situations that are designed to promote creative productive giftedness emphasize the use and application of knowledge and thinking processes in an integrated, inductive, and real-problem-oriented manner. The role of the student is transformed from that of a learner of prescribed lessons and consumer of information (however advanced) to one in which he or she uses the modus operandi of the firsthand inquirer. I have written in some detail about this transformed role of the learner (Renzulli, 1982a), and I only say at this point that it serves as the main rationale for the Type III dimension of the enrichment triad model discussed previously.

The idea for creative productive giftedness and the three-ring conception of giftedness came from the broad range of research I have reviewed on the nature of human abilities (Renzulli, 1978, 1982b, 1986) as well as numerous case studies about people of unusual accomplishment (both young people and adults) who would not have been identified or served in special programs if one relied solely on cognitive ability test scores. These observations have also led me to another conclusion about the temporal and situational nature of creative productive giftedness, and especially the creativity and task commitment components of the three-ring conception. Whereas lesson learning giftedness, which is mainly accounted for in the above average ability circle of the three-ring conception, tends to remain stable over time, persons do not always display maximum creativity or task commitment. Highly creative and productive people have peaks and valleys of high-level output. Some persons have commented that the valleys are as necessary as the peaks because they allow for reflection, regeneration, and the accumulation of input for subsequent endeavors.

Similarly, creative productive giftedness tends to be contextual or domain specific. Although there certainly have been a small number of "Renaissance" men and women who have gained recognition for work in several fields, the overwhelming number of persons who have been recognized for their outstanding accomplishments have almost always achieved in a single field or domain. There is no focus in the triad theory to encourage young people to major in a field at a very young age, although some of them do develop lifelong interests, and these interests should not be discouraged. Rather, the focus is to encourage bright young people to explore interests both vertically and horizontally, and if there is an encouragement toward anything, that thing is the joy of authentic inquiry, creativity, and an emerging sense of self as a person who can be a force in his or her selected field of study.

The temporal and situational nature of creative productive giftedness has resulted in some misunderstanding and criticism about the three-ring conception (Jarrell & Borland, 1990; Jellen, 1983, 1985; and Kontos, Carter, Ormrod, & Cooney, 1983) and some efforts on my part to address of this phenomenon (Renzulli, 1985, 1988b, 1990a; Renzulli & Owen, 1983). A good deal of the misunderstanding and related controversy lies in the difficulty of defining a complex concept without creating a semantic atrocity or dwelling on rhetorical arguments such as the differences in meaning between words such as *gifted* and *talented*. In my early writing on the topic, I made an attempt to clarify the concept by adding a figural representation in the form of three intersecting circles. This Venn diagram was intended to convey figurally the dynamic properties of the concept, that is, those properties pertaining to motion, interaction, continuous change, and energy rather than a fixed or static state. However, my best efforts at both semantic and figural communication have, nevertheless, resulted in interpretations that clearly were not intended. Consider, for example, a comment by Tannenbaum (1986) in which he states "Renzulli does not specify that giftedness requires the interplay of all three attributes in his model" (p. 31). I do indeed specify this, and it was for this very reason (i.e., interaction) that I chose to present the model figurally in the form of three overlapping rings. The primary purpose of a Venn diagram is to portray this type of interactive relationship.

The issue of performance versus potential is probably the aspect of my work on the conception of giftedness that is most frequently discussed in the literature. As an example, consider a discussion of the three-ring conception in a popular book for parents by Webb, Meckstroth, and Tolan (1982). However, first, allow me to highlight an important phrase from the original definition (Renzulli, 1978): "Gifted and talented children are those possessing *or capable of developing* [italics added] this composite set of traits and applying them to any potentially valuable area of human performance" (p. 261; italics were not in the original but perhaps should have been). My intention was to convey the message that candidates for special services need not manifest all three clusters but rather that students are identified as capable of developing these characteristics. Webb et al. (1982) seem to have overlooked or chosen to ignore the words that were highlighted in the previous quotation because in their book, they state the following:

> Another way of stating the Renzulli model is that superior ability, itself, is not enough—there must be high motivation to use that ability, and it must be expressed in creative ways, or to an unusual degree. Because it insists on the clear *expression* of giftedness, use of the Renzulli model overlooks many gifted children who, for a variety of reasons, are unwilling to demonstrate their talents in the ways being measured. (p. 49)

Similar statements can be found in the textbook literature (Davis & Rimm, 1985, p. 12; Gallagher, 1985, p. 8; Maker, 1982, p. 232), and there is a general tendency to conclude that the three-ring conception fails to take account of "gifted underachievers." Thus, for example, Gagne (1985) states "The factor that makes Renzulli's model inapplicable to underachievers is the presence of motivation as an essential component of giftedness" (p. 105); and

Davis and Rimm (1985) state "This model excludes underachievers" (p. 16). Similar statements focus on creativity. For example VanTassel-Baska (1998) comments, "… witness Renzulli's definition of giftedness, which excludes those children who do not display evidence of creativity" (p. 384).

Because, to my knowledge, none of the preceding commentators conducted any research on the broadened conception of giftedness or programs using the triad model or the three-ring conception of giftedness, I am left with the uneasy feeling that their conjecture is more journalistic than scientific. In point of fact, one of the few intervention studies in the research literature that shows highly favorable results for underachieving gifted students (Baum, Renzulli, & Hebert, 1995) is a study that selected participants based on the three-ring conception and used the enrichment triad as a direct intervention for counteracting underachievement.

The major reason for the interpretations I discussed previously undoubtedly lies in the type of research that led me to the conclusions that are summarized in the research rationale for the three-ring conception of giftedness (Renzulli, 1978, 1986). Because this research dealt mainly with factors that contributed to the development of creative and productive behavior in adults, an obvious but not necessarily valid conclusion on the parts of some writers is that these same traits should be required of children to gain admission to programs for the gifted. It is, therefore, only a short leap in logic to the kinds of statements I quoted previously and the belief that young people, regardless of ability, will be overlooked if they do not display task commitment or creativity. Clearly, this was not what I intended, and in fact, the three-ring theory drew on many anecdotal experiences with young people who developed exactly the same kinds of creative productivity that can be found in the literature about accomplished adults. However, to understand the rationale and the practical implications (for identification) of the three-ring conception, one must examine another major concept underlying the theory. This concept is the important distinction between two types of information that allow one to examine and estimate human potential.

If scores on IQ tests and other measures of cognitive ability only account for a limited proportion of the common variance with school grades, we can be equally certain that these measures do not tell the whole story when it comes to making predictions about creative-productive giftedness. Before defending this assertion with some research findings, I briefly review what is meant by this second type of giftedness, the important role that it should play in programming, and, therefore, the reasons practitioners should attempt to assess it in their identification procedures; even if such assessment causes one to look below the top 3% to 5% on the normal curve of IQ scores.

Creative-productive giftedness describes those aspects of human activity and involvement for which a premium is placed on the development of original material and products that are purposefully designed to have an impact on one or more target audiences. Learning situations that are designed to promote creative-productive giftedness emphasize the use and application of information (content) and thinking processes in an integrated, inductive, and real-problem-oriented manner. The role of the student is transformed from that of a learner of prescribed lessons to one in which she or he uses the modus operandi of a firsthand inquirer. This approach is quite different from the development of lesson-learning giftedness that tends to emphasize deductive learning; structured training in the development of thinking processes; and the acquisition, storage, and retrieval of information. In other words, creative-productive giftedness is simply putting one's abilities to work on problems and areas of study that have personal relevance to the student and that can be escalated to appropriately challenging levels of investigative activity. The roles that both students and teachers should play in the pursuit of these problems have been described elsewhere (Renzulli, 1982a, 1982b).

Why is creative-productive giftedness important enough for one to question the "tidy" and relatively easy approach that traditionally has been used to select students on the basis of test scores? Why do some people want to rock the boat by challenging a conception of giftedness that can be numerically defined by simply giving a test? The answers to these questions are simple and yet very compelling. The research has indicated that there is much more to the making of a gifted person than the abilities revealed on traditional tests of intelligence, aptitude, and achievement. Furthermore, history has indicated it has been the creative and productive people of the world, the producers rather than consumers of knowledge, the reconstructionists of thought in all areas of human endeavor, who have become recognized as "truly gifted" individuals. We know of the Einsteins, Edisons, and Carsons of the world because of what they did, not because of how they scored on tests! Also, it is these kinds of inquirers and creators that should be the major focus of who we serve in gifted education programs. History does not remember persons who merely scored well on IQ tests or those who learned their lessons well.

Status and Action Information

Status information consists of test scores, previous grades or accomplishments, teacher ratings, and anything else one can "put down on paper" beforehand that tells something about a person's traits and potentials. Status information is undoubtedly the best way for identifying students with high levels of schoolhouse giftedness, and it can also be used to identify a talent pool of above average ability students with potentials for creativity and task commitment. However, the temporal and contextual nature of creativity and task commitment in real and present problem situations require that one look for these behaviors within contexts where such behaviors are displayed, developed, and hopefully encouraged.

Action information, which has been described in detail elsewhere (Renzulli, Reis, & Smith, 1981), can best be defined as the type of dynamic interactions that take place when a person becomes extremely interested in or excited about a particular topic, area of study, issue, idea, or event that takes place within the school or the nonschool environment. These interactions (e.g., connections, insights, relations, discoveries, contacts) occur when students encounter or are influenced by persons, concepts, or particular pieces of knowledge. They create the proverbial "Ahas" that may become triggers for subsequent involvement. It is for this reason that I included Type I enrichment (general exploratory experiences) and Type II enrichment (group training activities) in the triad model. The influence of the interactions between and among the enrichment components may be relatively limited, or they may have a highly positive and extremely motivating effect on certain individuals. If the influence is strong enough and positive enough to promote further exploration and follow-up on the part of an individual or group of students with a common interest, then one may say that a dynamic interaction has taken place. These ideas, however good they may sound, must eventually be borne out in research settings, so I now turn the reader's attention to research about the theories and strategies for using the research in the acceptance finding process.

THE ROLE OF RESEARCH IN THE CHANGE PROCESS

No single research study can ever verify or negate a complex theory, especially a theory that has multidimensional application processes. To translate the previously mentioned theories into practice, my colleagues Reis, Smith, and I (Renzulli et al., 1981) developed an identification system and service delivery model that respects the tenants of the theories and that could be used as the bases for a variety of empirical studies. These studies have been summarized elsewhere (Renzulli & Reis, 1994) and are periodically updated at the Web site (www.gifted.uconn.edu/sem/rrsem.html). The essence of the identification system is to provide general or targeted (by ability level, domain, or interest area) "talent pools" of students with a broad variety of general enrichment experiences (Types I and II in the enrichment triad model as well as opportunities to follow up on regular school curricular experiences and noncurricular interests) and to use the ways in which students respond to these experiences to determine who and in which areas of study students should revolve into Type III enrichment opportunities. In addition to the general enrichment provided in special program situations, we also trained classroom teachers to use a form called the

"Action Information Message" so that they could serve as referral agents whenever students reacted in highly positive ways to regular classroom experiences (Renzulli et al., 1981).

Although this approach to identification and programming departs significantly from traditional practices, its effectiveness has been documented by a series of research studies and field tests in schools with widely varying socioeconomic levels and program organizational patterns. The most important study (Reis & Renzulli, 1982) conducted in the early stages of our research used a population of 1,162 students in Grades 1 through 6 in 11 school districts. Reis and Renzulli (1982) study examined several variables related to the identification system based on the three-ring conception of giftedness and the effectiveness of the triad model. The talent pools in each participating school were designated (but not divided) into two groups. Group A consisted of students who scored in the top 5% on standardized tests of intelligence and achievement. Group B consisted of students who scored between 10 to 15 percentile points below the top 5% and/or who were rated highly by teachers using the "Scales for Rating the Behavioral Characteristics of Superior Students" (Renzulli, Smith, White, Callahan, & Hartman, 1976). Both groups participated equally in all program activities, and they were not aware of their group designations.

Reis and Renzulli (1982) used an instrument entitled the Student Product Assessment Form (SPAF; Reis, 1981; Reis & Renzulli, 1982) to compare the quality of products emanating from each group. This instrument provides individual ratings for eight specific characteristics of product quality and seven factors related to overall product quality. The validity and reliability of the SPAF were established through a yearlong series of studies that yielded reliability coefficients as high as .98. A double-blind method of product coding was used so that judges did not know group membership (i.e., Group A or B) when evaluating individual products. No significant differences were found between Group A and Group B on the quality of students' products. These findings lend support to the concept that students who are above average but not necessarily superior in general ability are capable of producing high-quality products when they participate on an equal basis in a programming model that focuses on creative productivity. Reis and Renzulli (1982) concluded that there was justification for inclusion of a broader spectrum of students in this type of program than the traditional top 5% on which traditional programs focus.

Reis and Renzulli (1982) used questionnaires and interviews to examine several other factors related to overall program effectiveness. The data indicated that feelings about the triad program—gathered from classroom teachers, administrators, students in the talent pools, and their parents—were generally positive. Many classroom teachers reported that their high level of involvement in the program had favorably influenced their teaching practices and their overall attitudes toward gifted programs in general. Parents whose children had been placed previously in traditional programs for the gifted (Group A) did not differ in their opinions about the programs' value and effectiveness from parents whose children had been identified as gifted under the expanded three-ring conception criteria, and resource teachers—many of whom had been involved previously in traditional programs for the gifted—overwhelmingly preferred the expanded talent-pool approach to traditional reliance on test scores alone. Posttreatment questionnaires and interviews indicated, among other things, that resource teachers especially appreciated working with students who showed a greater diversity of interests and creative ideas. In fact, several resource teachers in the experimental study said that they would resign or request transfers to regular classrooms if their school systems reverted to traditional identification practices.

Additional research in the early stages of theory testing (Delisle & Renzulli, 1982) examined academic self-concept and locus of control. Delisle and Renzulli's study established the importance of nonintellective factors in creative production and verified earlier research related to the three-ring conception of giftedness. Using a stepwise multiple regression technique to study the correlates of creative production, Gubbins (1982) found that above-average ability is a necessary but not sufficient condition for high-level productivity. The roles of task commitment and time commitment and the importance of student interests were verified. Several factors related to improved productivity were identified. A study of student, parent, and classroom teachers' attitudes toward the model (Delisle, Reis, & Gubbins, 1981) revealed support for this approach and a high degree of cooperation among all persons involved in the implementation of this type of program. These studies have also shown that a more flexible approach to identification helped to minimize attitudes of elitism and promoted a "radiation of excellence" (Ward, 1961) throughout the buildings in which the model was implemented.

THE POLITICS OF EDUCATIONAL RESEARCH

Knowing that yet another research study and derivative articles seldom have an impact among policymakers led the researchers of the National Research Center on the Gifted and Talented to develop a research-into-action strategy that paid off in a far shorter period of time than the usual trickle-down effect of most research. Amidst much fanfare and publicity, a meeting was organized that included the superintendents who agreed to allow the previously mentioned research (Reis, 1981; Reis & Renzulli, 1982; Gubbins, 1982) to take place, state department of education (SDE) personnel (in the areas of both gifted education and research/evaluation), and the state commissioner of education. Members of this group agreed to have SDE personnel monitor the research, and they agreed to make changes in state identification regulations if the research warranted such change. The commissioner's involvement was critical, and this research could not have gone forward without the support of a person at the highest level who was regarded as a courageous and progressive leader. The research results clearly supported a more flexible approach to identification of students for gifted programs, but when it came to changing regulations, the SDE personnel started to get a bit indecisive! However, when the research team reminded them of the original agreement and said that we would send the report directly to the commissioner if they would not, quick action resulted! Within a week, a letter and executive summary of our research was sent to every superintendent and gifted program director in the state informing them that our identification system was a legally allowable alternative. In the years that followed, many schools adopted the identification system, and because the research was conducted in what many considered to be a leading state in gifted education, we were able to have an influence beyond our own state borders. Some of the influence resulted from research articles, articles written for practitioner audiences, and numerous presentations on the state gifted conference circuit. One thing we learned about the change process is that a little research goes a long way in influencing policy, and when well packaged in the form of practitioner-friendly examples of effective adaptations of the model, it goes even further. Also, the procedural research is further enhanced when practitioners are provided with practical, inexpensive, well-researched instruments that can be used in theory-driven identification and service activities. Teacher rating scales (Renzulli et al., 1976) and interest (Renzulli, 1977b), learning styles (Renzulli, Rizza, & Smith, 1997), and expression style inventories (Kettle, Renzulli, & Rizza, 1998) that are compatible with the theories make it easier for practitioners to use recommended models and thus serve to facilitate theory into practice.

The identification system I described previously is the one that is most consistent with the two theories that are the subject of this chapter, but translating theory into practice sometimes involves accommodations that take into account state and local policies that require having "names on a list" before any services are rendered. To address this political reality, a modified identification model was developed that does respect preselection requirements but that also asks schools to "leave some room" in their preselected body of students who can gain entrance on the basis of nontest criteria (Renzulli, 1990a). An article dealing with this identification system was published in a nongifted field journal (Renzulli & Smith, 1990) because I felt it was, once again, necessary to reach out to a larger and more responsive audience than might be found in the gifted establishment.

Navigating the Rocky Road : From Frustration To Application

Although submitting the three-ring conception of giftedness article to the *Phi Delta Kappan* (Renzulli, 1978) was an act born out of disappointment and frustration, it had an unexpected effect! Many persons in general education, especially school administrators, who previously had unfavorable attitudes toward programs for the gifted began to raise questions about greater flexibility in identification. Sometimes these attitudes were based on "philosophic" concerns about equity and fairness in the allocation of resources. Practical issues accounted for the unfavorable attitudes of others. Scheduling problems, pushy parents, the costs of individual testing, and conflicts between classroom teachers and teachers of the gifted led many educators to look for alternatives to traditional approaches for identification and programming, and in overseas nations, especially in Western Europe and some of the Asian countries, the socialist democracies were cautious about programs that categorized students along what they perceived to be class lines. Questions were raised with gifted education professionals at local and state levels about the possibility of different approaches and requests for reprints of the *Phi Delta Kappan* article (Renzulli, 1978) and permission to reprint it in collections of readings far exceeded my fondest expectations.

High levels of continuing interest caused me to establish an institute in the summer of 1978, and once again, enrollment far exceeded my expectations. Although the institute attracted a small number of skeptics and persons who were sent by school districts against their will, the majority of participants were liberal-minded educators who were seeking greater flexibility in identifying students and providing services—I called them positive malcontents! The institute, named Confratute (intended to convey the best aspects of a *conf*erence and an inst*itute* with a measure of *frat*ernity blended within) continues today after more than 26 years and has a cumulative enrollment approaching 20,000 participants. Although persons attending Confratute are made aware of the theoretical and research underpinnings of this work, the major focus is on practical strategies for implementing the theories in a variety of school settings. To this end, expert practitioners serve as the faculty for Confratute—persons with extensive experience in implementing the model, the majority of whom work in schools delivering services on a daily basis. Many Confratute faculty members were former participants in the summer program, and several have gone on to pursue graduate degrees at the University of Connecticut. Both participants and faculty have become, in effect, local, state, and sometimes even national emissaries for the types of services advocated in the theories underlying our work. It is not unusual to find them making presentations at conferences, conducting workshops for school districts, submitting articles to research and teacher-oriented professional journals, teaching college courses, and serving on committees that influence policy and practice in their respective states and school districts. Equally important are the unique approaches, materials, and innovations that many of these persons have contributed to practical implementation strategies, and even in this regard, communication is a critical ingredient. Through newsletters, Web sites, and invitations to practitioners to participate in various training venues, valuable information enhances the practical application of the theories and causes dedicated professionals to feel part of a "movement" that is having an impact on schools and students.

LESSONS LEARNED ABOUT TRANSLATING THEORY INTO PRACTICE

As I indicated earlier, translating theory into practice is all about organizational and policy change and the strategies necessary to enlist the support of practitioners who are ultimately responsible for implementing theory-driven change in an authentic fashion. Change that has its origins in the academic world usually occurs in one of two ways! A person or group has what they consider to be a big, bold, and obviously important idea, and they set the wheels in motion to slay Goliath by influencing policymakers and capturing the minds and hearts of those who they are convinced will benefit from the idea. Grand theories and systems, usually put forth by individuals from powerful institutions with high degrees of source credibility, come into the academic marketplace and become the stuff out of which great movements arise, and sometimes controversy is spawned. The major change strategy is the publication of books or articles in influential journals and keynote presentations before major professional societies. This type of change begins as a behemoth and steamrolls its way to acceptance or garners much scrutiny and controversy in the academic community. Gardner's (1983) book on multiple intelligences is an example of the first, and Herrnstein and Murray's (1994) book on the bell curve (come to mind) is an example of the second occurrence. If the work has aspirations for change among practitioners (e.g., therapists, educators, counselors), then another level of acceptance finding must be pursued. A high degree of academic source credibility and a strong research base are decided advantages in the change process (every administrator likes to gain support for newly adopted initiatives by arguing that "research says," especially if this research is initiated at a highly prestigious university), but winning the hearts and minds of practitioners requires another level of change strategies. This level includes understanding teachers' ways of knowing, providing information that makes sense to practitioners, developing personal relations that show respect on the part of the researcher toward practitioners (i.e. not talking down to them), and being willing to make modifications based on their tacit knowledge about the ways schools operate. Personalities are as important to promoting effective change as are good science and elegant designs!

A second approach, and the one that I believe has led to the widespread use of my work, is more modest in its origins and focuses on a bottom-up strategy. The main audience for persuasive communication vehicles has been teachers, gifted program coordinators, and building principals. Articles in "softer" journals such as *The Elementary Principal* and *Educational Leadership,* and presentations at practitioner rather than researcher conferences certainly call attention to the research base that supports the theories, but the main message is the what and the how of practices based on the theories. These articles and presentations have described and provided numerous examples about actual implementations of the theories. A recurring theme is what teachers have done to bring about various types of student involvement.

This second approach to persuasive communication does not ignore the importance of theory and research but usually presents it in a practitioner friendly way (less technical jargon, tabular summaries of research, classroom examples that illustrate a theoretical concept). It is almost always targeted toward journals that teachers and other practitioners read, even though they may be less prestigious than the scholarly journals that launch new initiatives mentioned in the first approach I mentioned previously. Make no mistake, this bottom-up approach has reached policymakers and brought about changes in regulations at district and state levels, but it is the success stories and the practitioner satisfaction rather than the hard-core theory and research that has usually influenced their ultimate adoption of a theory.

In conclusion, Keynes understood the change process when he wrote:

The real difficulty in changing

the course of any enterprise

lies not in developing new ideas

but in escaping from the old ones.

—*John Maynard Keynes* (1936, p. xxxiii)

REFERENCES

Albert, R. S. (1975). Toward a behavioral definition of genius. *American Psychologist,* *30,* 140–151.

Bandura, A. (1977). Self efficacy mechanism in human agency. *American Psychologist,* *37,* 122–147.

Barron, F. (1969). *Creative Person and Creative Process.* New York: Holt, Rinehart & Winston.

Baum, S. M., Renzulli, J. S., & Hebert, T. P. (1995). Reversing underachievement: Creative productivity as a systematic intervention. *Gifted Child Quarterly, 39*, 224–235.

Bloom, B. (Ed.). (1964). *Stability and change in human characteristics.* New York: Wiley.

Bloom, B. (Ed). (1985). *Developing talent in young people.* New York: Ballantine.

Bloom, B. S., & Sosniak, L. A. (1981). Talent development vs. schooling. *Educational Leadership, 39*(2), 86–94.

Boring, E. G. (1963). History, psychology, and science: Selected papers. New York: Wiley.

Bruner, J. S. (1966). *Toward a theory of instruction.* Cambridge, MA: Belknap Press of Harvard University.

Bruner, J. S. (1990). *Acts of meaning.* Cambridge, MA: Harvard University Press.

Busse, T. V., & Mansfield, R. S. (1980). Renzulli is right. *Gifted Child Quarterly, 24,* 132.

Csikszentmihalyi, M. (1991). *Flow: The psychology of optimal experience.* New York: HarperCollins.

Davis, G. A., & Rimm, S. B. (1985). *Education of the gifted and talented.* Englewood Cliffs, NJ: Prentice Hall.

Delisle, J. R., Reis, S. M., & Gubbins, E. J. (1981). The revolving door identification model and programming model. *Exceptional Children, 48,* 152–156.

Delisle, J. R., & Renzulli, J. S. (1982). The revolving door identification and programming model: Correlates of creative production. *Gifted Child Quarterly, 26,* 89–95.

Dewey, J. (1956). *Child and the curriculum and the school and society.* Chicago: University of Chicago Press.

Gagne, F. (1985). Giftedness and talent: Reexamining a reexamination of the definitions. *Gifted Child Quarterly, 29,* 103–112.

Gallagher, J. J. (1985). *Teaching the gifted child* (3rd ed.). Boston: Allyn & Bacon.

Gardner, H. (1983). *Frames of mind: The theory of multiple intelligences.* Needham Heights, MA: Allyn & Bacon.

Gubbins, J. (1982). *Revolving door identification model: Characteristics of talent pool students.* Unpublished doctoral dissertation, University of Connecticut, Storrs.

Herrnstein, R. J., & Murray, C. (1994). *The bell curve: Intelligence and class structure in American life.* New York: Free Press.

Holland, J. L., & Astin, A. W. (1962). The prediction of the academic, artistic, scientific and social achievement of undergraduates of superior scholastic aptitude. *Journal of Educational Psychology, 53,* 182–183.

Jarrell, R. H., & Borland, J. H. (1990). The research base for Renzulli's three ring conception of giftedness. *Journal for the Education of the Gifted, 13,* 288–308.

Jellen, H. G. (1983, November 14). *Renzulli-itis: A national disease in gifted education.* Paper presented at the Illinois State Conference on the Gifted, Peoria, IL.

Jellen, H. G. (1985). Renzulli's enrichment scheme for the gifted: Educational accommodation of the gifted in the American context. *Gifted Education International, 3,* 12–17.

Kettle, K., Renzulli, J. S., & Rizza, M. G. (1998). Products of mind: Exploring student preferences for product development using My Way ... An Expression Style Instrument. *Gifted Child Quarterly, 42,* 49–60.

Keynes, J. M. (1936). *The general theory of employment, interest and money.* Cambridge, MA: Macmillan Cambridge University Press.

Kontos, S., Carter, K. R., Ormrod, J. E., & Cooney, J. B. (1983). Reversing the revolving door: A strict interpretation of Renzulli's definition of giftedness. *Roeper Review, 6,* 35–38.

Maker, J. (1982). *Teaching models in education of the gifted.* Rockville, MD: Aspen.

McCurdy, H. G. (1960). The childhood patterns of genius. *Horizon,* 32–41.

Montessori, M. (1964). *Absorbent mind* (Claude A Claremont, Trans.). New York: Dell.

Montessori, M. (1967). *Advanced Montessori method*. Cambridge, MA: R. Bentley.

Nicholls, J. G. (1972). Creativity in the Person Who Will Never Produce Anything Original
and Useful: The Concept of Creativity as a Normally Distributed Trait. *American Psychologist, 27,* 717–727.

Reis, S. M. (1981). *An analysis of the productivity of gifted students participating in programs of gifted students participating in programs using the revolving door identification model.* Unpublished doctoral dissertation, University of Connecticut, Storrs.

Reis, S. M., & Renzulli, J. S. (1982). A research report on the revolving door identification model: A case for the broadened conception of giftedness. *Phi Delta Kappan, 63,* 619–620.

Reis, S. M., Westberg, K. L., Kulikowich, J., Caillard, F., Hebert, T. P., Purcell, J. H., Rogers, J., Smist, J., & Plucker, J. A. (1992). *Technical report of the curriculum compacting study.* Storrs: The National Research Center on the Gifted and Talented, University of Connecticut.

Renzulli, J. S. (1977a). *The enrichment triad model: A guide for developing defensible programs for the gifted and talented.* Mansfield Center, CT: Creative Learning Press.

Renzulli, J. S. (1977b). *Interest-a-lyzer.* Mansfield Center, CT: Creative Learning Press.

Renzulli, J. S. (1978). What makes giftedness? Reexamining a definition. *Phi Delta Kappan, 60,* 180–184, 261.

Renzulli, J. S. (1982a). Dear Mr. and Mrs. Copernicus: We regret to inform you … *Gifted Child Quarterly, 26,* 11–14.

Renzulli, J. S. (1982b). What makes a problem real: Stalking the illusive meaning of qualitative differences in gifted education. *Gifted Child Quarterly, 26,* 147–156.

Renzulli, J. S. (1985). A bull's eye on my back: The perils and pitfalls of trying to bring about educational change. *Gifted Education International, 3,* 18–23.

Renzulli, J. S. (1986). The three ring conception of giftedness: A developmental model for creative productivity. In R. J. Sternberg & J. E. Davidson (Eds.), *Conceptions of giftedness* (pp. 53–92). New York: Cambridge University Press.

Renzulli, J. S. (1988a). The multiple menu model for developing differentiated curriculum for the gifted and talented. *Gifted Child Quarterly, 32,* 298–309.

Renzulli, J. S. (Ed.). (1988b). *Technical report on research studies related to the revolving door identification model.* Storrs: Bureau of Educational Research, The University of Connecticut.

Renzulli, J. S. (1990a). A practical system for identifying gifted and talented students. *Early Childhood Development, 63,* 9–18.

Renzulli, J. S. (1990b). Torturing data until they confess: An analysis of the three ring conception of giftedness. *Journal for the Education of the Gifted, 13,* 309–331.

Renzulli, J. S., & Owen, S. V. (1983). The revolving door identification model: If it ain't busted don't fix it, if you don't understand it don't nix it. *Roeper Review, 6,* 39–41.

Renzulli, J. S., Smith, L. H., & Reis, S. M. (1982). Curriculum compacting: An essential strategy for working with gifted students. *The Elementary School Journal, 82,* 185–194.

Renzulli, J. S., & Reis, S. M. (1985). *The schoolwide enrichment model: A comprehensive plan for educational excellence.* Mansfield Center, CT: Creative Learning Press.

Renzulli, J. S., & Reis, S. M. (1994). Research related to the schoolwide enrichment model. *Gifted Child Quarterly, 38,* 7–20.

Renzulli, J. S., & Reis, S. M. (1997). *The schoolwide enrichment model: A how-to guide for educational excellence.* Mansfield Center, CT: Creative Learning Press.

Renzulli, J. S., Reis, S. M., & Smith, L. (1981). *The revolving door identification model.* Mansfield Center, CT: Creative Learning Press.

Renzulli, J. S., Rizza, M. G., & Smith, L. H. (1997). *The learning styles inventory.* Mansfield Center, CT: Creative Learning Press.

Renzulli, J. S., & Smith. L. H. (1990). A practical system for identifying gifted and talented students. *Early Child Development and Care, 63,* 9–18.

Renzulli, J. S., Smith, L. H., White, A. J., Callahan, C. M., & Hartman, R. K. (1976). *Scales for rating the behavioral characteristics of superior students* (Rev. ed.). Mansfield Center, CT: Creative Learning Press.

Roe, A. (1952). *The making of a scientist.* New York: Dodd, Mead.

Simonton, D. K. (1978). History and the eminent person. *Gifted Child Quarterly, 22,* 187–195.

Simonton, D. K. (1994). *Greatness: Who makes history and why.* New York: Guilford.

Snelbecker, G. E. (1974). *Learning theory, instructional theory, and psychoeducational design.* New York: McGraw-Hill.

Sternberg, R. J. (1984). Toward a triarchic theory of human intelligence. *Behavioral and Brain Sciences, 7,* 269–316.

Sternberg, R. J. (1985). A componential theory of intellectual giftedness. *Gifted Child Quarterly, 25,* 86–93.

Sternberg, R. J. (1999). The theory of successful intelligence. *Review of General Psychology, 3,* 292–316.

Tannenbaum, A. J. (1986). Giftedness: A psychosocial approach. In R. J. Sternberg & J. E. Davidson (Eds.), *Conceptions of giftedness* (pp. 21–52). New York: Cambridge University Press.

Terman, L. M. (1916). *The measurement of intelligence.* Boston: Houghton Mifflin Co.

Treffinger, D. J. (1987). [*Critical issues in gifted education*]. *Journal for the Education of the Gifted, 10,* 324–331.

VanTassel-Baska, J. (1998). *Excellence in educating gifted and talented learners.* Denver, CO: Love.

Wallach, M. A., & Wing, C. W., Jr. (1969). *The talented students: A validation of the creativity intelligence distinction.* New York: Holt, Rinehart & Winston.

Ward, V. (1961). *Educating the gifted: An axiomatic approach.* Columbus. OH: Merrill.

Webb, J. T., Meckstroth, E. A., & Tolan, S. S. (1982). *Guiding the gifted child.* Columbus, OH: Ohio Psychology Publishing Company.

Zuckerman, M. (1979). Attribution of success and failure revisited: or The motivational bias is alive and well in attribution theory. *Journal of Personality, 47*(2), 245–287.

11

Multiple Intelligences: Developments in Implementation and Theory

Mindy L. Kornhaber
Pennsylvania State University

Howard Gardner
Harvard University

Theoretical perspectives generated by social and behavioral researchers are often left on the sidelines of educational practice. Gardner's (1983/1993) theory of multiple intelligences (MI) suffers no such neglect. Gardner (1983/1993) first published the theory in his 1983 book, *Frames of Mind: The Theory of Multiple Intelligences* (Gardner, 1983). That book has now been translated into 11 languages. Educators throughout the United States, and from Europe, Australia, South America, and Asia have written to us to say they are applying the theory. They are doing so at every grade level from prekindergarten through college, for students in regular classrooms and schools, and in those designed for students with learning disabilities, gifted students, juveniles in detention centers, adults lacking literacy skills, and other special populations.

The main "problem" with MI is not a dearth of translation into practice. Rather, the extensive implementation of the theory has itself led to at least two other conundra. The first conundrum entails figuring out why MI—a theory about the mind, not educational practice—has been so widely translated even in the absence of an organization to promote it or Gardner-produced, "off-the-shelf" materials to support its use. The second conundrum concerns quality control. Given that the theory was not accompanied by suggestions for how to apply it in schools, it is hardly surprising that educators' translations vary enormously in quality. What, if anything, can be done to complement the theory with some reasonable guidelines for its use now that it is actually in widespread practice?

We begin the chapter by briefly describing the theory. We then take up the two conundra generated by the unanticipated, mass implementation of MI: First, why is MI adopted? Answers to this question offer potentially useful insights for other theories and research that are aimed at influencing educational practice. Second, we address the issue of quality control. We do this both theoretically by considering the contribution of disciplinary understanding to quality practice and empirically by presenting research aimed at identifying and disseminating sound practices associated with MI. We conclude by exploring the possibilities for, and intersections between, future developments in MI theory and practice.

THE THEORY OF MI

Gardner's (1983/1993) endeavor to develop and promulgate MI had two starting points. First, Gardner (1983/1993) sought to organize into a useful and defensible framework the extant data on cognitive development and brain organization. Second, Gardner (1983/1993) focused on the enormous diversity of human end states—adult roles undertaken across human cultures—and sought to develop a theory of intelligence that helped to explain this diversity. Gardner (1983/1993) wanted to understand, for example, what set of mental functions might explain the diverse accomplishments of mathematicians and shamans, Romantic poets, and Puluwat navigators (see, e.g., Bate, 1963; Gladwin, 1970; Hardy, 1967; Harner, 1990).

In its original version, the theory stated that there were a number (originally seven, now eight) of "relatively autonomous" intelligences. This view contrasted with the notion of one, overarching general intelligence, "g" that had by then dominated psychometric thinking for nearly 80 years (Spearman, 1904). Opposition to g was not new. However, both the evidence for g as well as volleys against it were driven by efforts to explain and analyze data from intelligence test batteries (e.g., Guilford, 1967; Horn & Cattell, 1966; Thomson, 1939; Thurstone, 1938; Vernon, 1950). In contrast, Gardner's (1983/1993) theory was not centered around psychometric approaches. It originated out of a set of criteria by which he assessed candidate abilities or intelligences that together enabled humans to undertake varied adult roles. These criteria included:

- Potential isolation of the intelligence by brain damage as in cases of brain injury that may impair language comprehension but leave musical functioning intact.
- The existence of special populations, such as prodigies and autistic savants, who manifest one or two exceptional capacities, whereas other capacities may be normal or even impaired.
- Evolutionary history and plausibility, which indicate current mental functions evolved from selection pressures (e.g., human ancestors likely needed skill in making sense of the behaviors of others).
- One or more core operations that process information particular to that intelligence (e.g., in music, pitch discrimination and rhythm are core functions, whereas syntax and phonemic distinctions are central to language).
- Susceptibility to encoding in a symbol system: Intelligences help to convey important cultural information; symbol systems have been developed to make such information readily transmissible (hence, maps, musical notation, gestural notation, mathematical notations, and writing).
- A distinct developmental history culminating in identifiable expert end states. Intelligences are manifested in cultural activities, which have their own developmental histories (e.g., the development from early manifestations of musical ability to professional musician has different paths and milestones than the development of a socially aware child into a clinical psychologist).
- Experimental psychological tasks aimed at teasing apart different mental operations through observations of how people process two simultaneous activities. The ability simultaneously to walk and talk indicates separate processing abilities for motoric and language capacities.
- Psychometric findings, which have often yielded evidence for separable spatial and linguistic capacities, and newer investigations also support an independent capacity for social/emotional intelligence (Rosnow, Skedler, Jaeger, & Rind, 1994).

Using these criteria, Gardner (1999a) has now identified eight intelligences. Gardner (1999c) defines an intelligence as "a psychobiological potential to process information that can be activated in a cultural setting to solve problems or create products that are of value in a culture" (pp. 33–34). The eight intelligences, very briefly, are

1. Linguistic intelligence features sensitivity to language in spoken and/or written forms, the ability to learn languages, and to use language in pursuit of one's goals.
2. Logical-mathematical intelligence concerns the capacities for mathematical operations, logical analyses, and scientific investigation.

3. Musical intelligence facilitates composition, performance, and appreciation of musical patterns.
4. Bodily-kinesthetic intelligence involves the use of all or parts of the body to solve problems or fashion products.
5. Spatial intelligence entails the perception, use, and transformation of spatial information.
6. Interpersonal intelligence enables individuals to recognize and make distinctions among others' feelings and intentions.
7. Intrapersonal intelligence helps individuals to understand themselves and to use this understanding effectively to manage their own lives.
8. Naturalist intelligence allows people to distinguish among, classify, and use features of the environment.

Some Finer Points

Despite these separable descriptions of the intelligences, Gardner (1983/1993, 1999a) emphasizes that in the absence of brain damage, all individuals possess all the intelligences as part of their species membership. What differs among individuals is the relative strengths and weaknesses in their "profiles of intelligence." In addition, Gardner underscores that the intelligences are harnessed together to master academic disciplines and to carry out real-world activities. For example, a musician certainly relies on musical intelligence to interpret and perform a musical composition. However, controlling one's voice or instrument entails bodily-kinesthetic intelligence, and stage presence demands interpersonal intelligence. Recently, Gardner (2003) has distinguished a third dimension of the concept of intelligence: the manner in which a practitioner uses her skill or expertise in the service of a goal. An individual with musical intelligence can give a performance of a work that is either intelligent or not, depending on his or her goals and how these goals are or are not achieved (Gardner, 2003).

It is worthwhile to note that Gardner's list of intelligences is provisional (Gardner, 1983/1993, 1999a). Additional intelligences could be added if they meet most or all of the eight criteria we noted previously (Gardner, 1999a). As we discuss in more detail in this chapter's conclusion, Gardner also sees modifications of the theory as appropriate responses to growing understanding of the conceptual distinction between intelligence and disciplinary understanding and to more recent breakthroughs in neuroscience.

TWO CONUNDRA

Gardner (1983/1993) put forth MI with the aim of reorganizing psychology's conception of intelligence. Psychologists were typically not swayed (e.g., Herrnstein & Murray, 1994; Scarr, 1985). The theory's arm-length reception among mainstream psychologists stands in marked contrast to that offered by teachers and other educational practitioners. Within a very few years of the theory's publication, individual teachers began to apply the theory in their classrooms. Then, in 1987, a group of public school teachers in Indianapolis organized the Key School, the first school based on MI. Although this group actually did meet with Gardner to discuss their ideas, their implementations were largely of their own design. It was a pioneering effort, and like many such efforts, it drew largely on intuitive ideas and personal experience. Similarly, the later torrent of individual teachers and whole schools that adopted MI based translations on their own instincts or those suggested by consultants or staff developers who had independently devised their own ideas (and small industry) about the forms that MI-influenced practice should take. At this point, as we noted previously, MI appears to have been put into practice on six continents and been adopted for every imaginable student population. Indeed, the theory has taken on the quality of a "meme" (Dawkins, 1976), an idea that has been passed along so frequently that it has become part of the culture (Gardner, 2004).

That educators and staff developers so readily took to MI is remarkable in light of how little guidance for its use was offered. The book in which Gardner (1983/1993) first published the theory, *Frames of Mind: The Theory of Multiple Intelligences,* offers perhaps six paragraphs of direct information on this topic (see Gardner, 1983/1993, pp. 386–392, passim). Even these are notably abstract. For example, Gardner (1983/1993) briefly mentions that assessment should entail monitoring youngsters as they work with "inherently engrossing materials" (p. 386) and that such assessments, over perhaps a month's time, may enable teachers to develop better matches between educational regimens and individual students. The paucity of information relevant to practitioners is also reflected in the book's index. A scan of that reveals no entries for such fundamentals as curriculum, instruction, pedagogy, teachers, or testing. Furthermore, unlike other research-based ideas that have influenced education—such as Accelerated Schools (Levin, 1999), the School Development Program (Comer, 1988; Comer & Emmons, 1999), or Success for All (Slavin, Madden, Dolan, & Wasik, 1996)—MI provided no guidelines about such practical matters as professional development, school governance, organizational structures, or community involvement. Nor did its founder institute a field staff to support the implementation of his ideas and to evaluate their use.

These obvious lacunae, in conjunction with the theory's widespread adoption, raise our first conundrum: Why is MI so broadly adopted? What is it about MI that makes it attractive to practitioners across an enormous variety of cultures, educational settings, and student populations? What lessons might be learned from understanding this question that could be useful to other educational researchers and theorists whose work is actually intended to influence practice?

The second conundrum is related to the first. It concerns quality control. Of course, with the exception of a few research-driven programs that tightly dictate curriculum and how it is to be doled out by teachers, quality control is generally a problem for research and scholarship that enter the classroom. Yet, this is especially so for MI. Because its implementation is driven by the ideas of the educators and consultants who adopted it, the quality of "MI practice" varies accordingly. Observers of the MI "scene" have thus offered both glowing reports and sweeping condemnations. This situation raises another set of questions: What practices are being used in schools that associate MI with improvements for students? Relatedly, once these practices are identified, is it possible now to begin to influence—corral?—the enormous diversity of MI practices so that they support important educational aims?

Both conundra have spurred empirical investigations of practice. These investigations, which we describe following, provide new and grounded understandings of why and how MI operates in the educational world.

WHY IS MI ADOPTED?

Two investigations have been launched to help shed light on the question of why MI is adopted (Kornhaber, Fierros, & Veenema, 2004; Kornhaber & Krechevsky, 1995). Kornhaber and Krechevsky (1995) sought to provide an initial description of the state of MI in educational practice. The Kornhaber and Krechevsky study sample consisted of nine diverse sites. The sample was in no way random. It was drawn from a collection of site-initiated correspondence with Gardner or his associates at Project Zero or from information reported to Gardner by visitors to the sites. To be selected, each site was required to have been using MI in classrooms for at least 2 years. The sites ranged in scope from a single teacher who had been intensively using MI since shortly after its publication to several schools within a large northeastern urban school district in which central office staff had supported the theory's adoption. One site was a middle school. The rest served elementary-age populations.

Data for the study came from several sources including interviews, documents, and observations. The initial information was gathered through semistructured individual phone interviews with the primary person responsible for the theory's adoption in the site. This was sometimes an individual teacher, sometimes a central office administrator, but typically a principal. The interview asked for background information about the site and surrounding school district, about how the educator first encountered MI, and how MI was implemented. There were also questions about approaches to curriculum, assessment, pedagogy, materials, parent conferences, school structure, and organization. Following these interviews, most sites sent written materials. These varied across sites, spanning report card forms, grant proposals, newspaper articles about the site, program descriptions, and one initial evaluation. In addition, Kornhaber and Krechevsky visited each site for about a day. The visits entailed classroom observations; many informal conversations with faculty, administrators, and students; and teacher interviews. A total of 91 teachers were interviewed. The teacher interviews paralleled the substance of the earlier phone interviews.

This study revealed that educators adopted the theory for a relatively small set of reasons.

MI Validated What Educators Already Know About Learning. Educators commonly mentioned that their everyday observations were very much in line with the theory's idea that people learn in a variety of ways. That a Harvard psychologist's theory validated their experiences encouraged educators to plumb the theory's implications for practice. As one administrator explained, "I think teachers—good teachers anyway—have been making provisions for those kids [different kinds of learners], but feeling a great sense of guilt.... Now they can keep the door [to their classrooms] open."

MI Complemented Educators' Existing Philosophies and Beliefs. For example, educators felt that MI aligned well with a constructivist philosophy and with beliefs about educating the whole child and that all children should experience success in at least one area. A teacher explained that after reading *Frames of Mind* (Gardner, 1983/1993), she thought, "I finally read somebody who's done something that validates what I've always believed."

Educators Already Used Some Practices That Fit With the Theory. Some of the practices educators were already using enabled them to draw on a range of intelligences. These included project-based curriculum, arts-integrated approaches, thematic units, learning centers, and experiential, "hands-on" learning. One administrator noted, "A lot of what I think MI is about—and a lot of the manifestations—we were doing. So, it fits us really, really well."

MI Provided a Framework for Organizing Educators' Practice. Teachers, like other skilled practitioners, have a repertoire of methods, materials, and knowledge that is accessed intuitively (Polanyi, 1958; Schön, 1983). MI offered teachers a handy way of categorizing and understanding the contents of their repertoire. An administrator noted that MI was "providing us with an intellectual framework and common language." Kornhaber (1994, 1999; Kornhaber & Krechevsky, 1995) has earlier referred to this as MI's "closet-organizing effect."

Educators Reported That MI Helped Extend Their Practice.   When a closet organizer is put in place, it is possible to see more clearly both what's been categorized and also what is missing. As one teacher put it, "unless you put things into terms, you aren't necessarily going to be able to do as much effective work on it." In essence, educators reported that MI provided a framework that supported systematic reflection on, and development of, their practice.

In a related study, Kornhaber (1994, 1999) drew on a subsample of three sites from the first investigation. The aim of this study was to test, on a limited basis, the null hypothesis that MI might be a name-only phenomenon. If teachers already had some synchronous practices and beliefs, and if MI stipulated nothing in particular that had to be done, it was possible that teachers said they "did MI" without actually changing anything. In essence, was the theory just a faddish label under which teachers continued to do just what they had always done?

The three sites were picked because they offered a "best case scenario" (Light, Singer, & Willett, 1990, p. 225). Essentially, this kind of sample is selected because it is most receptive to the innovation in question. Such sampling is useful when it is unclear that the innovation—in this case, MI—makes any difference at all. The sites were two elementary schools and one middle school that served primarily middle-class, White students. Each had highly experienced teachers, good support for the arts, and a curricular focus that went beyond basic skills.

Teacher and principal interview data for each school was coded as either "consistent with prior practice," an "extension of prior practice," or "change from prior practice" in the areas of curriculum, assessment, pedagogy, and school structure. Coded text for each area was placed in matrices yielding a visual display of stasis, extension, or change. This revealed that for each of the three schools, there was at least extension or change in two or more of the four areas.

In this best-case scenario sample, MI is not simply a fad sitting atop existing practice but is a stimulus for developing or changing practice. This analysis also indicates that the extent to which MI might be associated with school change intersects with the pre-MI state of practice within the schools themselves. For example, in "School 1," an extremely experienced staff, with access to abundant art resources, had been drawing on constructivist and whole-child philosophies for many years. Thus, MI was well within its "zone of proximal development" (Vygotsky, 1978). In that school, MI supported an extension of practice in the areas of curriculum, pedagogy, assessment, and school structure (e.g., additional collaboration) rather than outright change. In contrast, "School 3" initially implemented MI as a program within a traditional elementary school in which teachers had long relied on textbooks, and instruction was centered on work that drew on linguistic and logical-mathematical intelligences. For School 3, MI presented a substantial stretch in practice. The early-adapting teachers who migrated to the MI program initiated new organizational structures, adopted wholly new assessments, and drafted new curriculum, which eventually traveled through much of the rest of the school.

The findings from these two studies (Kornhaber, 1999; Kornhaber & Krechevsky, 1995) offer some useful ideas for other theory and research aimed at practice. These studies suggest that MI—and perhaps other theory and research that align to some degree with teachers' existing beliefs and practices—may be more readily adopted than those that call for wholesale change. In essence, such theory and research are within the organizational zone of proximal development of the school as well as those of individual teachers (Kornhaber, 1994; Vygotsky, 1978). Therefore, the ideas from research and theory may act as a scaffold to extend existing practice (Wood, Bruner, & Ross, 1976). In the case of MI, the scaffolding of the theory enables educators to organize their intuitive repertoire, reflect systematically on it, and thereby build on what they do.

Ideally, theory and research that speak to educators should not only be within their grasp but also develop their practice in ways that are clearly shown to advance students' learning. MI may fulfill the former better than the latter, in part because it was not devised as a vehicle to advance learning and has been dependent on implementers' ideas. In contrast, some other recent reforms fulfill the latter more so than the former: Such reforms may advance students' skills, especially as measured by tests, but they call on educators to adopt approaches that are out of range of existing practice and belief. Therefore, they are harder to implement on a wide scale without a significant degree of externally imposed structure, support, and/or control.

WHAT IS QUALITY PRACTICE INVOLVING MI?

Theoretical Considerations

Had MI been launched with the aim of shifting practice, it would no doubt have been useful to determine in advance of its dissemination whether the theory had a constructive influence on student learning. Then, too, it would have been helpful to produce research-based guidelines and materials for educators who wished to use the theory in ways that were associated with benefits for students.

Yet, events did not unfold in this fashion in part because Gardner was always more interested in the theoretical and scientific questions raised by the theory than in curriculum materials that might support its implementation. This preference reflects both Gardner's own expertise and his skepticism about "pre-cooked" materials. Even as educators' interest in the theory became apparent, Gardner resisted developing materials. Gardner maintains that educators should be regarded as professionals who themselves are in the best position to decide how to adapt new ideas into the classroom. Gardner, Feldman, Krechevsky, and Chen (1998a, 1998b, 1998c), and others, have produced some materials in conjunction with Project Spectrum. This effort merges assessment and curriculum to ascertain the profile of intelligences in young children. Although these materials are available (Gardner et al., 1998a, 1998b, 1998c) and have been translated into several languages, neither Gardner nor his colleagues ever sought to establish Spectrum classrooms or schools or, indeed, any kind of institutions based on MI theory. Instead, they have very largely stuck to producing frameworks that educators can adapt in light of local circumstances and standards.

Although Gardner refrained from developing materials and programs, he has fleshed out what good practice entailing MI might mean from a theoretical standpoint: As he turned his attention to the educational uses of MI, he became convinced that the theory should never in itself constitute or guide educational ends. The ends, an enterprise in values, need to be determined first. These can vary from, for example, preparing individuals for the workplace or helping them to become intellectually well-rounded and from instilling religious or moral values to enhancing one's respect for diversity. Only after such ends have been determined can the advantages of an MI approach be assessed.

Gardner's (1999b) own educational philosophy indicated that an important end for precollegiate education is disciplinary understanding. In Gardner's formulation, disciplines are distinguished from subject matters. The latter reflect what can be captured within a textbook and assessed by end-of-chapter tests or their equivalent. In contrast, when a person masters a discipline, he or she learns to think in specified ways. Historians approach the issue of causality differently from scientists or novelists; what count as data differs for statisticians, musicologists, or cultural anthropologists. Thus, disciplinary understanding goes well beyond memorizing definitions, or examples, or solutions to a problem. An individual who understands an idea or theory can apply it appropriately in a new circumstance or understand why it does not apply.

An MI approach to disciplinary understanding entails in-depth study of a small number of topics. Only with such focus is it possible to acquire disciplinary modes of thinking and to apply knowledge of a topic to a new question or challenge. With a commitment to "uncovering" rather than covering curriculum, it becomes reasonable to approach topics in many ways, use multiple comparisons and analogies, and express key ideas in a number of symbolic languages. These three "moves" take clear advantage of people's MI and their capacities to represent knowledge in multiple media and symbolic codes. So, for Gardner and his colleagues (e.g., see Blythe, 1997; Boix-Mansilla, & Gardner,

1999; Gardner 1999b; Wiske, 1997), the melding of MI to disciplinary (and, eventually, interdisciplinary) understanding represents the optimal educational use of the theory at the precollegiate levels.

Empirically Driven Considerations

Although Gardner (1999b) has advocated using MI to acquire disciplinary understanding, and some educators appear to use it in that way, it is also clear that educational programs enacted in the theory's name often have not followed that path. Some have been deeply problematic. In a particularly flagrant case, educators in an Australian state made claims about the intellectual strengths and weaknesses associated with each of the resident racial and ethnic groups and proposed educational programs in line with this erroneous assumption. Gardner appeared on television to denounce the educational enterprise as "pseudo-science." In response, the initiative was cancelled shortly thereafter.

Given such wide variation in quality, it seemed worthwhile to explore what educators were actually doing when they implemented MI and associated the theory with benefits for students. The identification of such practices was the main aim of the Project on Schools Using MI Theory (SUMIT). SUMIT also sought to disseminate information about these practices to educators in the field (Kornhaber et al., 2004).

Data collection for SUMIT took place in two phases: an initial broad collection through phone interviews followed by a more in-depth collection entailing 10 site visits each lasting 2–3 days. The phone interviews were conducted with 41 schools, 39 of which were public, and all but 7 were elementary. The schools were located in 18 states and one Canadian province. They were diverse for socioeconomic status and ethnicity: One-third of the schools had substantial percentages (40% to 100%) of students on free or reduced meals, and one fourth of the schools had student populations that were between 50% and 100% African American and/or Latino students. The sample was culled from an initial population of over 60 schools. This population was gathered through files of correspondence to Gardner in which educators' claimed that MI improved student outcomes and through referrals from 10 of the busier, freelance MI consultants who were asked to recommend schools in which they thought MI "was working." Forty-four schools met our initial criterion; namely, that were identified as having used MI for at least 3 years. Of these, 41 both agreed to participate and actually completed the lengthy phone interview (which typically lasted somewhat more than an hour). Most participants were the school's principal, although in a few instances, a lead teacher was the key respondent for the school. All interviews were recorded and transcribed verbatim. The 10 sites that we visited had also used MI for at least 3 years, had received one or more external awards for excellence, and were chosen to reflect, en masse, a great diversity in student populations. All 10 sites were regular (i.e., noncharter, nonmagnet) public schools (Kornhaber et al., 2004).

The telephone interview addressed four areas: the school's students, staff, and community; the methods used to introduce the school to MI; curriculum, assessment, and organizational practices; and outcomes associated with the use of the theory. Kornhaber and Krechevsky's (1995) earlier investigation had made it clear that MI is "not adopted in a vacuum" but is in play together with many different ideas, philosophies, theories, and programs. Therefore, when interviewees reported outcomes, their reports were probed to tease out whether the change was one the respondent felt was associated with the school's adoption of MI or whether it was wholly unrelated to MI. For example, the probe after one school reported improvements in student discipline revealed that this gain was more likely attributable to a social skills curriculum the school had forcefully implemented (Kornhaber, Fierros, & Veenema, 2004).

Through close readings of the interview transcripts, the research team established coding parameters, demonstrated an interrater reliability of .83 (Cohen's kappa), then initially coded all transcripts for outcome information. This revealed that the schools reported positive associations between MI and four outcomes: Nearly 80% of the schools reported improvements in standardized test scores, of which nearly half of the schools associated the improvement with MI. Second, 80% reported improvements in student behavior, with slightly more than half associating this improvement with MI. Third, 80% reported increased parent participation, with 60% associating the increase with the school's adoption of MI. Finally, 80% reported a range of improvements for students with learning disabilities (e.g., improved learning; improved motivation, effort, or social adjustment), with all but one of the schools associating this improvement with MI (Kornhaber et al., 2004).

Clearly, this study is a qualitative one based on semistructured interviews and observations at selected research sites. Although supportive data were sometimes available, the investigators relied primarily on the reports of the individuals with whom they spoke (Kornhaber et al., 2004). These suffer limitations akin to all other self-reports (Neisser, 1986; Schwarz, 1999). Thus, the findings must be regarded as provisional, pending more carefully controlled conditions. Nonetheless, Kornhaber and her co-investigators have some confidence in their findings because interviewees' remarks across these diverse schools were consistent in spite of the fact that there was little, if any, interaction among the sites (Kornhaber et al., 2004).

In addition to consistent comments linking MI to improvements in test scores, student behavior, parent participation, and the education of students with learning disabilities, there are logical connections to associate the theory with such outcomes. For example, improvements in test scores might come in part from "uncovering" the curriculum: Many schools reported striving to engage students through various media and symbol systems in in-depth units, a practice that Gardner, from a theoretical vantage point, has argued would advance disciplinary understanding. For instance, one teacher associated increased achievement with her school's implementation of MI in this fashion: "I think children have more opportunities to achieve better … because they have different modalities and different ways to express themselves." That only about half the schools reported such gains may also not be surprising. Almost none of the schools sought to raise test scores through direct test preparation but instead focused on what they considered best practice. In addition, small cohort sizes in some schools made for fluctuating scores and a lack of clarity about testing gains (see Kane & Staiger, 2002).

Improvements in disciplinary problems can be logically linked to efforts to engage students whose strengths might lie outside the traditional academic intelligences: linguistic and logical mathematical. In addition, as we discuss following, the theory also supported school cultures in which a wide range of learners were more likely to be respected and to have opportunities to make constructive contributions. If fewer students are intellectually or socially alienated, then fewer students are likely to act out.

Parent participation has been associated with student achievement (Epstein & Connors, 1992; Henderson, 1987; Henderson & Beria, 1994). One reason that MI may foster increased parent involvement is that by going beyond the traditional "academic intelligences," the theory helps to value parents from across the school-performance spectrum. Relatedly, the theory embraces a diversity of adult end states, not only those requiring an academic pedigree. These aspects of the theory may help a wider range of parents to feel comfortable interacting with teachers and contributing to school activities. In the schools we investigated (Kornhaber et al., 2004), parents from many walks of life—from trainmen on the Long Island Railroad to pottery makers and professors—had all been called on to talk about or demonstrate what they do. As one principal remarked, "MI has given us real reasons to have parent volunteers." For example, in a unit involving the history of the surrounding town, many parents came in to school to share knowledge of local history and culture. Another possible explanation is the schools often went to a good deal of effort to educate parents about the theory and to make the school as a whole accessible to parents across the socioeconomic and academic spectrum.

The schools in the SUMIT study (Kornhaber et al., 2004) reported both academic and social or emotional improvements for students with learning differences. These were often linked together. For example, one principal noted that students with learning differences "feel good about being able to choose and play on strengths, while they're also working on weaknesses in other areas so that they can become effective." Interviews, and later classroom observations, revealed that youngsters with special needs were commonly working constructively within regular classrooms and typically with the same high level of engagement as other students. The frequent reports of improvements for students with learning disabilities were especially intriguing, and Kornhaber and her colleagues (Kornhaber et al., 2004) probed respondents to uncover what particular practices were being used with these students. The answer was consistent: We are not doing anything differently than we are for our regular students. The practices that had been adopted appeared to serve all students.

Following these findings, Kornhaber, Fierros, and Veenema (2004) then asked: what practices were the schools using? Analysis of coded interview data revealed a set of six organizational practices commonly shared across this very diverse set of schools. Site visits helped to confirm that these practices were regularly in play in the schools. We call these practices "compass points" and regard them as guidelines for orienting practice and charting progress to incorporate MI in a constructive fashion (Kornhaber et al., 2004).

Compass Point Practices

Culture.   The cultures of the schools in the SUMIT study shared four salient qualities that support diverse learners (Kornhaber et al., 2004). First were deeply held beliefs that all children have strengths and can learn. As a principal from British Columbia put it, "[We are] not thinking of any child as a loser, but rather thinking of them all as successful and [our task is] finding ways for each of them to represent their learning." Alongside this belief, educators promoted, and acted on, the value that all members of the school community were to be cared for and respected. Educators felt that MI either fostered or enhanced this value: "I think kids really have a respect for each other and an empathy for each other, because they realize that they have strengths and weaknesses." In our site visits, we saw several remarkable acts of compassion between students, and notably between students with and without disabilities. A third salient quality was hard work on the part of the adults in the schools. A principal from a Seattle suburb asserted that using MI "does take extra effort. It takes time in preparation and extra dedication." Teachers in these schools often invested a good deal of energy to develop new curriculum, share ideas, and create unusually rich classroom environments. The fourth aspect of the culture of these schools was that despite much hard work, there was also a sense of joy and excitement about learning. It was typical of our 10 site visits to see classrooms of students who were eagerly and actively engaged.

Readiness.   While many reforms advocate the sorts of cultures we found (e.g., Comer, 1988; Comer & Emmons, 1999; Levin, 1999; Sizer,

1984), they differ with respect to ideas about optimal speed of implementation (see Fullan, 1990; Levin, 1999). In the schools we investigated, MI typically moved into classroom practice gradually. There was a "readiness" period of a year to 18 months between the introduction of the theory into the school's conversation and its application in several classrooms. The SUMIT investigation confirmed the earlier findings (Kornhaber, 1994, 1999) that introducing MI required some degree of change in practice as well as culture. We believe that this period of readiness enabled teachers to tackle more complex approaches to curriculum and instruction.

Principals, or other school leaders, also played a vital role in supporting this gradual change during the readiness period. They did so in several ways: hiring teachers amenable to MI, organizing professional development activities such as teacher study groups, visits to other classrooms within the school or to another school using MI, and funding attendance at workshops or conferences. School leaders were also essential in promoting a vision for the school during the readiness period as one in which students' diverse abilities should be respected and could be productively engaged. In several cases, they sustained this vision even as district offices reemphasized back-to-basics and test-based accountability measures. For example, a principal of one urban school kept her MI-influenced, project-based approach even after a visiting school board member expressed great dismay that the children weren't able to spit out multiplication facts on her command. In another urban school, the principal described her job in part as protecting teachers from central office demands so that they could keep working in ways that benefited students. Although each of these schools outperformed similar schools in their district, they received little, if any, encouragement from central office staff and principals in other schools in their district. We came to label these and other kindred reports as "you can't be a prophet in your own land."

Collaboration. Teachers in these schools often had formal arrangements that facilitated collaborations such as team teaching or common planning time. These collaborations yielded rich educational experiences for many different learners. For example, in a school in Brewster, New York, a third-grade teacher in a full inclusion room and the school's speech and language teacher regularly took turns leading brief segments during the same lesson. They did this to engage both students who struggled with language and those who were working on grade-level. In Maine, two teachers and the principal collaborated to create a hands-on archaeology dig for fifth graders, which drew on the narrative strengths of the social studies teacher and the scientific methods advocated by the science teacher. In Kentucky, several teachers joined their primary classrooms to provide dramatic readings of such classics as *Charlotte's Web* (White, 1952) Alongside these formal collaborations, there was an abundance of informal, "pickup" collaborations. A new teacher in one of the schools remarked, "people were just offering me help all the time ... I never thought for a minute that I couldn't walk into anybody's room and ask them for anything." In addition, teachers tended to appreciate each other's strengths and to draw on them to complement their own teaching. Accordingly, arts teachers and librarians frequently served as key collaborators in fleshing out large units rather than as people who facilitated classroom teachers' prep time. One of the upshots of so much collaboration appears to be that teachers gained new skills and knowledge. For example, in the third-grade inclusion room mentioned earlier, both teachers reported that they could each lead a lesson directed at the other's target students.

Choice.   To foster student engagement in content, teachers often al-lowed students to make choices in how they wanted to acquire and demon-strate their knowledge. In the earliest grades, choices were often facilitated through learning centers. For example, kindergarten and first-grade class-rooms often had an area for building, another for dramatic play, music, computers, nature, and reading. The materials in these areas were some-times linked to a larger thematic unit such as "spiders" or "community." As students got older, the choices were typically structured to tap meaningful work in particular disciplines or domains. For example, in an investigation of Pittsburgh's rivers, students could begin the day's work by starting in the area of their choice: building models of river landscapes, generating and testing hypotheses about how rivers flow using a working model of a stream, or reading about rivers. Later, they rotated to one of the other activities that engaged different strengths and forms of representation. Alongside curriculum activities, students often had choices in the way that they demonstrated their learning. For example, in a classroom in Albuquerque, students could present a standard book report, offer a dramatic representa-tion of it, develop a poster session, or devise some other venue. However, students' choices in demonstrating their knowledge were also regulated. A principal in Illinois described this clearly: "We honor children's choices, but we also control that. We tell students, 'the last four times you did ... a visual representation. Let's see if we can't have you do something in another for-mat.'" Through choice in these schools, a wide range of learners could be constructively engaged through their strengths and stretched to develop new knowledge, skills, and forms of representation.

Tool.   SUMIT and our earlier studies (Kornhaber, 1994, 1999; Kornhaber & Krechevsky, 1995) reveal a common, initial approach to im-plementing MI: Do everything in seven (or eight) ways. However, typically after a year or two, educators modified this strategy. A principal in Maine described his school's transition in these terms: "We are way over that kind of thinking." At that point, educators judiciously integrated some intelligences into lessons and units rather than superficially drawing on all of them in every circumstance. In so doing, the theory became a tool for educating students rather than an end in and of itself. The use of MI as a tool is clearly illustrated by this New York City principal's remark: "[We use] MI to support what we need to do for kids, [rather than] manipulating what we do with kids to support MI." Similarly, a principal in Pittsburgh commented, "We never said that today we are going to do art because we want to do multiple intelligences." Instead, the school offered arts-enriched instruction so that students had many ways to engage and represent their learning. As these examples illustrate, MI did not serve as a curriculum template in these schools. Rather, it offered educators a way to think about opening up the curriculum to more learners. Only in a very few schools was MI explicitly described to the students. Even then, it was taught largely as a vehicle for helping students to understand that they had a variety of strengths and many possible ways to learn. These instrumental uses of the theory align with Gardner's (1999b, 1999c) notion that the theory should provide a means to educational goals rather than serve as an end in and of itself.

Arts.   The arts played a prominent and vital role in nearly every school in the SUMIT study (Kornhaber et al., 2004). The great majority of schools had at least a part-time visual art and music teacher who taught these art forms as separate disciplines. Dance was sometimes taught by physical education teachers. Several schools secured a variety of grants and community partnerships to bring theater, opera, and museum experiences to the students. The arts were also widely integrated into the regular classroom curriculum. In a study of Pittsburgh's rivers, the art and classroom teacher collaborated so that on a field trip to the rivers, students could record their observations both in writing and through chalk sketches. In addition, students used clay and other modeling materials to construct three-dimensional representations of the rivers at various points from their respective sources in the countryside to their course through the city. In a New Mexico school, art prints were used to help build first- and second-graders' vocabulary. For example, in one classroom, first and second graders generated perhaps a dozen synonyms for describing the young women's position in the grassy foreground of Wyeth's "Christina's World." They also gained some understanding of art as art, learning to recognize a variety of painting styles such as impressionism, cubism, and realism, and techniques (e.g., chiaroscuro). The presence of the arts in these schools was likely not simply a reflection of the largely elementary-age sample: The importance of the arts shone through even in the secondary schools and even in two elementary schools in which there was no art teacher. In one such school, several classrooms resembled museums or ateliers in which prints, student-produced paintings and models, and art books occupied every imaginable space. In the other, the fire marshal had ordered a potentially hazardous overabundance of artwork to come down from the corridors. These examples illustrate that even in the absence of resources, the arts are not seen as "frills." They are essential as ends in and of themselves, and they serve as a powerful means for learning and representing other disciplinary content.

Through SUMIT's research and the empirical work we described earlier, we have gleaned a much clearer idea of the practices in place in schools and classrooms in which educators associate MI with benefits for students. Clearly, many of these practices, especially caring and respectful school cultures and teacher collaboration, overlap with good school practice generally (see e.g., Comer, 1988; Comer & Emmons, 1999; Sizer, 1984). However, there are also some clear distinctions. One is that MI supports the development of supportive school cultures by providing a framework for recognizing and appreciating different intellectual strengths. In addition, the powerful presence of the arts is rare in research-to-practice reforms. The place of the arts aligns with Gardner's theoretical ideas about using MI well, specifically about gaining disciplinary understanding through the use of multiple media and multiple forms of symbolic representation (Gardner, 1999b, 1999c).

Our research design does not allow us to say MI causes schools to use the compass point practices. Clearly, in some schools, a predilection for arts was already in place when the educators encountered MI; in other schools, that was not the case. Similarly, in some schools, there was a civil and respectful environment in operation prior to the introduction of MI; in other schools, there were problems with school climate that educators tackled by drawing on MI. What we can say from this investigation is that the compass point practices infuse schools that are committed to implementing MI in ways that benefit a wide range of students and that we think it is worthwhile for schools to incorporate these practices.

Although SUMIT's work has identified the compass points, that endeavor is no more a spur to their adoption than is any other research intended for translation into practice. There is some possibility that the compass points could ride into practice on MI's wide and popular coattails. Even so, one of the lessons to be drawn from the highly variable quality of MI in schools is that it is simply not sufficient to enter practice by publishing research-based frameworks that are attractive to educators.

To shift practice constructively—in ways that benefit learners—other supports are needed. A number of other reforms have recruited a staff to support such efforts (e.g., Comer, 1988; Levin, 1999; Simon & Gerstein, 1999; Slavin et al., 1996). Lacking that, we believe it is vital for such frameworks to be complemented by detailed and concrete illustrations that are both within practitioners' zone of proximal development and that support the development of disciplinary understanding. Such examples have now been produced out of SUMIT's research using a process of extensive redrafting that drew on feedback from teacher focus groups and trial runs in numerous professional development settings (Kornhaber et al., 2004). These examples clearly describe how real educators have orchestrated the compass points, the kinds of teaching strategies they employ, the materials and room arrangements they use, the kinds of products that students produce, and the curriculum activities and assessments that support such products. That publication is intended to improve MI-influenced practice and guide it in directions that are associated with benefits for students. Drawing on a decade of investigations of MI and of school reforms more generally, we think that the compass points framework coupled with these examples can enhance teacher practice. We hope, but cannot yet say, that this framework plus examples can actually help to advance students' understanding on a broader scale. Of one thing we are certain: To the extent that this research is adopted at all, it will be translated in some as-yet-unanticipated ways.

FUTURE DEVELOPMENTS IN MI THEORY AND PRACTICE

One question that has yet to be considered in exploring the translation of MI theory into practice is what should happen to current MI-influenced practice if the theory were to change? In some cases, the changes in the theory may be modest and readily assimilated. If Gardner adds one or two intelligences to the theory, as he did in the case of the naturalist (Gardner, 1999a), it would be easy enough to enhance the list and create new materials. However, more dramatic changes can be easily envisioned. For example, on the basis of research, it might be determined that the lines between the intelligences have been inappropriately drawn. Perhaps musical and spatial intelligences are closely related or should even be combined into a single intelligence. Or perhaps the relationship between bodily-kinesthetic and spatial intelligences needs to be rethought. Such changes might prove more difficult to incorporate into materials and pedagogies, and it is unknown to what extent educational practice will respond.

Indeed, at present, Gardner is rethinking several aspects of the theory. For example, the relationship between intelligences and domains and disciplines is a far more vexed issue than had been originally appreciated. The assumption that mathematics involves chiefly logical-mathematical intelligence or that musicians draw chiefly on musical intelligence may be wrong or at least oversimplified. Implications for interdisciplinary education are also on the table. Knowledge of genetics, brain structure and functioning, and evolutionary psychology has grown exponentially in the past decades as has scientists' understanding of neural plasticity, particularly during the early years of life. The brain basis of the several intelligences needs, at a minimum, to be restated. Finally, although MI theory was originally developed to counter theories of general cognitive capacities, the whole relationship between specific and general faculties may need to be rethought in light of emerging information about the neural bases of intellectual capacities and the early development of cognition (e.g., Hauser, Chomsky, & Fitch, 2003).

As theorists and researchers, we are delighted by these new lines of work. Should time and energy persist, new formulations can and should be assimilated into MI theory and its successors. However, such changes could wreak havoc with practices that were based primarily on an earlier version of the theory—a version that was right for its time but that is now being superseded by a more sophisticated, differentiated version of the theory. This change of affairs may leave the average educational practitioner confused and perhaps alienated. Or it may kindle new thinking and attention from educators in the field. Such possibilities serve to remind us of the often complex and challenging relationship between scholarly research and applications in the real world.

ACKNOWLEDGMENT

We thank those who have generously funded the work reported in this chapter, particularly the Geraldine R. Dodge Foundation, the Schwab Foundation for Learning, the Spencer Foundation, and the Van Leer Foundation.

REFERENCES

Bate, W. J. (1963). *John Keats*. Cambridge, MA: Harvard University Press.

Blythe, T. (1997). *The teaching for understanding guide*. San Francisco: Jossey-Bass.

Boix-Mansilla, V., & Gardner, H. (1999). On disciplinary lenses and interdisciplinary work. In S. Wineberg & P. Grossman (Eds.), *Interdisciplinary curriculum: Challenges to implementation* (pp. 17–38). New York: Teachers College Press.

Comer, J. (1988). Educating poor minority children. *Scientific American, 259*(11), 42–48.

Comer, J., & Emmons, C. (1999). The school development program. In J. H. Block, S. T. Everson, & T. R. Guskey (Eds.), *Comprehensive school reform: A program perspective* (pp. 245–256). Dubuque, IA: Kendall/Hunt.

Dawkins, R. (1976). *The selfish gene*. Oxford, England: Oxford University Press.

Epstein, J. L., & Connors, L. J. (1992). School and family partnerships. *The Practitioner, 18*(4), 3–10.

Fullan, M. G. (1990). Staff development, innovation, and institutional development. In B. Joyce (Ed.), *Changing school culture through staff development: 1990 yearbook of the Association for Supervision and Curriculum Development* (pp. 3–25). Alexandria, VA: Association for Supervision and Curriculum Development.

Gardner, H. (1993). *Frames of mind: The theory of multiple intelligences.* New York: Basic Books. (Original work published 1983)

Gardner, H. (1999a). Are there additional intelligences? In H. Gardner *Intelligence reframed* (pp. 47–66). New York: Basic Books.

Gardner, H. (1999b). *The disciplined mind: What all students should understand.* New York: Simon & Schuster.

Gardner, H. (1999c). The theory of MI: A personal perspective. In H. Gardner *Intelligence reframed* (pp. 27–46). New York: Basic Books.

Gardner H. (2003). Three distinct meanings of intelligence. In R. J. Sternberg, J. Lautrey, & T. Lubart (Eds.), *Models of intelligence: International perspectives* (pp. 43–54). Washington, DC: American Psychological Association.

Gardner, H. (2004). Multiple intelligences after twenty years. In H. Gardner *Frames of mind: The theory of multiple intelligences.* New York: Basic Books.

Gardner, H., Feldman, D., Krechevsky, M., & Chen, J.-Q. (1998a). *Building on children's strengths: The experience of project spectrum.* New York: Teachers College Press.

Gardner, H., Feldman, D., Krechevsky, M., & Chen, J.-Q. (1998b). *Project spectrum: Early learning activities.* New York: Teachers College Press.

Gardner, H., Feldman, D., Krechevsky, M., & Chen, J.-Q. (1998c). *Project spectrum: Preschool assessment handbook.* New York: Teachers College Press.

Gladwin, T. (1970). *The east is a big bird: Navigation and logic on Puluwat Atoll.* Cambridge, MA: Harvard University Press.

Guilford, J. P. (1967). *The nature of human intelligence.* New York: McGraw-Hill.

Hardy, G. H. (1967). *A mathematician's apology.* Cambridge, England: Cambridge University Press.

Harner, M. (1990). *The way of the shaman.* San Francisco: Harper.

Hauser, N. D., Chomsky, N., & Fitch, W. T. (2003). The faculty of language: What is it, who has it, and how did it evolve? *Science, 298*(22), 1569–1579.

Henderson, A. (Ed.). (1987). *The evidence continues to grow: Parent involvement improves student achievement: An annotated bibliography* (National Committee for Citizens in Education Special Report). Columbia, MD: National Committee for Citizens in Education.

Henderson, A., & Beria, N. (1994). *A new generation of evidence: The family is critical to student achievement.* Washington, DC: National Committee for Citizens in Education.

Herrnstein, R. J., & Murray, C. (1994). *The bell curve: Intelligence and class structure in American life.* New York: Free Press.

Horn, J., & Cattell, R. B. (1966). Refinement and test of the theory of fluid and crystallized general intelligences. *Journal of Educational Psychology, 57,* 253–270.

Kane, T., & Staiger, D. O. (2002). *Volatility in school test scores: Implications for test-based accountability systems.* Retrieved January 3, 2003, from http://www.dartmouth.edu/~dstaiger/Papers/KaneStaiger_brookings2002.pdf

Kornhaber, M. (1994). *The theory of multiple intelligences: Why and how schools use it.* Unpublished manuscript, Harvard Graduate School of Education, Cambridge, MA.

Kornhaber, M. (1999). Multiple intelligences theory in practice. In J. H. Block, S. T. Everson, & T. R. Guskey (Eds.), *Comprehensive school reform: A program perspective* (pp. 179–191). Dubuque, IA: Kendall/Hunt.

Kornhaber, M. L., Fierros, E., & Veenema, S. (2004). *Multiple intelligences: Best ideas from theory and practice.* Needham Heights, MA: Allyn & Bacon.

Kornhaber, M., & Krechevsky, M. (1995). Expanding definitions of teaching and learning: Notes from the MI underground. In P. Cookson & B. Schneider (Eds.), *Transforming schools* (pp. 181–208). New York: Garland.

Levin, H. (1999). Learning from accelerated schools. In J. H. Block, S. T. Everson, & T. R. Guskey (Eds.), *Comprehensive school reform: A program perspective* (pp. 17–32). Dubuque, IA: Kendall/Hunt.

Light, R. J., Singer, J. D., & Willett, J. B. (1990). *By design: Planning research on higher education.* Cambridge, MA: Harvard University Press.

Neisser, U. (1986). Nested structure in autobiographical memory. In D. C. Rubin (Ed.), *Autobiographical memory* (pp. 71–88). Cambridge, England: Cambridge University Press.

Polanyi, M. (1958). *Personal knowledge: Towards a post-critical philosophy.* Chicago: University of Chicago Press.

Rosnow, R., Skedler, A., Jaeger, M., & Rind, B. (1994). Intelligence and the epistemics of interpersonal acumen: Testing some implications of Gardner's theory. *Intelligence, 19,* 93–116.

Scarr, S. (1985). An author's frame of mind: [the book]. *New Ideas in Psychology, 3*(1), 95–100.

Schön, D. (1983). *The reflective practitioner: How professionals think in action.* New York: Basic Books.

Schwarz, N. (1999). Self reports of behaviors and opinions. In N. Schwarz, D. Park, B Knauper, & S. Sudman (Eds.), *Cognition, aging, and self reports* (pp. 17–43). Philadelphia: Psychology Press.

Simon, K., & Gerstein, A. (1999). The coalition of essential schools: A principle-based approach to school reform. In J. H. Block, S. T. Everson, & T. R. Guskey (Eds.), *Comprehensive school reform: A program perspective* (pp. 52–71). Dubuque, IA: Kendall/Hunt.

Sizer, T. (1984). *Horace's compromise: The dilemma of the American high school.* Boston: Houghton Mifflin.

Slavin, R. E., Madden, N. A., Dolan, L. J., & Wasik, B. A. (1996). *Every child, every school: Success for all.* Thousand Oaks, CA: Corwin Press.

Spearman, C. (1904). General intelligence, objectively determined and measured. *American Journal of Psychology, 15,* 201–293.

Thomson, G. H. (1939). *The factorial analysis of human ability.* Boston: Houghton Mifflin.

Thurstone, L. L. (1938). *Primary mental abilities.* Chicago: University of Chicago Press.

Vernon, P. E. (1950). *The structure of human abilities.* London: Methuen.

Vygotsky, L. S. (1978). *Mind in society: The development of higher psychological processes.* Cambridge, MA: Harvard University Press.

White, E. B. (1952). *Charlotte's Web.* New York: Harper.

Wiske, M. S. (Ed.). (1997). *Teaching for understanding: Linking research with practice.* San Francisco: Jossey-Bass.

Wood, D., Bruner, J., & Ross, G. (1976). The role of tutoring in problem solving. *Journal of Child Psychology and Psychiatry, 17,* 89–100.

Author Index

Subject Index